IDENTIFYING AND PRICING
ORIENTAL RUGS

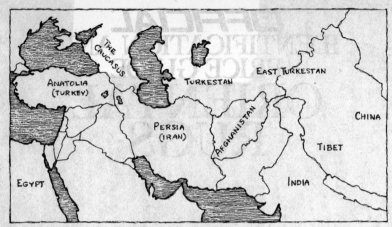

Map of principal oriental rug-producing region.

THE OFFICIAL®
IDENTIFICATION AND PRICE GUIDE
ORIENTAL RUGS

JOYCE C. WARE

Line drawings by Wilson P. Ware

FIRST EDITION

HOUSE OF COLLECTIBLES • NEW YORK

© 1992 by Joyce C. Ware

All rights reserved under International and Pan-American Copyright Conventions.

Published by: House of Collectibles
201 East 50th Street
New York, New York 10022

Text design by Holly Johnson

Distributed by Ballantine Books, a division of Random House, Inc., New York, and simultaneously in Canada by Random House of Canada Limited, Toronto.

Manufactured in the United States of America

ISBN: 0-876-37882-3

First Edition: March 1992

10 9 8 7 6 5 4 3 2 1

For Jeano,
dear sister, loyal friend, valued mentor:
"Güle güle"

CONTENTS

CONTENTS

ACKNOWLEDGMENTS

A gratifying number of busy people granted me generous amounts of time for the interviews that underlie the advice given in these pages. Among them were Michael Craycraft, whose Adraskand Gallery in San Anselmo, California, is a mecca for collectors of tribal and rustic weavings; Elsie Nazarian of Nazarian Brothers, Washington DC, able administrator of a distinguished family business committed to customer service; Peter Scholten of Boalsburg, Pennsylvania, rug dealer and aficionado who has shared his observations with me at many a Skinner auction; and Peter Pap of Dublin, New Hampshire, whose elegant new gallery includes an area devoted to collectible rugs in which collectors can browse undisturbed.

I am also indebted to Marian Miller, Seyfullah Turkkan, Kesang Tashi, George Jevremovic, and Chris Walter for the loan of rugs and photographs of rugs featured as contemporary collectibles, and the London office of Christie's for the loan of the transparency of the "Maggie and Jiggs" silk Kashan carpet.

The rug sales at the major auction houses are an important source of rugs for collectors to see and handle as well as buy, and the rug experts I interviewed were more than equal to their demanding jobs. Keith Wayne, late of Christie's, was particularly generous with his time, and the photo commitments he made to me were honored with impressive efficiency by Kathleen Guzman, President of Christie's East. Mary Jo Otsea of Sotheby's proved to be expert not only at her oriental rug specialty but also in her pursuit of permissions for the photos I requested. The photos I sought from Skinner's were supplied by Jo Kris, who continues to choose and display rugs with the discernment collectors have come to expect of that Bolton, Massachusetts, gallery. Thanks, too, to Michael Grogan, president of Grogan and Company in Boston, who responded courteously and promptly to my photo requests, and to Tim Vos of Butterfield & Butterfield in San Francisco, who sent me back home to Connecticut with a packet of informative brochures and a tape of thoughtful answers to my long list of questions.

No collecting guide would be complete without guidance from experienced collectors. Those mentioned in the pages that follow are not only articulate about our shared obsession but also able to maintain a commendable degree of objectivity. DeWitt Mallary of New York collects

Baluch and Turkoman weavings and writes about the rug scene for *Hali*, the international quarterly periodical about oriental rugs and textiles. Wells Klein, also of New York, specializes in Caucasian weavings, as does Rosalie Rudnick of Boston, who has come a long way since I first met her at a Skinner auction about ten years ago. Wilton and Martha Mason of Chapel Hill, North Carolina, provided excellent company on trips to rug weaving centers and collections in Romania and Turkey.

In the course of a study trip organized by Dr. Harald Böhmer on behalf of the DOBAG weaving cooperatives in western Anatolia, I was privileged to discuss rugs with Jon Thompson, a widely respected rug scholar, as kind as he is witty, and Cornelia Montgomery, currently acting as a specialist consultant for Peter Pap's New Hampshire gallery. Islamic arts scholar Walter Denny and Holly Chase, who writes and lectures about rugs and textiles, were the leaders of a rug-related tour through eastern Turkey, and Dennis Dodds of the Maqam Gallery hosted a similar tour through Romania, Hungary, Austria, and Turkey.

Closer to home, I have been provided valuable insights by dealers Louise Woodhead of Brookline, Massachusetts, and Steven Maeck and Lee Beshar of New York. Collectors Tatiana Divens, Roger Hamernik, and Kathleen Gallagher march to the same collecting drum as I, as does Richard E. Newman, whose incomparable restorations of tribal and rustic rugs include a very old and beautiful Caucasian rug of mine.

Other acquaintances who may be unaware of their contributions are Sally Sherrill and Rosalind Benedict, whose scholarship is of the highest order; George O'Bannon, former editor of *Oriental Rug Review* and mentor to a legion of collectors; and John Edelmann, whose Saturday morning auction sales and free picnic lunches enlivened the New York rug scene in the early 1980s.

Special thanks are due my good friend Gayle Garrett of The Rug Project in Washington DC, who was always ready to listen and intelligently advise; my agent, Adele Leone, and my editors, Dorothy Harris and Karen Shapiro, who made it all possible; and my talented husband, Wilson, who ended up doing three times as many pen and ink sketches as originally estimated.

ORIENTAL RUGS

INTRODUCTION

The term "oriental rug" is an arbitrary catchall for a wide variety of knotted-pile and flat-woven textiles produced in a vast area stretching from North Africa to China. Included in this territory are Turkey (Anatolia), Iran (Persia), Afghanistan, Pakistan, India, and three historically significant weaving areas that are now part of the Soviet Union: the Caucasus, Turkestan, and East Central Asia. Beautiful carpets were also made in Spain and Egypt, and an important modern industry has developed in Romania in addition to the distinctive floral-patterned kilims for which it has long been known.

A genuine oriental rug is made by hand. Some machine-made rugs, such as the popular American-made Karastan, are of good quality and certainly far superior to plain-colored carpets printed with oriental-type patterns, but both are required by law to be designated and advertised as oriental *design*.

The vast majority of rugs offered for sale by dealers or at auction are 20th- or late-19th-century examples. Only a small minority of these can be considered either collectible or antique, and although the terms are often thought to be synonymous, they are not. In fact, some rugs being made today with hand-spun wool and vegetable colors are more collectible than century-old rugs defaced by unstable synthetic dyes.

If you are less interested in rugs for their own sake than as an element of a decorative ensemble, the faded look characteristic of old unstable dyes or the untraditional palette of a computer-designed new rug may very well suit you. The true collector, however, views rugs primarily as works of woven art. Collectors may use commercially designed decorative carpets in high-traffic household areas, but they are no more likely to confuse that practical choice with collectible rugs than they would a paperback thriller with Tolstoy's *War and Peace*.

The dating of oriental rugs is often a matter for lively debate, and since some collectors value age above all other factors, the outcome can be of considerable monetary importance to buyer and seller alike. The classification of age, however, depends in large measure upon who does the determination. The international auction houses, like Sotheby's and Christie's, consider as antiques rugs woven 100 or more years ago. More conservative authorities apply that desirable label only to rugs predating the introduction of synthetic dyes in the area in which they were woven, in some cases as early as 1860. In the trade, a rug becomes an antique in about 80 years; semiantique if it predates World War II, and "old" if made at least 25 years ago.

Perhaps at this point you should ask yourself why you picked up this book in the first place. If your interest in rugs begins and ends with the wish to furnish your home with a few attractive pieces, or if you just want to know more about the rugs you already have and how to care for them, this book will help you accomplish that worthwhile goal.

Dyed-in-the-wool rug collectors, on the other hand, acquire over the years more pieces than can conceivably be used or displayed at any one time, the overflow crowding the foot lockers and closet shelves that in other households are used for out-of-season garments and sporting gear. Since I fall into that category myself, I hope what follows will help others steer clear of some of the pitfalls awaiting the unwary rug collector in the course of enjoying collecting's many delights.

The first hard lesson most collectors learn is that the coveted object bought expensively today, perhaps even excitingly dueled over at auction, is worth in dollars only what the next buyer will pay for it. With that in mind, here are a few basic truths:

1. Collectors who, for whatever worthy reason, haven't time to spare for visiting museum collections, attending exhibitions, or prowling auction previews, should put themselves in the hands of a reputable dealer. When it comes to rugs, beautiful pictures and scholarly articles just aren't enough. You have to see the colors, feel the wool, and examine the structure, preferably in the company of collectors more knowledgeable than yourself. In short, you have to develop an eye.

2. Connoisseur collecting is expensive. World-class antique rugs of exceptional color, design quality, and condition are not picked up for pocket change at a tag sale, local antique show, or rural auction. The rare exceptions are just that, very rare. Adjust your collecting sights to your pocketbook. It can be just as rewarding, and you'll sleep better. Besides, as Joseph Alsop shrewdly observed in *The Rare Art Traditions*, "the line between 'worth having' and 'not worth having' is always shifting, since collectors with limited means are constantly exploring all the things 'not worth having' for possible prizes when a new collectors' category finds favor."

3. Only buy rugs that please you. News of a high price paid for a so-called rare rug, which may have little otherwise to recommend it, invariably brings hitherto unknown but similar pieces out of attics and into the auction rooms where the rarity bought for a quick killing quickly becomes a drug on the market.

4. Finally, be prepared to make mistakes. Everyone does. Experts loftily advise beginners to collect only what they like and to buy only

the best examples. Obviously, we all hope to scorn the mediocre, but the catch is that if it takes a trained eye to distinguish the best from the good, the novice is often hard put to choose between the run-of-the-mill and the embarrassingly awful. It's not easy to admit to our mistakes, but admit them we must: do not blame the dealer who "talked you into it," or the catalog description that misled you, or the poor light, or auction fever. The decision was yours.

Since we learn much more from our mistakes than we do from inspired choices, consider the cost of yours as tuition. Let us hope the school you are about to enter offers more pleasure than hard knocks, but be ever mindful of the motto emblazoned above its gates: *Caveat Emptor*.

A LITTLE BIT OF HISTORY

Since the materials used in rug making are rather perishable, the art undoubtedly antedates the existence of known specimens. In 1949, a Russian archaeologist found a very well preserved, finely knotted carpet at Pazyryk in the Altai mountains of eastern Siberia that was dated to between the fifth and third centuries B.C. Although newer information argues for a later dating, the skillfully balanced design, well-drawn pictorial motifs, and fine craftsmanship of this astonishing rug is *prima facie* evidence that the art of knotted textiles was well developed much earlier than the evidence available before the Pazyryk excavations had led scholars to assume.

The oldest known Islamic rug, known as the Fustat (Old Cairo) Carpet, alleged to have been excavated in Egypt, has been carbon-dated to the seventh to ninth centuries A.D. Acquired in 1986 by the Fine Arts Museums of San Francisco, its sadly faded colors and fragmentary design will no doubt fuel scholarly surmise and discussion for years to come.

After the invasion of Egypt by Islamic armies in 640 A.D. and the domination of varying areas of Spain by the Moors from North Africa from the 8th century through the 15th century, the arts in both areas

The Pazyryk carpet, oldest-known knotted pile rug.

became influenced by the Islamic tradition. The best-known Egyptian weavings produced during this period are the Mamluk carpets of the 15th and 16th centuries, which, unsurprisingly, have stylistic links to both Anatolian and northwest Persian weaving of the same period. Their distinctive iridescent coloration and geometric patterning were succeeded by curvilinear designs after the occupation of Cairo by the Ottoman Turks in 1517.

Early Spanish rug design was also derived largely from eastern Islamic patterns except for the custom of knotting into the field of carpets the crests of the noble Spanish families who commissioned them. The earliest surviving examples, dating from the 15th century, are reminiscent of Egyptian work. Later, Anatolian influences prevailed, and still later, in the 16th and 17th centuries, European baroque patterns were commonly employed.

The production of pile carpets diminished in both Egypt and Spain in the 18th century, and although superb early examples may be seen in museum collections—especially noteworthy is the glowing silk Mamluk in the Osterreichisches Museum für Angewandte Kunst in Vienna—they are rarely available in the market except as fragments. There is no significant modern production in Spain, but Persian-design rugs of superb quality are being made today in Egypt, thanks to a recent revival of workshop weaving there.

The peak of the rug weaving art was reached under the patronage of the Safavid dynasty in Persia, 1499–1722. Carpets and other textiles—as well as paintings, ceramics, ironwork, and calligraphy—attained a level of extraordinary virtuosity during this period, but not as a result of the expression of individual creativity within the weaver's cultural tradition, which is prized by many collectors today. On the contrary, the highly sophisticated designs of these carpets woven in court-sponsored manufactories were created by master artists. It was a combined achievement of artistry and craft possible only in a society in which, since time itself was of little value, weavers were expected to take as much time as was necessary to produce the desired result. In terms of delicacy of ornament, subtle coloration, and mastery of technique, these glorious carpets have never been equaled.

Wonderful carpets were also made in India in the Mughal dynasty's workshops during roughly the same period, 1500–1738. "The art was borrowed," says Islamic art scholar Walter Denny, "but as with the Japanese and baseball, it was taken up with enthusiasm: Indian rugs of the classical period are the largest, most finely knotted, and most brilliantly colored carpets ever made." These classical Indian carpets employ exquisite floral motifs—more realistically drawn than those on

Persian models—arrayed together with bizarre animals on distinctive claret-red grounds. Except for the flat-woven dhurries, Indian weaving later became entirely dominated by Persian designs, and although these rugs may be attractive as furnishing pieces, they lack the cultural expression that make a rug collectible. The same holds true for India's sizable contemporary production, which consists largely of Persian-design knock-offs offering good value but unlikely ever to interest collectors.

Rug making in the area now known as Turkey is particularly well documented thanks to the long-established custom there of giving carpets to mosques as tokens of piety and thanksgiving. In urban centers and remote villages alike, they accumulated over the centuries, layer upon layer, awaiting discovery by scholars and removal to Turkish museum collections for documentation and conservation. The earliest carpets, whose fragments have been dated to the 13th- and 14th-century Seljuk dynasty, were large coarse weavings with textile-like repeat patterns bordered by barbarically bold motifs. Ottoman court carpets, like their Persian and Indian counterparts, used silk and fine wools for their elaborate, floral-based patterns. The arched prayer rug design has been an enduringly popular format throughout Turkey, from the finely knotted silks produced in Hereke workshops to refined village products like the tulip-decorated Ladiks and the brightly colored geometricized versions produced on cottage looms. The use of cheap European synthetic dyes wreaked havoc in the Turkish cottage weaving industry from about 1870 through most of the 20th century, but the reintroduction of vegetable dyes and hand-spun wool in the early 1980s (see chapter on contemporary collectibles) has spurred a lively revival of dealer and collector interest in these handsome traditional rugs.

By the 14th and 15th centuries, rugs began being imported by Venetian merchants, first from Anatolia—now Turkey—and later from the Caucasus, where a thriving cottage industry produced carpets with distinctive large-scale floral and stylized dragon designs. European fascination with the brilliant color and bold geometric designs of the early Anatolian rugs is confirmed by their frequent depiction in the contemporary paintings of Previtali, Bassano, Lotto, and Holbein. In fact, the names of the two latter artists have been applied to the designs of the Anatolian carpets they favored as accessories. It is interesting to note that these paintings show rugs being used as table covers at least as often as floor decoration.

The turmoil resulting from frequent hostile invasions in both Persia and Anatolia during the 18th century contributed to a decline in court carpet production in these important weaving areas. Rulers seeking to preserve their thrones have more on their minds than aesthetics. As a result, the rugs of this period of most interest to collectors originated in villages and nomadic tents throughout the Middle East and Central Asia.

Among the tribal populations of these rugged hills and windswept plains, where life was affected much less by distant troubled courts than by local harvests and seasonal treks to pasturage, the need for sturdy domestic woven goods remained constant.

As one travels east, the appearance of rugs characteristic of the various weaving areas from East Turkestan to China begins to differ from the type most Westerners think of as oriental rugs, even though many of the motifs seen in the classical Persian, Indian, and Turkish carpets originated in ancient China, arriving in the West in the wake of invading Mongol hordes in the 12th century and along the famed silk routes stretching from China to the Mediterranean.

East Turkestan rugs tend to be transitional in type, borrowing colors and designs from rug-making neighbors both to the east and to the west. The best of the Tibetan rugs, a Chinese-influenced art of relatively recent date, possess a unique vigor and charm, especially the so-called tiger rugs.

Although Chinese rugs were not introduced to the West until about 1900, there is reason to believe that pile rug making was an established art there as early as the 12th century. The rather sparse use of unfamiliar symbolic figures and the subdued Chinese palette characteristic of these interesting rugs lacked initial appeal to Western eyes more accustomed to the colorful swirling patterns of the carpets long associated with the term "oriental." In recent years, however, sophisticated collectors have come to appreciate their subtle artistry, and the prices of antique pieces have risen accordingly. Today, vast quantities of both silk and wool rugs are produced in government-controlled workshops in Chinese and Persian designs. Although they provide good value as attractive, reasonably priced furnishing rugs, the slick, cookie-cutter sameness of these modern reproductions virtually rules out any collector interest in the foreseeable future.

European interest in oriental rugs revived in the late 19th century, due largely to the popularity of paintings by Western artists fascinated by the exoticism of Middle Eastern scenes. Unfortunately, the resulting revitalization of the Eastern carpet industry was accompanied by a new and not altogether happy twist. Although earlier rugs had also been commercially produced and exported, the colors, the sizes, and even the designs of this later and much larger production were often dictated by foreign importing firms to suit the needs and tastes of Western buyers. Further, the well-intended systems of quality control introduced by these importers resulted in bale after bale of a uniformly well-made but artistically uninspired product.

This development, although of no particular significance to the buyer of a decorative furnishing rug, contributed to the current collector inter-

est in village and tribal weavings. These homely items produced solely
for practical domestic use retained a vitality and relative purity of design
well into this century. In fact, although unrest in the Middle East has
hampered it, tribal research has been one of the most popular areas of
study for rug scholars and enterprising collectors interested as much in
the weavers' materials, techniques, design sources, and day-to-day lives
as they are in the rugs they make.

For More Information

Until recently, books about oriental rugs were published for the most
part in costly limited editions authored by gentleman collectors who acquired their information and rug collections in the course of adventure-
some journeys through rug-producing areas. Other books, less
expensively illustrated and even more myth-laden, were written by rug
dealers more interested in intriguing a naive potential rug-buying public
than imparting accurately researched information. Happily, this situation
has radically altered in the past 15 years.

Although the best of the scholarly rug books are expensive, particularly those well supplied with good color plates, there are now available—thanks to the rapid advance in rug scholarship—several reasonably
priced, competently written, well-illustrated guides.

An annotated list of recommended titles is included in the Resource
Guide. If some of the more expensive titles are beyond your reach, inquire about borrowing them through your state interlibrary loan system
before settling for an outdated third-rater gathering dust on the shelves
of your local library. There has been a lot of nonsense written about
rugs, and if you are just beginning to study them, it will be less confusing
in the long run if you start with recognized authorities. They, too, may
contradict each other on occasion, but at least their contradictions are
based on informed reasoning.

THE MARKETPLACE

THE AUCTION HOUSE

Once upon a time, dealers in old and antique rugs were the principal buyers of auctioned goods. The few collectors who prowled the dealers' auction house turf could pick up for peanuts the wonderful tribal trappings, rugs, and kilims that until the late 1970s were of little interest to anyone except the cognoscenti. Decorative carpets, too, especially those with "unfashionable" colors and patterns, could be had at wholesale prices. This is no longer the case. In fact, a dealer who today acquires rugs from an estate or through trade is sometimes able to price them for less than they might bring at auction. There are several reasons for this topsy-turvy situation.

In recent years the major auction houses have taken to wooing the retail dealers' customers; some even allow prospective buyers to see how a particular decorative carpet will look in their homes before deciding whether to bid. Pleased by the opportunity to eliminate the middleman and unbothered by commercial concerns about profit and loss, these customers routinely top the dealers' bids. If a rug becomes the object of obsessive desire, the winning bid may leave the dealers reeling with shock.

Such was the case at Sotheby's in New York on January 20, 1990, when an oversize, palely pretty Persian Sultanabad carpet with an already hefty estimate of $80,000–$120,000 soared in the heat of competitive bidding by private parties to $181,500. Although the victor in such duels is often awarded with applause for providing lively entertainment, astronomical bids fueled by ego rarely affect day-to-day market pricing.

Another class of wild-card bidders are the decorators prepared to pay large prices to get their wealthy clients the "design statement" their newly decorated lodgings require. A third cause of inflated bids is auction fever, a mouth-drying, palm-dampening affliction that compels its hapless victims to bid well beyond a carefully predetermined limit. And finally, there's simple ignorance, such as a novice collector's inability to distinguish a 20th-century version of an antique Caucasian Kazak from the real thing.

It is not my intent to discourage budding collectors from attending auctions. Not only are they fun, but the previews of the rug-only sales held two or three times a year by the major houses provide the only opportunity for hands-on study of as many as 200 to 400 good rugs of all types at one's own pace. Close inspection of museum holdings, no matter how wonderful they may be, is hampered by a universal no-touch policy and a color-conservation level of lighting more suited to owls than people.

For their major sales the big auction houses publish illustrated catalogs, available singly or by subscription, that allow serious collectors to track prices and trends. Sotheby's recently broke new ground with the addition of widely praised structural analyses of the collector pieces in the front half of their catalogs. Most houses offer rugs at mixed-furnishings sales as well. Few of these are of collectible interest, but alert buyers can sometimes pick up for a bargain price good rugs that either have condition problems or were consigned by owners unwilling to wait for the next major sale.

Each house has its own style; each has an informed—but not infallible—staff of experts happy to provide detailed objective advice, either in person at previews that allow interested parties ample time—from two to six days—for firsthand inspection or over the phone to persons unable to attend them. Usually, a selection of photos can also be provided to potential absentee bidders, and many pricey rugs have been acquired in this fashion; but unless I were sure the auction house expert advising me "sees" rugs as I do, I would not be inclined to bid on a rug that I or a knowledgeable friend or agent had not personally inspected. And I never rely on the catalogs alone; catalog descriptions sometimes inadvertently omit crucial information about condition. A poor black-and-white photograph can make a rug appear less desirable than it actually is, and given the inaccuracies of color reproduction, the full-page plates of major offerings can be misleading, too.

Always remember that no matter how posh the setting, auction sales, unlike purchases made through retail dealers, are final. Except in the very rare instance of a grossly inaccurate representation, there are no returns, no exchanges. In fact, Keith Wayne, who steered Christie's rug department through almost a decade of successful sales, told me he prefers uncertain buyers to go the retail route.

OTHER AUCTIONS

Small regional and country auctions pose additional hazards. They rarely have experts on staff, and except for the measurements marked on the tag, the information supplied is often inaccurate. It is true that wonderful buys of decorative carpets and the occasional esoteric collectible can sometimes be made, especially if a rug ring is operating, but bargains of any kind are unlikely at auctions at which two or more rings compete for the same rugs.

A "ring" or "pool" is an impromptu organization of dealers attending an auction—including "pickers" who supply dealers—who agree not to bid against one another, the purpose being to buy the rugs offered at the lowest possible price. One of the ring's members is chosen to bid for the group; later the ring holds its own postsale auction as a result of which some will receive rugs and others will receive money as their reward for agreeing not to compete. Although rings—rugs, silver, whatever—are illegal in many states, they continue to be an outsize thorn in every auctioneer's side.

On-site auctions of estates at a distance from urban centers offer keen-eyed collectors the best opportunities, but sometimes rugs that local dealers are desperate to unload are accomodatingly placed in parlors and hallways to "round out" sales. Ask the auctioneer if the displayed rugs originated in the estate being auctioned. I have found that a direct question of this sort vests me with sufficient authority to rate a truthful answer.

Lies, however, are the stock-in-trade of the weekend motel sales known as short-notice auctions. Friends are forever calling me up about these events, anxious that I not miss this great opportunity to add to my collection. You've probably seen the ads: Important Public Auction! Shipment Cleared from U.S. Bonded Warehouse to Be Disposed of at Nominal Price for Immediate Cash Realization!

I attended one of those sales once out of curiosity and was fascinated by the techniques employed to lull suspicion and flatter bidders. No preview time was allowed, but early arrivals could hastily inspect rugs as they were carried in, and any attribution one cared to guess at was respectfully accepted and one's knowledge complimented. For the most part, the rugs were either 25- to 40-year-old worn examples of types that were mediocre to begin with or else shoddy new goods.

In the beginning of the sale, one or two rugs were regretfully set aside because the highest bids received for these "fine pieces" were too low. This reassured an audience made up of bargain-seeking but basically decent people that they would not be taking unfair advantage of dealers down on their luck. Winning bidders were occasionally complimented for their sagacity in choosing the "antique" rug they had just bought. "A very good buy, sir," the auctioneer would solemnly say, and oh, how the buyer beamed!

By the end of the sale, half of the audience had made "very good buys," including the rugs set aside at the beginning of the sale and whisked out later to "give away" tearfully at prices half again as high as the usual retail price. Again, no returns and no refunds, not even when you belatedly discover in the cold light of day that a significant portion of the pattern has been touched up with paint to hide the wear and bleeding dyes.

ANTIQUE SHOWS

Weekend antique shows occasionally offer interesting rug-buying opportunities, but if a rug dealer is among the exhibitors, chances are that any attractive rug bargains in other booths will have been snapped up before the public is admitted. On the other hand, the booths of knowledgeable dealers who regularly make weekend forays out of their home turf—Peter Pap of New Hampshire and Lawrence Kearney of Massachusetts, for example—allow busy collectors a wonderful opportunity to see a much better than average selection of rugs close to home. Dealers who participate in antique shows will be happy to supply you with a list of upcoming events and bring to any show you plan to attend rugs suited to your furnishing needs or collecting interests (consult the lists of dealers in the Resource Guide).

Many antique show promoters have a policy of admitting early buyers on payment of from $10 to $60 above the standard entrance fee. For the most part, these premium-paying buyers are dealers able to spot a promising item out of the corner of a practiced eye and make an immediate decision. In this company, he who hesitates is lost. A novice collector who rushes to judgment under these pressured circumstances risks making very expensive mistakes. A bargain prize may later reveal synthetic dyes, unnoticed areas of wear, moth damage, and patches.

FLEA MARKETS AND TAG SALES

Flea markets and garage tag sales are rarely worth a rug collector's notice. In-house estate tag sales sometimes offer treasures, but if the ad you see makes your mouth water, you can be sure dealers and other collectors will be similarly affected.

First come, first served is the order of the day at country estate tag sales. Numbers are handed out to the prospective buyers in the order of their arrival, and they are usually admitted in small groups to guard against pilferage. Dealers will drive considerable distances if the sale is exceptionally promising, often arriving just before the sale begins, whereupon offers of handsome sums to those first in line—$200 to $400 is not uncommon—allow them to sweep in with their purchased low numbers ahead of scores of outraged standees. In the case of rugs, all it takes is one carload of well-heeled dealers to pick a sale clean in the first 15 minutes.

ORIENTAL RUG DEALERS

Auctions and estate sales deserve a place on the collector's agenda, but the most reliable way to assemble a rug collection worthy of the name is through dealers who specialize in old and collectible rugs. Department stores stock new goods only; the average retail rug dealer does too, although dealers may occasionally receive old rugs through trade or from local estates. Any good pieces thus acquired are usually promptly shipped off to the big metropolitan auction houses, so nearby dealers should be asked to call you when anything interesting comes their way.

Specialty rug dealers tend to cluster on the two coasts and in or near major metropolitan centers elsewhere. Until the mid-1970s, most rug dealers were either immigrants or first-generation Americans whose knowledge of weaving was bred in the bone. Dealers with a Middle Eastern family background continue to dominate the oriental rug market, but they have been joined by a group of art- and scholarship-oriented, collector-cum-dealer Westerners whose first introduction to the glories of oriental weaving was often a result of overseas assignments by organizations like the Peace Corps. The former editor of *Oriental Rug Review*, George O'Bannon, is a notable example of these latter-day, home-grown enthusiasts.

Whatever their background or approach, specialty dealers will first send you photos and descriptions of rugs of the type you express interest in acquiring and then ship to you for firsthand inspection any pieces you are considering buying. If you are unknown to the dealer, a returnable deposit of part or all of the price may be required for this service. (Dealers, unlike auction houses, often absorb the cost of shipment if you purchase the rug sent you on approval, but if you return it, you should expect to pay the entire cost of shipping and insurance.)

Because their stock consists primarily of one-of-a-kind antique and semiantique pieces, specialty dealers eschew the 60%-off sale events beloved of Main Street and shopping mall dealers in new orientals. They consider themselves, and rightly so, as dealers in art rather than floor coverings. If you enjoy bargaining, by all means give it a whirl, but don't expect across-the-board, end-of-season types of reductions.

BUYING RUGS ABROAD

If you are planning a trip to a rug-weaving area, this could be a marvelous buying opportunity if you heed certain cautions:

1. If you buy from a dealer unaccustomed to shipping overseas, try to bring your rug purchases home with you. You'd be amazed at the compact package a determined dealer can make of even a fairly good sized rug.

2. Unless you are very knowledgeable, you should consider confining your choice to new rugs.

In the Turkish bazaars, old-looking rugs of any age are invariably touted as antiques, and all dyes are sworn to be natural. It is assumed that if you don't know what you're looking at, you deserve to be cheated. Fine antique Turkish rugs exported generations ago can be purchased for less in the United States than in Turkey—and more safely, too, now that countries around the world have become understandably sensitive to the loss of their cultural artifacts to Western museums and collectors. You could be fined and even detained if you attempt to take antiques home with you, and although this is less likely to occur in the case of rugs, why take the chance when the new vegetable-dyed Turkish rugs and kilims are such worthy and economical buys? (See chapter on contemporary collectibles.)

For More Information

In the Resource Guide in the back of this book is a list of dealers either known to me personally or recommended by collectors whose judgment I respect or who regularly advertise in *Oriental Rug Review* and *Hali*, periodicals that specialize in rugs and textiles. Subscription information is included in the Resource Guide.

The members of oriental rug societies can also provide names of dealers likely to have rugs and trappings of interest to you. Membership in these societies is well worth seeking. Experienced collectors enjoy advising beginners, and the newsletters most rug societies publish usually include notices of rug-oriented events and tours and offer the best of the new rug books at a discount price to their members. See the Resource Guide for locations and the addresses to write to for membership information.

THE STRUCTURE OF ORIENTAL RUGS

The clearest, most succinct definition of handmade rugs I have ever come across and that I doubt can be improved upon is contained in a book called *Hand-Woven Carpets* by A. F. Kendrick and C. E. C. Tattersall, originally published in 1922:

> The whole field of hand-made carpets can be divided into two great classes—those with smooth faces and those with a pile. Both classes are textile fabrics, which means that they consist essentially of two sets of threads—the warp and the weft—which cross each other at right angles and are interwoven so as to make a coherent tissue. The smooth-faced carpets consist of warp and weft alone; the pile carpets have, in addition, short extra pieces of thread knotted to the warp threads so that their free ends stand up and form a surface similar to that made by the blades of grass in a meadow.

THE LOOM

Carpets, like other textile fabrics, are woven on a frame or loom. The degree of complexity of a loom varies according to the type, size, and sophistication of the article to be woven and the domicile of the weaver. Obviously, city workshop weavers will use larger and more elaborate looms than the womenfolk of nomadic tribes use, but the essentials remain the same: two stout beams kept apart by sidepieces, or in the case of nomadic weavers, by stakes driven into the ground.

The warp threads, which absorb the greater share of the stress created by the weaving process, are generally thicker and stronger than the weft. They are strung vertically upon the loom and lie parallel to the two side beams and to each other.

Once the warp has been strung, the weft threads may be woven through, over and under alternate warp threads, with each weft reversing the course of the previous weft, just like darning a sock. Unlike darning, however, a one-by-one process of interweaving weft and warp would become tedious in the extreme when translated to the large scale of a carpet. To avoid this, a stout rod is passed through the warp threads just

17

as a weft thread would be, above the area where the actual weaving is taking place. The rod divides the warp threads into two sets, or planes, forming a space called a shed between them, with all of the odd-numbered warps lying in one set and all of the even-numbered warps in the other. This manipulation of the warp threads into two sets allows the weft thread, which may be wound on a shuttle, to be thrust through the shed in one motion.

For the alternate passage, or shoot, of the weft, the position of one set of the warp threads relative to the other must be reversed. To achieve this, all of the warp threads at the back of the shed are attached with short, equal lengths of cord to another rod, an arrangement that, in toto, is known as a heddle. When this rod is drawn forward, the attached warps are pulled in front of the other set to create a reversed space, or shed, through which the next shoot of the weft is passed. (Consult the glossary at the end of this chapter for definitions of unfamiliar terms.)

THE NOMADIC HORIZONTAL GROUND LOOM

Nomadic weavers use the simplest looms because they may have to pack up their work many times during the weaving of a single rug. The horizontal beams over which the warp threads are wound are held in position by stakes driven into the ground rather than by rigid upright sidepieces. The tension of the warp threads is maintained by securing one of the warp beams to the stakes by pairs of stout ropes that can be tightened by twirling a stick placed between them. This far-from-ideal method of control makes it impossible to duplicate even the same degree of imperfect tension at each successive setting up of the loom, which is why the dimensions of nomadic weavings are seldom true. But even the most primitive nomadic looms usually have some sort of device to separate the sets of warp threads to facilitate the passage of the weft from one edge to the other.

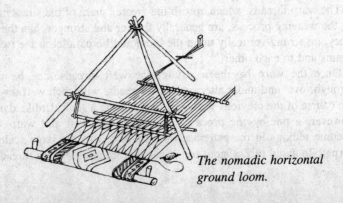

The nomadic horizontal ground loom.

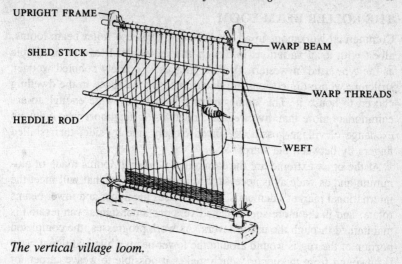

UPRIGHT FRAME

SHED STICK

HEDDLE ROD

WARP BEAM

WARP THREADS

WEFT

The vertical village loom.

THE VERTICAL VILLAGE LOOM

The typical village loom is only slightly more sophisticated than the horizontal type. Constructed from roughly fashioned timbers, they are housed in family dwellings so that the womenfolk may weave rugs—sometimes for household use but usually for the purpose of adding to a family's meager income—between the daily rounds of domestic duties.

The permanency of its placement and the addition of rigid vertical side pieces make it easier to maintain an even warp tension on these looms, but the length of a rug is predetermined by the distance between the upper and lower beams, a limitation shared with the nomadic horizontal loom.

Rugs are almost always woven from bottom to top: as work on a horizontal ground loom progresses, the weaver sits upon the part she has completed; but a weaver using the simplest type of vertical loom sits in front of the loom on a plank that is raised higher as the work progresses, a distinct drawback if one is working indoors in a poorly ventilated room that is dimly lit at best.

Both of these limitations are ameliorated by the Tabriz loom. Although similar to the village upright loom in its essentials, the warps strung around the upper and lower warp beams are looped so that, as the weaving progresses, the warp tension can be readily loosened and the completed portion drawn up behind the lower beam. This allows the weaver to remain seated at the same level throughout the weaving process and offers the additional advantage of doubling the possible length of the article being woven.

THE ROLLER BEAM LOOM

Commercial workshops in all rug-weaving areas use roller beam looms, albeit with local variations in design and materials. It can be as simple as the type used in western Turkish villages, a crudely cobbled wooden structure whose dimensions are determined by the space in the dwelling chosen to house it. This domestic version is rarely wide enough to accommodate more than two weavers, relatives or neighbors who enjoy an exchange of village gossip as, seated closely side by side, their skilled fingers fly between the warps.

At the other extreme are the Romanian workshop looms made of aluminum and as wide as is necessary to produce carpets that will meet the international market's demands. In both cases the upper and lower beams rotate, and in the more sophisticated versions a constant, even tension is maintained through the use of levers. As work progresses, the completed portion of the rug is wound around the lower beam while additional warp is unwound from the upper, which makes it possible to weave carpets of any length desired.

THE MATERIALS

The materials most commonly used to make oriental rugs are sheep's wool, cotton, silk, camel hair, and goat hair. Linen has great strength and has occasionally been used as warp threads in fine rugs. Hemp or jute occurs only in very cheap, coarse products, made mostly in Southeast Asia, which often have considerable charm but wear poorly.

In the distant past, all rugs were made primarily to insulate against the cold. They were made entirely of wool and were as apt to be felted as woven, as in fact many nomadic rugs still are. Sheep wool is by far the most commonly employed fiber; camel and goat hair are used primarily in nomadic and tribal weavings. The soft, honey-colored ground in many old Baluch rugs is natural camel hair, which is sometimes also used for both the warp and weft yarns in their flat-woven articles. Goat hair is generally too coarse and stiff to be used for knotting, but it is frequently incorporated into woolen warp yarns for strength and is used by several tribes to create distinctive, hard-wearing edge finishes.

Although wool is often used for both warp and weft in tribal and village weavings, handspun in many cases, and is by far the most commonly used fiber for pile in rugs of all types, virtually all 20th-century workshop carpets have been made with millspun cotton warps and wefts. Although subject to dry rot in humid environments, cotton is strong, it can be evenly and finely spun, and it is more stable and lies flatter than wool. Cotton was used in the foundations of antique rugs made in China and Persia and in the wefts of some late-19th-century East Caucasian rugs. Because the presence of cotton as a foundation material is often a clue to both the place and date of manufacture, it behooves collectors to acquaint themselves with the structural specifics of the weavings of most interest to them.

Silk has been used as both a pile and foundation material in very fine carpets through the centuries and is sometimes knotted into wool pile to impart a lustrous accent. Although mercerized cotton may be substituted for silk highlights in small rugs and bags, its principal use is in cheap souvenir rugs misleadingly described as "art silk."

THE PREPARATION OF FIBERS FOR WEAVING

Animal and vegetable fibers have one thing in common: initially, they are all a relatively tangled mass of filaments arranged in random manner and mixed with a good deal of trash. The fibers must first be disentangled and picked clean of burrs and twigs and sorted to separate dark- and light-colored strands. Wool is then combed to remove the shorter fibers and arrange the more desirable longer fibers so that they lie parallel to one another in an orderly fashion so as to produce when spun a strong, smooth-surfaced yarn capable of withstanding the stress of weaving.

Camel and goat hair fibers are usually used in their natural colors with minimal treatment before spinning. Sheep fleeces are normally washed after shearing, although some nomadic groups omit this initial washing, which may account for the extraordinary luster of some tribal pile work.

SPINNING

The spinning of wool in Eastern cultures is usually done by women; sometimes children share the task, and in some weaving groups it is considered an acceptable occupation for men, too. Collectors with first-hand knowledge of rug-weaving cultures always mention spinning as the one constant: the people spin while tending their flocks and herds, riding to and from pasturage, walking to fields and orchards, tending babies—in short, whenever both hands are not required to perform some other task. Hand spinning is usually accomplished with a spindle, a very simple device predating the wheel and used in many forms since before recorded history.

After the initial thread is spun by twisting the fibers into a continuous strand, several strands are twisted together in the opposite direction of the initial spin to form the yarn. The number of combined threads and the tightness of their twist determine a yarn's thickness and strength: two to four stout strands are firmly combined, or plied, for the warp yarns; the weft is thinner and more lightly plied, and the wool used for knotting the pile is even more loosely plied to avoid a crimped appearance and maintain a lustrous surface.

In the past, cotton was rarely used by nomads or isolated villagers because it had to be purchased from the outside, but improvements in transportation have made it more commonly available; an all-wool, vegetable-dyed product is no longer synonymous with tribal weaving. The wool and cotton used in most commercial rug-weaving workshops is cleaned, machine-spun, and dyed under controlled conditions to ensure uniformity.

DYEING

The wool may be washed again after spinning and before dyeing if enough grease remains in the wool to make it difficult for the dye to be evenly absorbed. Yarns used for the warp are seldom dyed, although threads from different-colored fleeces may be plied together. Weft yarns are sometimes dyed, and while the natural shades of pile yarns are occasionally used for design elements requiring ivory, gray, tan, brown, and black, they are usually colored with dyes. Traditionally, and in a few areas still, dyes were derived from naturally occurring sources, but these have long since been succeeded by synthetic dyes, which more easily fulfill industry requirements in regard to cost control and standardization. (The next chapter will discuss dyes in greater detail.)

THE WEAVING PROCESS

THE WARP

The first step in rug weaving is mounting the warp on the loom. The closeness of the warp threads, which depends on the thickness of the yarn chosen for the warp, determines to a major extent the fineness of the weaving to be done. Usually one or more of the warp yarns at the edges of the rug will be stouter than the others. It is customary to leave these edge warps free of pile knots but strengthened and fastened securely to the body of the rug with extra turns of the weft yarns. After the rug is completed, the edges are further reinforced with wool, goat hair, or cotton yarns, the methods and materials employed for these edge finishes being yet another clue to a rug's origin.

THE WEFT

Before the knotting of the pile threads on the warp threads begins, a section of interweaving of the warp is usually done—at the bottom of the rug, where the weaving commences, and again at the top after the knotted portion is completed—for the purpose of anchoring and protecting the pile knots from erosion. These plain-woven ends may terminate in a simple fringe created by the ends of the warp threads when the completed rug is cut from the loom, or the warps may be knotted, braided, or fashioned into a coarse, decorative netting. In some rugs a narrow band of plainweave is simply turned under and sewn to the back of the rug; on old Turkoman rugs, the red skirts may be up to 10 inches in length and narrowly striped in blue or otherwise decorated. In the case of much old Baluch work, the woven end skirts are elaborately patterned, the pile colors being repeated in traditional geometric designs. These characteristic rug end and edge finishes, whether plain or fancy, deserve the collector's notice and should be respected, insofar as possible, when repairs are undertaken. A later section on repair and restoration will discuss this question in greater detail.

After the initial band of plainweave has been completed and the first row of knots tied to the warps, a weft thread or threads are inserted. If two wefts are used, a common choice, the thread is transported through the shed from one side of the loom to the other in a single shoot, and immediately brought back through the reverse shed. If only one weft is inserted, a technique characteristic of the Hamadan district of Iran, then the reversed-shed weft is returned after the completion of the succeeding row of knots. Rugs like the South Caucasian Kazaks may have three or four red-dyed wefts clearly visible between each row of knots; in others, like the 19th-century Persian Kermans and Bijars, one or more of the wefts are hidden from sight within the structure. To the expert eye, the color, placement, and number of wefts laid in between each row of knots is as distinctive as a fingerprint.

To lay in wefts so that the same degree of tension is maintained throughout requires enormous skill, and although we take a well-made rug for granted and complain of its high cost, most of us would be very hard put indeed to duplicate it with our fumbling Western fingers.

KNOTTING THE PILE

The knots used in creating pile rugs are not tied knots in the same sense as those used by sailors and fishermen to securely attach boats to docks and hooks to fishing line. Rather, they are made by looping around the warp threads lengths of yarn held securely in place, not by the fashion in which they are looped but by the pressure exerted both by the adjacent knots and by the wefts, which are first passed between each row of knots and then pressed down very hard against them with a coarse, comblike tool known as a beater.

Most weavers use their fingers alone to "tie" the yarn, which is then cut with a knife snugged into the palm of one hand to produce the tufts that make up the resilient pile surface. In some Iranian districts a tool known as a *tikh*, which combines a knife with a hooked end, is used first to pull the pile yarn through the warps and then to cut the yarn after the knot is completed. In no case do oriental rug weavers employ short, precut pieces of yarn for their knots. As the knotting progresses, the weaver may roughly shear completed portions to check on the correctness of the emerging design, but the final shearing is saved for a master craftman to accomplish after the completed rug is removed from the loom.

The two knots used in the majority of oriental rugs are the Persian, an asymmetrical knot known traditionally as the *Senneh*—after a Persian weaving town—and the Turkish, or symmetrical knot, described in older publications and among traditional collectors as *Ghiordes*, the name of a famed Turkish weaving center.

The Turkish knot is employed primarily in Turkey and the Caucasus; both Persian and Turkish knots are used in Iran, and the Persian knot is found in Indian, Chinese, and the majority of Turkoman rugs. The decision to use one or the other of these knots is more a matter of tradition than any inherent advantage one has over the other, although a number of authorities believe it is easier to execute very finely detailed curvilinear patterns with the Persian knot in one of its several variations. With rare exceptions, the same type of knot is used throughout a single rug; occasionally, however, a Persian-knotted Turkoman will be found to have Turkish knots along its edges.

Because of the confusion generated by attaching the names of countries to an element of rug structure that disregards national boundaries, you will find the straightforward descriptive terms, symmetrical and asymmetrical, more and more frequently used in oriental rug publications.

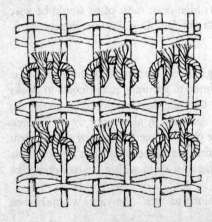

Symmetrical or Turkish knot with two wefts of equal tension passing between each row of knots.

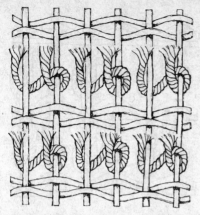
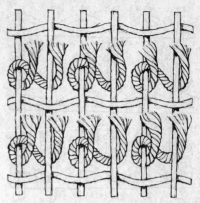

Asymmetrical or Persian knot opening to the left, with two wefts of equal tension passing between each row of knots.

Asymmetrical or Persian knot opening to the right, with one weft passing between each row of knots.

Both knots utilize adjacent warp threads: the yarn in the symmetrical Turkish knot lies across and on top of the pair of warps, the free ends passing around behind the warps and the two ends emerging together between them. In the asymmetrical Persian knot, one end of the yarn completely surrounds one warp thread while the other passes behind the second warp thread and comes up outside of it. Since the Turkish knot is symmetrically looped, the two little bumps or nodes it makes on the back of the rug almost always look about the same, although it may be coarser or finer depending on the particular rug. The space taken by a single Turkish knot is broader than it is high, which means that in a Turkish knotted rug there are fewer knots per inch horizontally than vertically.

Persian knots, because of their asymmetrical structure, may be looped so that the encircled warp thread is either the right or left thread of the pair. Knots opening to the left incline the pile to the right; knots open to the right incline it to the left.

In some rugs the tension of the wefts is deliberately varied so as to markedly displace one thread of the warp pair, thus pulling the emerging tufts of pile closer together. To more easily visualize this, hold up two fingers from one hand to represent the pair of warp threads, their knuckles becoming the two nodes of a single knot. When the fingers are in the same plane, both knuckle-nodes are clearly visible, but if you rotate your fingers from horizontal to the vertical, as if one finger-warp were being displaced by the pressure of a tightly drawn weft exerted upon it, then only one knuckle-node can be seen. Looking at the back of a rug, when

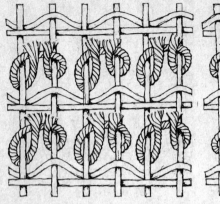 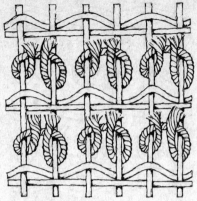

Symmetrical knots with two wefts
of varying tensions.

Symmetrical knots with two wefts
of varying tensions.

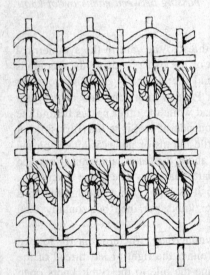 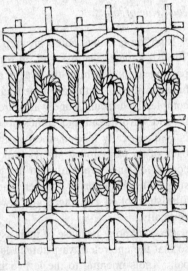

Asymmetrical knots with one loose,
one tight, weft.

Asymmetrical knots with two tight
wefts, one loose weft.

one of the knot nodes no longer lies parallel to the other, the result is a
series of squares created by one node rather than the rectangles two nodes
form. This allows the knot count along the rug's width to equal that of
the length, which in turn minimizes distortion of complicated designs
worked from an artist's drawing or cartoon.

As we have seen, there's more to the combination of warp, weft, and
pile knot than at first meets the eye. The sizes of the yarns, the position

of the warp, and the tension of the wefts affect a rug's construction and feel, the amount of detail possible in its design, and its wear characteristics. Is there such a thing as an ideal structure? The answer, of course, depends on the purpose a rug is intended to serve. For example, comparisons of collectible rugs on the basis of the density of the knot count fall wide of the mark, the fineness of a rug's knotting rarely being of primary interest to a sophisticated collector.

Three other types of knots are the *jufti*, the Tibetan, and the Spanish. The *jufti*, which is tied over four warps instead of two, is a wool-and-labor-saving variation of either the Turkish or Persian knot. It is sometimes interspersed with regular two-warp knots, but in either case its use is rarely acknowledged by the weavers who employ it and is considered a deceptive practice.

Tibetan weavers employ a unique looping technique in which a full row of loops is made at a time, each loop around a pair of warp threads and in combination with a guide rod that remains in place until wefts are inserted and beaten down, at which time the loops are cut and the guide rod removed. The Spanish knot, which is peculiar to antique Spanish carpets, completely encircles every other warp thread, the encircled thread alternating with each row.

A skilled weaver, working without interruptions, can tie up to a thousand knots in an hour. Rugs may be knotted by a single nomadic woman weaving traditional patterns from memory, by a group of weavers working from an artist's cartoon pinned to the loom above their flying fingers, or in a shop filled with looms of identical rugs woven in sections by teams of weavers following the knot sequence called out to them in a rhythmic drone. Even if each workshop weaver ties an average of 8,000 to 10,000 knots a day in the width of the carpet assigned her, only a few inches of a finely woven carpet can be knotted in a single day, and it can take a month or more to complete it.

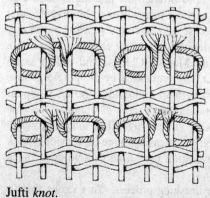

Jufti *knot.*

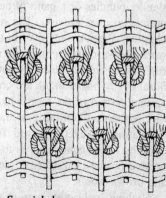

Spanish *knot.*

As a general rule, very finely knotted rugs are more expensive than those with an average knot count, but the breathtaking impact of superior examples of tribal weaving can induce collectors to part with very large sums to acquire relatively coarsely knotted, often quite small works of textile art.

The number of knots per square inch can vary from about 16 to 1,000, reaching an incredible 2,000 in a few extraordinarily fine Mughal prayer rugs. In the vast majority of carpets the number lies between 50 and 100; a knot count above 300 is uncommon, and little is gained aesthetically by increasing the count beyond 400 knots to the inch. If durability is an important consideration, a well-made carpet of middling coarseness will prove more satisfactory in service than a finely knotted one.

The wide variety of techniques employed throughout the weaving history of carpet-producing countries precludes a uniform knot-counting system. The only constant is that knots should be counted along the width first and along the length second. Always keep in mind, however, that although each pair of bumps in the rows you see across the width of a rug's back ordinarily represents one knot, only one bump will show in the case of a depressed warp structure, which is characteristically ribbed in appearance to a greater or lesser degree depending on the severity of the warp displacement. In written structural analyses of rugs, knot counts are expressed in terms of knots either per square inch or per square decimeter, which is 10 centimeters by 10 centimeters. There are approximately 2.54 centimeters to the inch.

FINISHING

Upon completion of the weaving of a rug, it is removed from the loom and finished either for domestic use or for the market. The warps may be cut and left as simple fringes or they may be knotted into either slender bundles or a band of netting to provide the pile knots additional protection from erosion. The roughly cut pile will then be given a final clipping: a quick once-over in the case of a nomadic weaver, but in city workshops a master craftsman undertakes a precise shearing suited to a rug's style and fineness of knotting. Modern Chinese and Indian pastel floral candy-box designs are commonly embossed by clipping a groove around certain of the motifs to throw them into opulent relief. Clipped, too, is the dark outlining of the traditional designs of much of the new generation of vegetable-dyed Turkish village rugs. The intent, frowned upon by many collectors, is to ape the pleasing three-dimensional look created by the characteristic deterioration over time of acid-dyed black and brown wools.

Washing is the final step in the finishing process. This varies from a simple cleansing with soap and water to treatment with chemicals to "soften" bright colors and to heighten the natural luster of the wool pile. Depending on the type and concentration of the chemicals used, the effect on the appearance and durability of the rug can range from mild to disastrous. A collector may accept a mild chemical wash in a furnishing rug, but any hint of past chemical treatment will adversely affect the desirability of an otherwise collectible piece.

FLAT-WOVEN RUGS

To repeat part of the definition quoted at the beginning of this chapter, flat-woven, or smooth-faced, rugs "consist essentially of two sets of threads . . . which cross each other at right angles and are interwoven."

Although some flat-woven work is very fine and intricately patterned—most notably the exquisite Senneh kilims—and some combine several techniques in a single piece, the examples most sought after by collectors are slit-tapestry kilims woven in simple, traditional geometric designs accented by bold figures and bands and blocks of brilliant color. They are the graphic art, the posters of the rug world, and enthusiasts consider the average pile rug fussy and insipid in comparison.

Authorities differ widely, sometimes heatedly, on how best to group and describe the various flat-weave techniques. For the beginning collector, understandably confounded by this large, bewilderingly complex class of weavings, I have adapted and updated Valerie Justin's introduction to the subject in her book *Flat-Woven Rugs of the World*, which is noteworthy for its clarity.

PLAIN WEAVE

Plain weave is produced by a simple alternate interlacing of the warp and weft. Depending on the thickness and spacing of the warp threads, the resulting fabric is said to be balanced, which means that neither the warp nor the weft predominates. If, however, either the warp or weft dominates, with one set of threads becoming more visible than the other, the result is known technically as a warp- or weft-faced weave.

Plain weave structure.

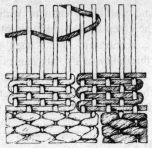

Tapestry weave used in kilims.

TAPESTRY WEAVE

Tapestry weave is a type of weft-faced plain weave used in kilims in which the warp is entirely concealed by beaten-down weft threads woven in color blocks rather than continuously across the width of the loom. These *dis*continuous colored wefts turning back into their own color blocks create a slit between the warps of one block and the adjoining color areas. This slit may be left open to serve as part of the design; it may be eliminated during the weaving by dovetailing the wefts from adjacent color areas on a single warp, or it may be sewn closed after the weaving is completed. Sometimes an added, or supplementary, weft in a contrasting color or sheathed in gold or silver is used to join and strengthen the slits, thus highlighting the basic design with added color or glitter.

Most flat-woven textiles have geometric designs, but curvilinear designs can be achieved by depressing the wefts unevenly with the beater, tightly pressing them in some areas and leaving them looser in others to express the soft curves of floral motifs. Known as eccentric wefting, outstanding examples of this tapestry-weave variation can be seen in the lovely Balkan-style floral kilims being reproduced today in western Turkey (see chapter on contemporary collectibles).

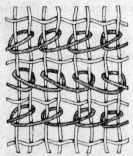

Soumak weave with shoots of weft alternating with warp-wrapping wefts.

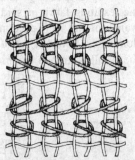

Soumak weave with shoots of weft alternating with warp-wrapping wefts.

SOUMAK WEAVE

In this technique, the wefts are not just interwoven with the warps; they actually wrap around them. Sometimes the rows of warp-wrapping wefts alternate with shoots of plain-weave wefts, in which case the wrapping wefts are considered supplementary rather than part of the basic structure.

Soumak warp-wrapping sequences can vary considerably from place to place and are dictated largely by tradition.

BROCADING

The term *brocade*, when applied to flat-woven articles, indicates the addition of *dis*continuous supplementary wefts or warps to a basic interwoven structure; therefore some soumak weaving in which the warp-wrapping technique, alternating with plainweave, is confined to a specific pattern or color area can be considered a type of brocading. Soumak brocade is usually a one-faced fabric in which the ends of the differently colored discontinuous wefts are left hanging loose on the back.

Other forms of brocading used in Turkey are the *cicim*, which often combines weft floats with brocaded accents easy to confuse with embroidery (see below), and the *zili*. The *zili* has many forms, the most distinctive of which presents a ribbed surface appearance.

WEFT-FLOAT

If continuous wefts are used to create a surface pattern, they are temporarily unincorporated into the basic structure by being "floated" on the back between pattern areas. The bands of weft-float decoration often seen on the skirts of old Baluch rugs provide an excellent example of this technique.

EMBROIDERY

The patterning techniques discussed above are employed during the weaving process. If decoration is added with a needle after the woven article is removed from the loom, the rug is said to have been embroidered.

A GLOSSARY OF RUG-WEAVING TERMS

Written descriptions of weaving and fiber manufacture often employ undefined technical terms bewildering to the layman. Below are definitions of the most commonly encountered puzzlers and a review of some of the terms used in this section.

Beating Up, Down, or In The process by which a weft or wefts are forced down tightly against a preceding row of knots. This is accomplished with a large multitined wood or metal forklike tool known as a beater.

Carding The process of brushing out, cleaning, and intermixing fibers with a pair of carders, which are paddle-like implements set with angled teeth of bent wire.

Cartoon A drawing on paper, usually graphed, showing a section of rug design. For large urban workshops, cartoons are prepared to order by artists, but a village weaver can buy cartoons at local markets and adapt them to suit her needs and fancies.

Combing Preparing wool for worsted (see below) spinning by combing out the short fibers and arranging the remaining longer fibers into smooth, parallel order.

Dovetailing To avoid slits in tapestry weaving, the discontinued wefts from adjacent color areas meet and share a common warp.

Fibers Commonly Used in Rug Making

   Cotton A soft fluffy vegetable fiber of almost pure cellulose with a flattened tubular structure. Although stronger wet than dry, moisture reduces its elasticity and, if prolonged, invites dry rot.

   Silk A protein animal product much finer and stronger than other animal fibers. A continuous silk filament of 400 to 1,000 yards can be reeled from a single silkworm cocoon.

   Wool and Hair An animal fiber made up of infinite numbers of small scales that allow it to bend without breaking. The quality of the fiber, whether from sheep, goat, or camel, depends on where the animal was pastured, its breeding and age, from what part of the animal and at what time of year the wool or hair was obtained, and whether it was alive or dead at the time of pulling or shearing.

   Animal fibers are stronger when dry than wet and although vulnerable to insect damage are not subject to dry rot.

Flat Weave A fabric created by the interweaving of horizontal threads (weft) with vertical (warp) threads in any one of a variety of interlocking techniques.

Fringe The cut warp ends of a rug removed from the loom.

Heddle The rods attached to the loom to which alternate warps are attached and drawn forward and back to create the space, or shed, to facilitate the passage of the weft threads.

Jufti A type of pile-making knot whose looping encompasses more than the usual single pair of warps. Although the resulting product is considered inferior, it is sometimes employed as a labor- and material-saving device.

Knots, Pile The knots most commonly used to loop pile yarns around the warps are the symmetrical Turkish knot, also known as the *Ghiordes*, and the asymmetrical Persian, or *Senneh*, knot. These knots and a few of their many variations are described and illustrated in the text preceding this glossary.

Pick Alternate term for shoot, the passage of one thread of weft through the warp threads. This passage of the pick may also be described as being "laid in the shed."

Ply See *Yarn Ply and Twist* below.

Rove or Roving A drawn out and slightly twisted roll or sliver of fiber ready for spinning.

Selvage The edges formed by the passage of the weft yarns around the bundles of warp threads that bound the sides, sometimes reinforced after weaving is completed by overwrapping with goat hair or overcasting in wool.

Shed The space formed by the separation of the warp threads into two planes and through which the shuttle passes carrying the weft thread. This space can be created either by use of a heddle (see above) or by a more primitive device known as a shed stick (see below).

Shed Stick A long flat stick threaded through alternate warp strings. By turning the stick on edge, a space yielding a reasonably satisfactory shed is formed.

Shoot See *Pick*, above.

Shuttle A device around which weft threads are looped to prevent the yarns from becoming entangled on the floor and to facilitate the passage of the weft through the warp shed. If several colors are used, a shuttle will be required for each.

Skirt The bands of plainweave on the ends of some types of rugs are known as skirts when their length exceeds approximately 3 inches. These skirts may be of a single color or striped or otherwise decorated with either pile or flat-woven motifs.

Spindle, Drop A device consisting, in one common version, of a shaft approximately a foot in length to which, near the bottom, a disk-shaped weight is joined. The shafts are usually wooden; the weights may be of wood or clay or fashioned from metal coins. Light of weight and eminently portable, it is the tool of choice for spinning yarns in the Middle East.

Spinning The process whereby animal or plant fibers are twisted into strong continuous strands suitable for weaving.

Warp The chief foundation thread of fabrics; also, the strong yarns running from end to end on a loom and interwoven with weft threads, which are usually thinner and more loosely spun.

Weft The thread or yarn interwoven with the warp threads and carried on a shuttle through a space, known as the shed, created between them.

In pile rugs, wefts are employed to separate and anchor the rows of pile knots and strengthen the selvedges. In flat-woven textiles, various techniques employ wefts that are discontinuous, supplementary, or floated, terms described in the preceding section on flat weaves.

Woof A term sometimes used for weft.

Woolen Woolen yarns are made from carded and interlaced short fibers, which, when spun, make a light, fluffy yarn unsuitable for rugs because of its inability to withstand the abrasive stress of the weaving process, much less the wear it would receive underfoot.

Worsted A process whereby long fibers of wool are combed parallel and spun into a strong, smooth-surfaced yarn. Oriental rugs are traditionally made from long, lustrous worsted-spun fibers, which acquire a characteristic paintbrush-like tip with wear. The term is also applied to a suiting cloth made from worsted-spun yarn.

Yarn Ply and Twist When fibers are spun into yarn, the twist of the threads is described either as "Z" or "S," depending upon the direction of the slant of the fibers. In the structural analyses supplied for rugs in some publications, the technical descriptions of warp, weft, and pile yarns

"S" and "Z" spun yarns.

needed to determine a rug's provenance appear in an abbreviated form. For example, a "Z2S" notation for a warp yarn indicates a makeup of two single Z-spun strands S-plied together.

The initial spun thread is termed a single. Combined singles are a ply; two singles twisted together are 2-ply; three singles, 3-ply, and so on. When yarn singles are plied, the twist is usually opposite to that of the initial twist of the singles. Plied yarns can also be twisted together—in the direction opposite to that of the initial ply—to produce the stout outer warps needed to strengthen the selvedges.

The tightness of the twist imparted to the yarn in the various stages of twisting and plying is determined, in part, by the use to which it will be put. Warp yarn, the principal foundation thread and subject to continual stress during the weaving process, is the tightest and stoutest; weft yarn, less so; and pile yarn, the least tight and thick of the three.

For More Information

A detailed examination of rug structures and the variety of weaving techniques employed in the oriental rug-weaving areas over the centuries far exceeds the scope of an introductory guide. Dozens of books have been written about flat weaves alone. The annotated list of books and periodicals in the Resource Guide will help you choose publications applicable to your particular area of interest.

DYES USED IN ORIENTAL RUGS

Rug enthusiasts can chat about the intricacies of warps, wefts, and knotting with a commendable degree of open-mindedness, and even an exchange of opinion about the provenance of a given rug may provoke only coolly discourteous disagreement. The topic guaranteed to transform discussion into a heated argument verging on naked aggression is natural versus synthetic dyes, probably because to scholars and many collectors the presence of synthetic dyes is *prima facie* evidence of inferiority.

Some respected experts maintain that since it is entirely possible to duplicate synthetically even the most subtle of natural shades, it is rather silly to dismiss a rug as unworthy of collection solely on the basis of synthetic dyes. They point out that when synthetic dyes were first introduced into remote areas, tribal weavers viewed their brilliance as special; the drawbacks as yet unknown, it was only their expense that limited their use to cotton and silk accents. As a clincher, these experts cite the fact that in some cases the only way to distinguish between a natural and a synthetic dye is through laboratory analysis, an expensive procedure sometimes necessary for scholarly research to establish beyond question whether or not a rug was made before 1860, the date when synthetic dyes were first known to be used in Middle Eastern rug-weaving districts.

But to the connoisseur, whose interest extends beyond technical minutiae to the historic and ethnic context in which carpets were woven, there is much more to the impression of color than the actual color itself. The shimmering pointillist effect of fine antique carpets is not the result of conscious planning or what we are now pleased to term quality control. Rather, it is to a significant degree a felicitous, accidental by-product of their manufacture.

The subtle shadings of pile color known as *abrash* occur because it is virtually impossible to avoid variations in color from one dye lot to another when using natural materials. Vegetable dye color is the product not merely of a particular plant variety but of the conditions in which it is grown—altitude, soil, moisture provided, and maturity at time of harvest—and the mineral content of the water with which the dyebath is prepared, all of which are largely a matter of circumstance. The qualities of the wool to be dyed—its natural color, degree of oiliness, and the varying thicknesses of hand-spun and plied fibers—also affect the way dye is absorbed and its color reflected.

In the past, since time was not a commodity, the weaver employing this vegetable-dyed wool could lavish upon each rug the care necessary to knot precisely the symbols and patterns reflecting her tribal or Islamic traditions, often including a few idiosyncratic touches of her own. Then, mellowed by sun and dust and smoke, the pile developed a patina through decades of respectful use. A truly old rug gains thereby an authenticity that, to the educated eye and sensibility, distinguishes one carpet from another no matter how similar they may appear to the layman.

Because the supply of natural dyes has always been limited and uncertain and their successful employment required considerable skill, the availability of synthetic dyes that could be measured and used with a precision impossible with vegetable dyes was not only encouraged but necessitated by the late-19th-century revival of the carpet trade. Carpets had been made for export before then, of course, but largely for a limited, wealthy clientele of discriminating aristocrats. The era of the pretty 9 × 12 designed for Western parlors had yet to arrive.

It was this later commercialization, aimed at an international market of comfortable middle-class folk, that introduced standardization in both carpet sizes and colors. After all, the reasoning went, how could a logical pricing structure be developed unless rugs without "unsightly" variations in color could be supplied to suit Western homes and tastes? Unfortunately, many of the early synthetic dyes were neither light- nor water-fast, and their use in otherwise well-designed, expertly knotted carpets was disastrous to the point where they were temporarily banned from both Persian and Turkish workshops. But synthetic dyes have improved enormously over the years, and both retailers and buyers can be justly satisfied with the choice offered by the variety of competently dyed rugs available in the market today.

Will a new, synthetically dyed carpet maintain its value? Assuming one chooses a quality piece to begin with, it undoubtedly will. Its relationship to an antique carpet made in a traditional context will remain that of a fine reproduction; but as time goes by, this distinction, including the ability to make it, may become blurred as copies more and more resemble the real thing.

I was amused recently to see in a department store a pile of identical scatter rugs that, from a distance, looked extraordinarily like 19th-century Turkoman tribal weavings. The color was the dark browny-red typical of old Yomud rugs; they had a subtle *abrash*, and even the border design was slightly irregular, as it often is in genuine nomadic work. These machine-made Belgian products would not fool anyone upon close inspection and were not intended to do so, but when the Middle Eastern rug workshops attain the sophistication of the Belgian and Dutch copyists and dyers, a new generation of hand-knotted reproductions will surely kindle hotter arguments than ever among future oriental rug enthusiasts.

NATURAL DYES

All dyes have a chemical makeup. The advantage of natural dyes is that even the most brilliant lack the uncompromising quality of modern synthetics as they are commonly employed by Eastern dyers, and time and sun will not appreciably mellow these almost aggressively fast dyes.

Natural dyes, even when expertly made and applied, yield by their very nature imprecise results that successful commercial synthetic dyes, again because of their very nature, do not. Although colors from natural dyes can be vibrant, they are not "pure" colors in the sense synthetic colors are because the decocted plants and insects contain many chemical constituents; therefore, although natural colors can be produced within specific ranges, it is rarely possible to exactly reproduce a particular hue. On the other hand, because of the naturally occurring chemical "overlaps," natural dyes are almost never disharmonious. If one considers this imprecision to be aesthetically superior, then synthetic dyes straightforwardly used will not satisfy, and synthetics manipulated to simulate the honest imprecision of natural dyes will deeply offend.

Part of the charm of natural dye materials lies in the romance of an art that was well developed by 2500 B.C. and in the sounds of names like indigo, saffron, and madder, which echo of the pyramids, Imperial Rome, Persian dynasties, and the black tents of nomads. Below is a list of the more commonly used natural dye materials—some dyestuffs are used universally; others are only locally available—and the metal salts, known as mordants, that are introduced to create a chemical bond between the dye and the fiber, as some dyes do not unite readily with animal fibers unaided. The name comes from the latin word *mordere*, which means "to bite."

INDIGO *(Indigofera tinctoria; Isatis tinctoria)*

Indigo is the most commonly used of all dyes, closely followed by madder. One oriental rug authority has said that these two dyes plus a few mordants and undyed dark and light wools make up the basic range of color. Exquisite rugs have been created from nothing more. Indigo has to undergo a complex process in a fermentation vat because the dye obtained from the leaves, indogotin, is not water-soluble. The natural and synthetic forms of indogotin, both of which may be obtained as a powder from dye supply houses, are chemically indistinguishable.

There are a number of ways of changing the insoluble blue powder to a solution. One traditional method, said to be the secret of the heavenly blue in some antique Turkoman carpets, is to steep the powder in the urine of very young boys. Whether this or a less exotic method is employed, the yarn is first dipped in the resulting greenish-yellow solution, then lifted out and exposed to the air, whereupon the coloring matter deposited on the yarn unites with the oxygen and turns blue. It is an entrancing process. Repeated immersions and airings deepen the blue to any desired shade. To produce greens and purples, indigo-dyed yarns may be mordanted with the appropriate metal salts and overdyed with yellow or red dyes, respectively.

MADDER *(Rubia tinctorum)*

Another of the most ancient dyestuffs, the plant from which madder is obtained grows both wild and under cultivation. Its color-fastness ranks very high. The dye is obtained from the red material beneath the outer bark of roots at least three years old. The roots are usually dried and powdered in order to release the color readily into the dyebath.

Madder yields a good clear red, varying in hue from orange-red to garnet to violet, depending on the proportion of the color-influencing compounds present in the plants used to make the dye and the minerals used for mordanting the wool. Madder rose is a beautiful clear, light, ruby red commonly seen in old Baluch tribal rugs; in the Melas area of Turkey, a strong pure orange is obtained from madder growing locally in the wild. A blue-toned red found in Chinese rugs is derived from a related plant, *Rubia codifolia*.

COCHINEAL *(Dactylopius coccus)*

Cochineal is a red dye obtained from an insect cultivated on cactus plants, principally in Mexico and Central America. One pound of cochineal powder contains about 70,000 of the dried insects. The Spanish introduced the dye to Europe in the early 1500s, but it was not used in Eastern carpets to any great extent until the 19th century.

The color, depending on the mordants used, usually has a cooler tonality than madder red and ranges from an orange-toned scarlet red through blue-toned crimson to purple. For a long time, the term *crimson* was applied solely to the bluish-red dye derived from either of two insects: the kermes, or oak shield louse, and the cochineal. Another insect-derived red dye is lac. Lac was used in early Persian carpets and extensively in India, but kermes-based dyes have not yet been found in any Eastern carpet.

WELD *(Reseda luteola)*

Weld, an annual herb growing about 3 feet high, is considered the best source of yellow dye and is almost as fast to light as indigo and madder.

All parts of the plant except the roots can be used; approximately 3 ounces of plant material is required for each ounce of wool. Depending on the mordants used, a bright yellow to gold to yellow-green may be obtained, and an indigo overdye results in a lovely medium green.

ISPEREK, OR ISPARUK *(Delphinium sulphuraeum)*

Although this milkwort is widely used as a yellow dye, the color obtained is apt to fade to cream upon prolonged exposure to light.

OAK *(Quercus,* in variety); TANNER'S SUMACH *(Rhus coriaria)*

Black and dark brown dyes are created when wool mordanted with iron salts are treated with the tannins extracted from these and other plant sources. The disadvantage is that the effect of the combined iron and tannin is corrosive, and wool thus treated tends to become brittle, especially when exposed to light for long periods. This effect is so well known that black-dyed wools used in reproductions of old rugs are often clipped to approximate an antique look.

There are many other plants used for dyeing, and to the very knowledgeable eye the colors they produce are as significant a clue to a rug's origin as its weave and design. Pomegranate, saffron, buckthorn, Persian berries, turmeric, and camomile produce yellows, and henna, a soft yellow-red. A green dye is extracted from ripe turmeric berries and from various combinations of dyes and mordants.

MORDANTS

Mordants, which provide the chemical bond necessary to fix dyestuffs to wool and silk fibers, affect color tones significantly. Tin is used to brighten a color; iron salts to darken or "sadden." Unfortunately, both of these agents can, unless carefully used, render wool harsh and brittle. Many old Baluch rugs exhibit an interesting but unintentional three-dimensional effect because of this corrosive quality, the dark browns and blacks all but disappearing long before the reds and blues show any signs of wear. Other minerals used for mordanting are alum, chrome, tannin, and carbonate of soda. This last, an alkali, can also adversely affect animal fibers.

Whether natural or synthetic dyes are employed, the Middle Eastern dyer traditionally colors the fibers after they have been spun into yarn. If mordants are used, the metal salts, having been dissolved in liquid, are applied first. The yarn is then dried and immersed in large vats of the colored dyeing solutions and allowed to remain for varying amounts of time depending on the shade desired. Succeeding uses of the same dyebath will produce paler and paler hues. When the wool is removed from the vats, it should be rinsed until the water runs clear, as even a normally fast color will bleed from the yarn at a later washing if it is insufficiently rinsed after dyeing. The wool is then dried again before collection or purchase by the weaver.

Natural colors are softened by prolonged exposure to strong light, and Western eyes used to the mellow look of even strongly colored old vegetable-dyed rugs are often jolted by the brightness of new vegetable-dyed wool, not to mention antique rugs, like those in the Black Church in Brasov, Romania, that have been shielded from light for centuries.

In old pieces made by some Turkoman tribal weavers, undyed natural brown wool is often found to have lightened over the years. Among the vegetable dyes, yellows—except those derived from weld—are particularly subject to fading. Greens achieved through an overdyeing of indigo and yellow often revert to blue on the front of the piece, where sun has faded the yellow, while the original green persists on the back. Indigo, which is deposited on fibers rather than bonded with them by mordants, is subject to slight color loss over time through abrasion.

SYNTHETIC DYES

By the end of the 19th century a method for the commercial synthesis of indigo had been developed, and this, coupled with an earlier synthesis of madder—a dye called alizarin—signaled an end to the commercial use of natural dyes in the West. However, although synthetics were introduced into rug-weaving areas as early as 1860, natural dyes were also used in Eastern rugs well into the 20th century, and a revival is well under way, most notably in Turkey.

The color-fastness of dyes to light and water has always presented dyers and chemists with major problems. In fact, the early history of organic chemistry consists largely of investigations of dye-making materials and methods. The first commercial production of a synthetic organic chemical was the dye mauveine, which was more or less accidently discovered in 1856 by a young British chemist, William Henry Perkin, through the oxidation of the coal-tar derivative, aniline. Unfortunately, mauveine and its early successors, all derived from aniline, proved to be notoriously fugitive.

Within ten years of the discovery of mauveine, a more brilliant color known variously as fuchsine (fooks-een) or magenta, became commercially available. Fuchsine rapidly supplanted the paler mauve, and its presence in late-19th-century rugs is best detected by its absence: old rugs with areas of pale dirty gray or beige on the face often retain a trace of the original magenta on the back.

When a dye fades, this does not mean the coloring substance vanishes into thin air. Rather, a chemical change, triggered by light or moisture or another incompatible substance, transforms the original dye into a new compound, which may be colorless, less highly colored, or differently colored. The principal objection to the early synthetics is that instead of merely softening to a paler hue, as the natural dyes do, the entire tonality of one or two colors shifted enough to destroy the color balance of the rug as a whole.

These unstable dyes were so unsuited to rug making that by 1910 their use was, as mentioned earlier, banned in Persian workshops and in some Turkish districts, although the policing of these bans was spotty and in remote areas virtually impossible. Nevertheless, large numbers of weavers returned to the use of naturally dyed yarns until later in the century when more reliable synthetic dyes became available.

Unfortunately, the bad reputation earned by the early dyes became unjustly attached to later synthetics as well, all of which became popularly and inaccurately known as "coal-tars" or "anilines" whether or not they were derived from coal tars or shared their undesirable characteristics. Not all synthetic dyes used today are reliable, but the color-fastness of the better varieties is good to excellent. Whether or not one likes the *quality* of the color thus obtained is a subjective judgment best left to individuals to make for themselves, but when cost is an issue, a new, well-made, synthetically dyed decorative furnishing carpet can provide many years of trouble-free service.

The chemical makeup of modern synthetic dyes is extremely complex, and an explanation of the system used to assign them into chemical family groups is not only beyond my ability to convey but unnecessary for the purpose at hand. More to the point is a simplified version of the pragmatic classification system used by professional cleaners and textile conservators charged with solving problems arising from the cleaning and restoration of valuable textiles.

The following definitions apply to animal fibers only. Cotton, or cellulose, presents the dyer with problems quite different from wool or silk; and since the use of dyed cotton as a pile fiber is very limited, it will be less confusing if it is eliminated from the discussion altogether.

DIRECT BASIC DYES

The aniline dyes are basic dyes, not in the "fundamental" sense of the word but rather because the color is absorbed directly from a neutral or weakly alkaline (i.e. base) solution, although sometimes a small quantity of acid is added to very hard water to facilitate absorption. As a class, the basic dyes are powerful, clear, and brilliant in hue and easily applied to wool and silk, but they have only fair to poor fastness to light, some fading so rapidly and markedly as to be known as fugitive. A late and relatively stable dye of this type is Rhodamine B, a bright fluorescent pink found in some late-19th-century Turkoman Ersari tribal rugs. The use of anilines was widespread in all of the traditional rug-weaving areas except among the Turkoman tribes of western Turkestan.

DIRECT ACID AND AZO-DYES

The first acid dyes, in which color is absorbed from an acid solution, were developed in 1862, but they did not become commercially available until the 1880s. They too are brilliant and easily applied to animal fibers, and although some acid dyes present the same problems due to lack of fastness as do the basic dyes, they were widely employed in the latter 19th century and in some areas still are.

Among the acid dyes used in the late 19th and early 20th centuries was Ponceau 2R, also known as Russian Red, which is a clear, bright red used extensively by Turkoman and Caucasian dyers. Although relatively fast to light, it sometimes stains the warps and may run when washed. Other acid dyes in common usage as determined by laboratory analysis were Amaranth, Crystal Scarlet, and Rocceline, a very unstable wine red found in late Yomud work. The dyes Orange II and Croceine Orange were used in the Caucasus and Turkey respectively to produce a fast color whose stridency persists long after adjacent areas of pile dyed with fugitive anilines have faded to beige or gray.

The wide variability in fastness is not surprising in light of the fact that there are three main classes of acid dyes, ranging from those freely soluble in water and possessing moderate fastness to the less soluble, more complex azo dyes with a high degree of fastness. To tribal or village weavers, simplicity of preparation and ease of application may be more desirable than long-range stability.

MORDANT AND PREMETALLIZED DYES

As we have seen, mordanting is employed extensively with dyes made from natural materials to facilitate their absorption and promote fastness, and the same principle applies to synthetic dyes. The azo dyes mentioned above displayed superior fastness when applied to mordanted wool, and in the 1940s a class of superior synthetics known as chrome or premetallized dyes was introduced to Eastern rug workshops. These dyes, which incorporate potassium bichromate as a mordant, are available in a wide spectrum of colors that are fast to light, water, and alkali. Chrome-dyed rugs considered too bright for modern Western tastes are often given a chemical wash to subdue their vibrancy.

Although antique rugs known to be dyed entirely with vegetable colors can also be very vividly colored, it is not the brightness of synthetics that connoisseurs consider objectionable but rather the uncompromising, hard-edged quality that results from their controlled, even, and thorough absorption.

DATING RUGS BY THE PRESENCE OF SYNTHETIC DYES

Many dealers and collectors can date rugs quite accurately by color alone, but this method can lead the overconfident novice badly astray. The following generalizations can be used as a rough guide to determining the age of rugs unless a substantial sum of money is riding on the judgment. In that case, the advice of an objective expert is always to be preferred.

To recapitulate, synthetic dyes were introduced into all of the rug-weaving areas around 1860–1870, except for rugs made by nomadic tribes too isolated to receive the dubious benefits of these wonders of organic chemistry. However, since rugs dyed entirely with natural materials were and are still being made, their exclusive use is not a guarantee of antiquity.

Mauve to Magenta

The earliest aniline dyes produced fugitive colors including a mauve, two magentas, blue, green, and purple. The original color may still be visible on the light-protected backs of areas of dirty gray-beige pile. If the pile is relatively unworn, the color may also be detected at the base of the knots. The presence of these dyes dates a rug to roughly 1865–1900. Purple dyes persisting on the face of a rug may be synthetic, but an aniline dye would have long since faded away.

Bright Orange

The acid dyes Orange II and Croceine Orange are characteristic of some late-19th- and early-20th-century Caucasian and Turkish rugs, particularly a well-made but depressing East Caucasian Shirvan type in which they are seen in conjunction with indigo blue, a faded-to-gray fuchsine or later type of listless purple, and a pale blue-green, the green and orange often staining the warps. Be careful, however, not to dismiss all strong orange hues as synthetic: madder, depending on where the plants grow, yields an authoritative orange, too.

Red

Even if one has had the opportunity to examine hundreds of rugs of all types and ages, there is no foolproof way to distinguish between the many natural and synthetic reds by color alone. Strident reds and pinks are apt to be synthetic, as are dark, dull wine reds, but a more reliable clue is bleaching at the tips of the pile fibers and dye runs ranging from blatant bleeding to faint pink blushes and staining of the warps and fringes. Bleeding red dyes have ruined quantities of carefully woven, handsomely patterned late-19th- and early-20th-century Turkoman rugs. Rugs of good quality made since about 1940 are apt to have stable reds, but inexpensive village pieces should be inspected for telltale blushes and stained fringes.

Blues

Natural indigo blues, as well as those prepared from the chemically identical synthetic indigo, are reliably light- and water-fast; but since they are pigmented colorings, they are subject as they age to partial removal through abrasion, particularly in flat-woven textiles. The process is gradual, and the effect is usually too slight to be considered aesthetically objectionable. A blue that bleeds is sure to be synthetic.

Yellows and Greens

Since yellows and greens obtained from most natural sources are subject to fading to one degree or another, uniformly vivid shades of either color should, as a general rule, arouse suspicion. On the other hand, if weld was the source, the older the carpet, the clearer and purer the yellow is apt to be.

CHEMICAL WASHES

The strident quality of synthetic dyes gave rise to the practice of using chemical washes to soften them. The strong reds in Mahals and Sarouks imported from Iran in the 1920s were first bleached to rose and then sometimes painted by hand to a then popular deep maroon. The candy-box pastels of post–World War II Kerman rugs and the golden Afghans of the 1960s were also created by chemical washes, and the majority of modern synthetically dyed carpets are routinely treated in this fashion to a lesser or greater degree depending on the desired effect. Although in some cases the color-mellowing, luster-enhancing result may be considered an improvement, the process tends to rob wool of its natural lubrication and, depending on the chemicals used, decrease its ability to withstand wear.

Always keep in mind that old rugs in mint condition will have clearer, fresher colors than a rug of the same age and type in average condition, and that the variations in hue characteristic of rugs made with natural dyes are, if not too pronounced, considered desirable.

Before deciding to buy a particular rug, you should view it in daylight. Any retail dealer reluctant to oblige you should be regarded with suspicion. Artificial light enhances the natural beauty of pile knotted with high-quality, lustrous wool, but daylight is preferred for judging the quality of the color and the detection of dye runs. It is not always possible to inspect a rug in daylight at auction previews, but if it is, insist on it even if the staff clearly considers you a nuisance.

For More Information

Several of the books and periodicals listed in the Resource Guide will provide you with additional information about dyes and the approximate dates of the introduction of synthetics into specific weaving areas, but nothing you read will be of much help to you in visually distinguishing synthetic from natural dyes. For this, you will need to see many rugs, preferably in the company of knowledgeable dealers or collectors. If an oriental rug society meets at a reasonably convenient distance from your home, you should apply for membership if only to take advantage of the frequently scheduled postlecture show-and-tell sessions.

ORIENTAL RUG SIZES, FORMATS, AND MOTIFS

Oriental rug formats and motifs are as traditional as the weaving techniques used to incorporate them into useful and decorative textiles. Creativity in the Western sense has little place in a culture that regards innovation as a threat to traditional values, and rugs hailed by Western collectors as unique invariably prove to be unusual variations on very old themes.

A successful rug as judged by Western connoisseurs usually excels in three areas:

1. The choice, clarity, and use of color.
2. The proportional relationship between the size of the rug and the elements within it—field, medallions, spandrels, borders—and of the elements to each other.
3. The selection, execution, and spacing of the motifs.

Until the last quarter of the 19th century, the sizes of rugs made as floor coverings were dictated by traditional manners of furnishing; in fact, size alone can indicate to a knowledgeable collector the probable age and intended use of a rug. In addition to rugs, weavers working at simple wooden looms provided the knotted-pile and flat-woven textiles needed in a variety of shapes and sizes for domestic storage, the transport of goods and crops, and decorative trappings suited to a way of life that was either wholly or seasonally nomadic.

In Persian dwellings, four narrow rugs were arranged in a long rectangle, one across the top with the other three placed side by side at right angles to it, the flanking pair typically narrower than the middle rug. This arrangement allowed for considerably more flexibility than the squarer room-size rug made later for the Western market, and these old rugs—cataloged by auction houses as "long" or "corridor" rugs—are often ideally suited to modern open-plan houses. The large triclinium or audience carpets sometimes seen at auction are a late-19th-century development aping the look of the traditional arrangement of four.

Aside from custom, another reason rugs tended to be long and narrow is that although the length of a carpet woven on a roller-beam workshop loom is limited only by the capacity of the beam, its width is fixed by

Traditional arrangement of carpets.

the width of the loom, which in turn is dictated by the space, rarely ample, available for it. The lengths of the great carpets in museum collections are generally two or three times their widths, and most antique rugs and kilims of Middle Eastern manufacture are similarly proportioned.

The sizes of smaller rugs made by village and tribal weavers were—and still are—determined by domestic as well as market considerations but are usually found to have proportions of 2 to 3—that is, roughly 1½ feet in length for every foot in width.

My choice of the adverb "roughly," by the way, was deliberate. A case in point is the *dozar*, the term long applied in the trade to rugs approximately 4½ × 7 feet—which, incidentally, is about the widest rug a woman weaving alone can comfortably manage. Although the *zar* is a traditional Persian unit of measure—a *dozar* is two *zars*—different villages had *zars* of different lengths, ranging between 41 and 44 inches. This degree of variance may seem odd by Western standards, but measurement in the weaving countries, according to Leslie Stroh, editor of *Rug News*, is like situational ethics:

> If you know that he knows that you know, then you *both* know, and the definition (of size) depends not on some abstract measure, but on the reality that both buyer and seller are confronting. There are small dozars and big dozars; there are dozars that actually measure correctly and dozars that do not . . . [yet all] come into the marketplace with both parties thinking of them as dozars.

Although equating long and narrow rugs with age is usually safe, the reverse is not necessarily true. The shape of some antique Chinese and Turkish rugs and Southwest Persian Afshar tribal rugs approach the square; it wasn't until the turn of the century, however, in response to a booming revival of Western interest in oriental rugs, that weavers throughout the rug-producing areas began making the squarer sizes that in terms of rug dimensions persist to this day.

Although it makes much more artistic sense to place a rug in a room so that the design and color, uncluttered by furniture, may be fully appreciated, the Western tendency has always been to blanket the floor with a rug upon which furniture is then plunked. For this reason, although in this country all sizes of hand-knotted floor coverings are customarily referred to as "rugs," the term "carpet" will be employed here for the large room-size rugs popular in Western homes.

This use of oriental rugs as a sort of patterned carpeting required a reworking of traditional designs, not all of which could be happily adapted to the new proportions; attempts to scale down for scatter rugs the dignified, spacious designs popular in room-size carpets were even less successful. In an effort to surmount these problems, artists commissioned by Western entrepreneurs began experimenting with combining traditional motifs in new ways; and once the barrier of tradition was breached, entirely new patterns soon followed. The most successful of these command good prices today: those commissioned by the Ziegler manufactories in Arak, Iran, the old Sultanabad of Persia, are an example of adapted designs; Sarouks featuring detached floral sprays represent new ones.

A bewildering variety of names can be found attached in the oriental rug literature to every size and shape of woven article. No standard terminology exists: each weaving area has its own name for articles whose purpose remains the same no matter where it is made, and further confusion results when these native terms are translated into the languages of Westerners writing about them. In addition, collectors have decided preferences, verging on snobberies, about the terminology used within their specialties.

Once a collector has chosen an area of concentration, a vocabulary of terms appropriate to it can soon be acquired via the literature and rug society lectures and in conversation with specialist dealers and other collectors. Here, in the interest of clarity, I plan to rely with as few exceptions as possible on descriptive and use-specific terms, beginning with rugs woven as floor furnishings. The fact that today's collectors may consider the best and oldest of them too rare or fine for such a plebian function is, for this purpose, irrelevant.

RUG SIZES

The units in which the measurements of a rug are expressed depend, if it is new, upon where the rug was made, or, in the case of old rugs, where the description is encountered. Foreign dealers and publications employ the metric system; American dealers and auction house catalogs supply dimensions in feet and inches, except for Sotheby's and Christie's in which both are given. For simplicity's sake, the sizes of the arbitrary groupings of rugs that follow are given in feet only; but readers should bear in mind that in the case of old rugs variations from exact dimensions are much more the rule than the exception.

MAT

Mats are small rugs, roughly 2 × 3 feet, used as bedside, doorway, and fireside rugs and room accents. Many mats used for these purposes were originally the topsides of covers for long, narrow pillows used on low couches or to support the back when sitting on a floor rug. In some cases the flat-woven backs are still attached. If the borders are unequal in width and if there are plain-woven tabs along one edge and a skirt along the other, the mat was probably the face of a bag used either for the transport or storage of goods.

SCATTER

Larger than a mat and smaller than an area rug, scatter rugs range from 2 × 4 to about 4 × 6 in varying proportions. Most of the old rugs in this category were produced by women weaving alone on home looms, and the naive, exuberant charm of the best of them is prized by collectors.

AREA (Dozar)

Approximately 4½ × 7 feet, rugs in this category can make a design statement far surpassing their modest, easily stored size. Included in this group are the enormously popular thick-pelted, boldly colored, geometrically patterned South Caucasian Kazaks as well as low-piled, elegantly detailed, jewel-toned Sarouk Ferahans.

LONG OR CORRIDOR RUG

These are rugs originally made for the traditional layout of four. They range in size from (a) 5–6 feet wide by 10–12 feet long, (b) 6–8 feet by 16–20 feet, and (c) 3–4 feet by 16–20 feet.

RUNNER

Although the narrowest of the long rugs are often used as runners, they are less likely than rugs designed for that specific use to have designs repeated in columnar fashion. Whichever type you choose, rugs used on stairs should be sturdily constructed and in good condition. A glossy, long-piled, loosely woven rug is unlikely to prove satisfactory for that purpose.

ROOM-SIZE

Rugs intended to cover most of the floor area of a given room range in size from a Western-size 8 × 10 or more traditionally proportioned 9 × 11 up to 24 × 14 feet; those exceeding that size are often referred to as palace carpets.

The large majority of older room-size carpets are of Persian manufacture; today they are as likely to be Indian, Pakistani, Romanian, or Chinese.

PRAYER

Prayer rugs always have an arch-shaped element at one end—rarely, both ends—representing the *mihrab* set in the wall of the mosque facing the holy city of Mecca and symbolizing the gateway to paradise. Prayer rugs have for centuries been a popular item of commerce and have been made mostly in scatter sizes in a variety of designs and materials, including extremely finely knotted silks intended as luxurious wall hangings.

Only a minority of the vast number of rugs made with the prayer format have been employed by the faithful for that purpose. Enjoined to use what is defined simply as a clean spot facing Mecca, a length of easily carried sacking or toweling serves the needs of many devout Muslims for the prayers they observe five times daily. Prayer rugs are, however, customarily used as such in mosques, which have been given them over the centuries as tokens of reverence and thanksgiving.

RUG FORMATS

PILE RUG FORMATS

Although the motifs used in oriental rugs can, when their variations are included, number in the hundreds, the ways in which these elements are organized can be reduced to six basic formats. A seventh, notable for its *lack* of organization, ends the listing.

Medallion

The classic court and urban workshop rug design features a single medallion or medallions centered in a bordered field. This format, which according to most authorities was derived from early embossed book bindings, was finely knotted in graceful curvilinear forms. The field may either be open—that is, without additional decoration—or swirled with readily recognizable vines, leaves, flowers, and trees. In the simpler,

Medallion format.

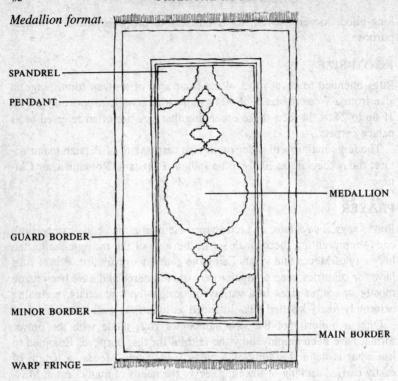

SPANDREL

PENDANT

MEDALLION

GUARD BORDER

MINOR BORDER

MAIN BORDER

WARP FRINGE

Sixteenth-century embossed bookbinding.

$$\begin{array}{rl} & = 1330 \\ \text{Add:} & \underline{583} \\ & 1913 \end{array}$$

$$\begin{array}{rl} & = 1328 \\ \text{Add:} & \underline{583} \\ & 1911 \end{array}$$

$$\begin{array}{rl} & = 1287 \\ \text{Add:} & \underline{583} \\ & 1870 \end{array}$$

The dating of old oriental rugs accords for the most part with the Islamic system, which begins with the Hegira, Mohammed's flight from Mecca to Medina in July of 622 A.D. Although the Moslem lunar year is eleven days shorter than our solar-based year, a reasonably accurate conversion can be achieved by adding 583 to the translated Islamic date, as shown above.

Arabic numerals with formula for dating inscribed rugs.
SKETCH AFTER FRANSES.

more coarsely knotted country-cousin versions produced on village looms, the graceful flower shapes assume simpler, more geometric forms; in tribal weavings they often verge on the abstract.

This is perhaps the appropriate place to address the problem presented by dated rugs. Workshop rugs with a curvilinear medallion format frequently have Arabic numerals dating their completion woven into an oblong border cartouche, but rustic rugs too are sometimes dated, with the numbers typically knotted into the field near the top of the rug as the weaving neared completion. Since age is valued in rugs, if the shape of the figures eludes easy identification, the reading of them will usually favor as early a dating as possible, and forging a date at the time of weaving or a later reknotting is by no means unheard of. A further complication is presented by illiterate weavers imperfectly copying dates they saw only as a filler motif.

Allover Designs

Removing the central focal point from a medallion format with a decorated field allows what had been a background design to expand into either a latticed or an unregimented pattern, which often appears to extend beneath and beyond the borders that arbitrarily contain it.

Compartment Rugs

In these, the field is divided into evenly proportioned boxed design units containing repeated motifs usually arranged in parallel, checkerboard-like, rows. The static quality of this format is often pleasingly relieved by variations in the size and color of the individual design units and their placement in relation to the others.

Repeat Designs

Turkoman rugs, the red-grounded "Bokharas" long a popular staple of the trade, are prime examples of rugs whose fields are patterned with motifs symmetrically repeated row upon row with little or no variation aside from alternations in color. The geometric figures, or *guls*, peculiar to each Turkoman tribe are more generously spaced in antique rugs than in later versions; and as a rule the later any type of rug with a repeating motif was made, the more cramped the motifs are apt to be.

Striking effects are achieved by strong contrasts in the colors of motifs in succeeding diagonal rows or in stepped patterning extending over the entire field.

Repeat motifs may either be contained within the borders or cut by them, in which case they may be considered to extend beneath and beyond the bounds imposed upon them.

Pictorial

Rugs depicting famous persons and scenes from history and legend have never been made in great numbers, and although often interesting or charming, as in the case of village weavers' naive representations of animals, they are rarely artistically successful. A notable exception is the exquisite 16th-century slit-tapestry silk Kashan piece depicting the Persian legend of Leila and Mejnoon, sold by Christie's in 1990 for the stunning price of $480,000. At least as stunning, in quite a different sense, is the mind-boggling "Maggie and Jiggs" silk Kashan rug, circa 1925, brought to my attention by an article in *Oriental Rug Review* and reproduced here with no further comment.

Prayer

The field below the arch, in which the faithful kneel, is sometimes open, sometimes flanked with pillars, and sometimes decorated with

"Maggie and Jiggs" silk Kashan carpet, sold in 1989 for $22,000.
PHOTO COURTESY OF CHRISTIE'S.

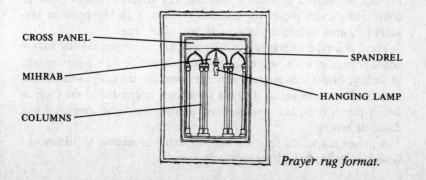

CROSS PANEL

SPANDREL

MIHRAB

HANGING LAMP

COLUMNS

Prayer rug format.

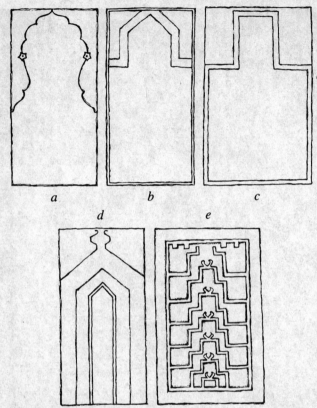

A variety of prayer rug styles: (a) Persian, 16th century; (b) Daghestan, Caucasus; (c) Baluch, Persia; Afghanistan; (d) Ersari Beshir, West Turkestan; (e) Turkish, stepped form.

objects associated with religious observance and symbols: incense burners, water jugs, lanterns representing the light of God, and the tree-of-life design beloved by Baluch weavers. The coupled-column Ottoman court manufactory prayer rug given to the New York Metropolitan Museum by James Ballard is considered particularly fine.

There is a type of prayer rug with multiple niches set side by side in single or parallel rows, which was probably developed for use in mosques: in Turkey, I have seen modern versions stretching the entire width of the interior. Known as *saphs*, they are sometimes referred to in the trade as family prayer rugs, but most authorities doubt they were ever used in a domestic setting.

A prayer rug with a series of stepped arches is peculiar to Turkey and is seen in both pile and flat-woven formats.

Sampler

Designs can pass from one weaving group to another in several ways: by direct observation, through graphed representations, and via sampler rugs, or *wagireh*, in which popular border and field motifs are randomly knotted. Sampler rugs are associated mainly with the Bidjar weaving area, and the best examples are vied for by collectors.

FLAT-WEAVE FORMATS

Kilims

Turkish kilims are characteristically either very long, in which case they were woven in two strips sewn together, or woven in a prayer format in scatter and area rug sizes.

Persian kilims are usually woven in one piece; the majority are reversible, and medium sizes are more common than the very long pieces associated with Turkey. Runners were made, too, but old examples are a rarity. The exquisite 19th-century kilims associated with the Kurdish weavers of Senneh are in a class by themselves: their intricate, delicate floral designs and relatively small size—many are woven in a prayer format—which makes them more suitable candidates for wall hangings than floor furnishings.

Old kilims made by Turkoman weavers are not often seen in the marketplace except for a narrow, shortish, tightly woven interlocked type associated with the Yomut tribe; it has red, white, and dark blue geometric motifs arrayed in rather compressed bands.

The more frequently available medium-sized, reversible kilims attributed to Caucasian weavers are remarkable for the clarity of their vivid, saturated colors.

Indian tapestry-woven rugs are known as *dhurries*. Because they are made of cotton, the name has become associated with inexpensive floor coverings of low durability, but quality pieces, some containing silk, have been woven for centuries. They are woven in one piece, and old *dhurries* of interest to collectors are generally of scatter to area size. An interesting group made in Indian prisons in the early 20th century features realistic fish, birds, and crocodiles crowded feathered cheek by scaled jowl in naturalistic settings. Clearly intended as hangings, these pieces have a horizontal format and run about 3 × 4 feet.

Soumak

Soumaks, wherever they originate, are usually of medium size and woven in one piece. Caucasian soumaks are the most frequently seen in the marketplace, and the designs, unlike those used for kilims, are clearly derived from much older knotted-pile rugs. Collectors particularly favor the designs influenced by early rugs with dragon motifs.

MIXED TECHNIQUES

Plain or balanced-weave textiles, in which the weft and warp have equal representation, are as likely as not to be combined with a variety of other techniques into distinctive structures whose names vary according to where they were woven. These include the elegant and somber mixed-technique covers (some one-piece, others made in two pieces later joined) characteristic of some Persian Baluch tribes: a group of large Turkoman rugs with plain-woven red grounds closely covered with a rectilinear repeat in weft-float brocading and a smaller type with stripes in variegated subdued colors alternating with wider bands of a stepped chevron design. Baluch and Turkoman flat-woven rugs usually have long skirts similar to those on their pile rugs.

One-piece mixed-technique rugs in small and medium sizes were woven throughout Turkey and Persia with every variety and combination of flat-weave technique represented; two-piece examples made by some tribal weavers approach the square. In Anatolia, prayer rugs were as frequently flat-woven as knotted in pile.

FORMATS FOR WEAVINGS OTHER THAN RUGS

Tent and Yurt Trappings

In the Middle East, tents used by nomadic and seminomadic tribes are large affairs, generally woven from dark brown or black goat hair and referred to in the literature, appropriately enough, as black tents. Yurts are similarly portable structures in which light-colored felt coverings are

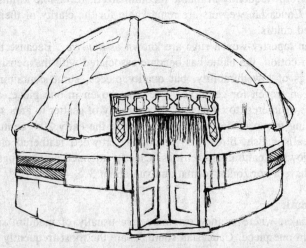

A yurt, a portable domestic structure covered with felts secured by a long, wide flat-woven band. The decorative weaving above the entrance is a kapunuk.

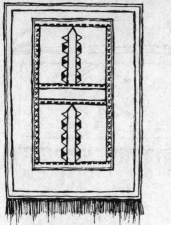 

Tent door rug (engsi).   *Door surround.*

wrapped around a round, domed framework and secured by very long flat-woven bands, which are sometimes lavishly decorated with motifs in knotted pile. Yurts and yurtlike dwellings are associated with Turkoman and Shahsavan tribes in northern Iran and tribal peoples throughout Central Asia.

Door Rugs. Because several versions of these interesting Turkoman weavings contain archlike elements, these pile tent entrance hangings used to be mistaken for prayer rugs. The unique layout is similar from tribe to tribe, but what it is intended to represent remains uncertain.

Tent Door Surround. A three-sided, usually tasseled Turkoman weaving whose form exactly follows its function, these are rarely seen in the market. Antique examples in reasonably good condition command high prices.

Meal Cloth. This is a long, narrow flat-weave with decorative borders, surrounding a field that is sometimes figured but more often left plain and undyed as a symbol of humility and reverence. To sit or walk on these cloths is frowned upon, as they are intended exclusively for the service of food.

Oven Cloth. In this instance, "oven" refers to a basin containing glowing coals placed under a low, square table covered by an old blanket or quilt on top of which is placed a richly decorated smaller square that may be either entirely flat-woven or ornamented in pile. The family warms itself by sitting around the table and under the heated blanket.

Storage Bags
Whatever the overall size of bags made to store bedding and other household articles, they are customarily longer than they are deep. When

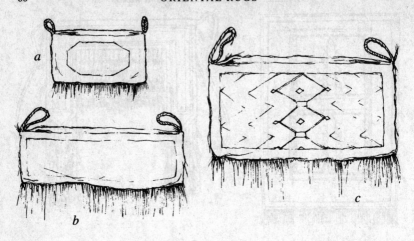

Tent framework-hung storage bags are made in a variety of sizes. These are the most common: (a) 1' × 2'; (b) 1½' × 3'; (c) 3' × 4½'.

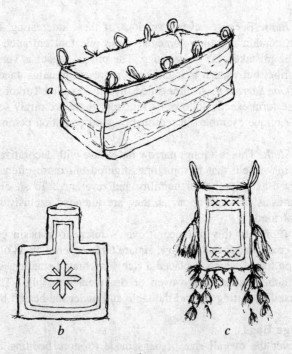

(a) Chest-type storage bag; (b) salt bag; (c) spoon bag.

fastened along the top edge, they can either be hung from woven-in loops from the tent framework or set side by side lengthwise along the wall or on low benches, where they serve as pillows. Either entirely flat-woven or with pile fronts and flat-woven backs, these bags frequently exemplify tribal weaving at its best. The faces are usually all that make their way into the market; an entire bag commands a premium.

Four-sided chest-type storage bags are found in all Iranian tribes except the Turkoman and Baluch; they are woven by girls of marriageable age to contain their dowries. Intact bags are rarely available; collectors are usually happy to settle for one beautifully woven side.

Salt Bag. This bag, used to store salt and other loose granular food-stuffs, has a wide body out of which rises a narrow chimney-like extension that serves as a spout and, flapped over, protects the contents from moisture and contamination. Its dimensions vary but are usually between 1 and 2 feet square.

Grain Bag. These bags, similar in shape and size to our flour sacks, are for the storage of grains for both family and domestic animals. Braided wool or goat hair loops at short intervals along the top allow the contents to be secured against rodents.

Spoon Bag. Narrow flat-woven or pile-faced small bags are used for storing spoons and spindles. Loops extending from each top corner allow the bag to be attached to the tent frame.

Bags for Personal Belongings

A variety of small, single-pouched bags are woven to hold combs, money, tobacco, and the like, which can be defined, depending on the

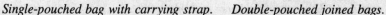

Single-pouched bag with carrying strap.   *Double-pouched joined bags.*

size, as vanity bags, satchels, and knapsacks. All bags of this type were made with a strap or handle, but accessories of this sort, including tassels and beads and decorative fringes, are often worn away over the years.

A bag format encountered with minor variations throughout the rug-producing area is a double-pouched type joined together by a flat-woven strip whose width indicates its use: if made to be carried over a man's shoulder or forearm the strip will be narrower than that on bags intended to be slung across the back of his donkey or horse.

Whatever the purpose, these bags, whether small or large, exhibit a greater variety in both design and weave than any other single class of Middle Eastern weaving. Collectors prize them for their artistry, and their small size allows them to be stored and maintained much more easily than a comparable number of rugs.

Animal Trappings

The bags described above have a practical function, but many of the trappings woven for horses and camels are intended as adornment pure and simple, especially those used at weddings, where they serve much the same purpose—albeit in a grander form—as the crepe paper ribbons seen streaming from American cars honking their way from church ceremony to restaurant reception.

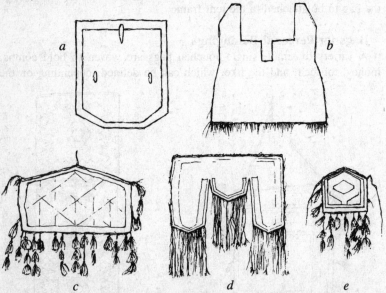

(a) Saddle cover; (b) horse cover; (c) one of a pair of camel-flank trappings used in wedding processions; (d) breast decoration for bride's camel; (e) knee cover for horse or camel.

Saddle Covers. The shape and finish of saddle covers varies widely, depending upon the style of saddle used.

Horse Covers. Horse covers are usually flat-woven, no doubt because a pile textile of sufficient size would be insufficiently flexible. Although the overall size may vary, the shape is generally the same from place to place. A Caucasian type with rows of stylized animals, either brocaded or soumak and usually fringed, are known as *vernehs*.

Camel Trappings. The most sought after are the five-sided bags—rarely, heptagonal—for decorating the right and left flanks of a Turkoman bride's camel.

Aside from the above, there is a wide variety of splendidly belled, tasseled, and shell-decorated trappings for the heads, chests, rumps, and even knees of both camels and horses. Proud indeed must be the rider whose mount is thus caparisoned. Although less commonly seen, the collecting of these artifacts is a pursuit ideally suited to those attracted by weavings both made and used in a tribal setting.

RUG MOTIFS

Scholars and collectors have pondered long and hard about the origins of rug motifs, and over the years various schools of thought have grown up on the subject. The conventional view, enormously simplified, is that oriental rug design originated from two distinct traditions:

1. The elegant, curvilinear floral forms developed by 15th-century Persian court artists, supplemented in the 16th century with designs derived from Chinese porcelains admired by contemporary Islamic collectors, and rendered, finely knotted, by skilled weavers in the palace workshops.

2. The rectilinear, generously scaled lattice-like and compartmented Turkish designs, similar to the carvings on early stone buildings, eminently suited to the limitations set by the rather large, square knots typical of Turkish weaving.

The nomadic weaver's idea of design is represented by the geometric infinite repeat, and among simple weavers the tendency to revert to this concept is very strong, even in the case of floral motifs borrowed from more sophisticated carpets.

Skeptics claim that these neat, well-documented theories fail to satisfactorily account for, among other anomalies, the patterning peculiar to the 15th–16th-century carpets produced in Egypt during the second Mamluk dynasty, not to mention the very early, astonishingly sophisticated Pazyrk carpet, which has a border of realistically drawn animals around a field of repeat geometric figures.

Further, although traditionalists claim Turkoman *guls* and the geometric devices on tribal rugs are, for the most part, highly abstracted versions of Persian floral motifs or ancient Chinese symbols, others convincingly interpret them as tribal totems. Out on the far edge of rug studies are the mystically inclined, who are currently engaged in a highly charged debate concerning their efforts to document the identification of tribal rug motifs with prehistoric cult mythology.

Collectors wishing to pursue the theoretical roots of rug design should consult the Bibliography at the back of this book. Presented here, prosaically and in visually confirmable terms, are the design progressions and variations of the motifs most commonly seen.

CURVILINEAR MOTIFS

Boteh

This pear-shaped or curled-leaf design with the bent-over top is encountered in all types of Persian and Caucasian rugs in an enormous variety of shapes and sizes, but rarely in Turkey, where it has never been part of the design vocabulary.

Boteh is a Persian word meaning "cluster of leaves"; a similar word, *buta*, is the name of a wild plant once used as kindling, and in Azerbaijan the motif is believed to symbolize the tongues of flame rising from its burning branches. Whatever the root—or roots—of this extremely popular motif may be, *boteh* is the name by which the figure is always referred, including in India, where it appears in the graceful form later popularized in the West by Paisley shawls.

Ten variations of the Boteh motif.

The *boteh* is used as a filler, or occasional, motif in the field designs of village and tribal weavings, but it is primarily a field motif. Sometimes it appears on the ground of a medallion rug, in which case it is small and its representation modest, as befits an allover secondary element, and sometimes in bold horizontal or diagonal rows in which the bent top may either face always in the same direction or alternate row to row. An interesting variation is found on old Persian Qashqai tribal rugs, among others, in which a flowering plant knotted in a *boteh*-like shape lends a blurred delicacy to a motif that in cruder, geometric forms can be strongly emphatic. In sum, I think it safe to say that no other motif has spawned weaving variations of more collectible interest.

Herati

The name applied to a pattern unit composed of a diamond-shaped floral center flanked by four curved leaves is derived from the city of Herat, which during the flowering of Persian carpet design was the most important urban center in what was then eastern Persia. During the 16th century its workshops produced wonderful carpets, many of which incorporated the leaf-and-flower unit now known as Herati. Stylistic links to the design can be found on 16th-century Cairene tiles, Ottoman carpets made in Cairo, Persian Kerman vase carpets, and early stone inlays in India.

The Herati pattern is used either as an allover design or as a medallion

(a) Herati motif; (b) Mina Khani; (c) Harshang motif; (d) Afshan motif.

rug background and, rarely, as a central figure on a bag face. It is seen at its best when the leaves and flowers are given room in which to flourish; when densely packed and finely knotted in subdued colors, it has about as much verve as a linoleum pattern. It is famously associated with Persian Ferahan rugs; tribal versions are apt to be distorted by compression.

Mina Khani

This name is applied to a lozenge-shaped arrangement of a central open rosette connected by a graceful lattice with four smaller and simpler flanking florettes. A favorite of Persian Kurdish weavers, it often appears in symmetrically repeated field designs on Veramin and Hamadan rugs. A version in which the flanking flowers are knotted in white and the central rosette supplied with a border of serrated leaves is seen on a type of Caucasian Shirvan known in the trade as blossom rugs. An even more striking effect is achieved on some Baluch rugs by floating the flanking white flowers—sometimes stylized, sometimes quite realistic—on a field of dark indigo blue or intense madder red, on which the lozenge-like rigidity of the pattern may be loosened and the lattice vines asymmetrically placed.

The Mina Khani is sometimes seen on bag faces, and a pretty variation featuring a spray of three white florettes is used as a border design.

Harshang or Crab Motif

This irregularly bordered flamelike design, seen on Caucasian and Persian rugs and occasionally in rectilinear form on Turkish rugs, derives from a blossom with leaflike projections, which was a staple on the earliest rugs in both Turkey and Persia. Some think the blocklike geometric pattern associated with Caucasian Star Kazaks is, in fact, an abstraction of the Harshang motif. The label ''crab'' was applied by weavers and dealers unfamiliar with the motif's historical progression.

Gol-Farang or Foreign Flower

This late-19th-century motif incorporating clusters of roses in full bloom was produced in direct commercial response to the French-influenced fashions popular in Czarist Russia. Realistic versions appear on Persian Senneh, Bijar, Baktiari, and Kerman rugs, in which the clusters may either be arrayed in rows as a field decoration or used as the central figure in a compartment design. An Afshar rug I once owned had a field repeat of lush, geometricized roses surrounded by a traditional tribal border.

These interesting rugs, somewhat of an acquired taste, are striking in Victorian settings.

Afshan

A floral motif directly adapted from an open, tulip-like flower presented on a bent stem was used as a flanking element for more important design units on 18th-century Caucasian rugs. An interesting version is seen on 19th-century Caucasian rugs, most notably Perepedils from the Kuba area, in which the flowers are simplified, the stem bent at right angles, and the whole conveying a strangely Chinese look.

Bid Majnun or Weeping Willow

This field design, which features willows, cypress, and poplars as well as vines and flowers, is one of the most appealing of the village weaver's repertoire. Although influenced by symmetrically formatted classic garden carpets, the Bid Majnun is at its best when informally arranged.

This motif is most frequently seen on Bidjar and other Kurdish rugs but is employed throughout the rug-weaving areas. An attractive Indian interpretation sold in 1990 at a Sotheby's auction in New York.

Tree-of-Life

The tree-of-life is a very old and universal motif symbolizing man's yearning reach from base, earthly life to the purity of paradise. In village and tribal versions the tree is usually reduced to a single vertical trunk stemmed with stylized, three-lobed leaves. A distinctive version found

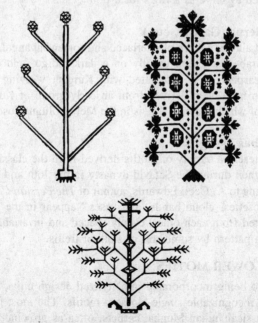

Three variations of the tree-of-life motif.

Zil-i-Sultan motif.

on many Baluch prayer rugs is more rectilinear than curvilinear; on workshop rugs, the artistry expressed in finely knotted and prettily arrayed blossoming naturalistic trees tends to overwhelm the symbolic significance.

Zil-i-Sultan

A classical Persian flower-and-vase repeat rendered either realistically or highly stylized as a field repeat design. Occasionally, the motif is much enlarged to serve as a rug's focal point.

Garus (Gerus, Garrus, etc.)

An elegant allover pattern of interlaced and somewhat angularized vine-and-flower arabesques seen usually on a dark indigo field on large to palace-size carpets. It is associated with Kurdish weaving towns and considered to have been derived from an early group of Kurdish rugs, an example of which, dated 1794, is in the Metropolitan Museum of Art.

Shah Abbas Designs

These represent a variety of motifs derived from the classical Persian carpets designed during the Safavid dynasty in the 16th and 17th centuries. According to A. Cecil Edwards, author of *The Persian Carpet*, these palmettes, rosettes, cloud bands, and vases "appear in the field of the carpet, isolated from each other, evenly spaced and invariably interconnected into a pattern by some sort of stalk or trellis."

OTHER FLOWER MOTIFS

In addition to being incorporated into stylized design units, flowers are also used as recognizable single-blossom motifs. The most realistic are found on classical Indian Mughal carpets, often as growing plants, and include the rose, poppy, tulip, carnation, peony, lotus, chrysanthemum, lily, geranium, and hollyhock. In a later group of Indian prayer rugs known as *millefleurs*, a veritable explosion of mixed blossoms fills the field of the *mihrab*. The tulip and carnation are popular motifs in Turkey, and the peony, chrysanthemum, and lotus are most strongly associated with East Turkestan, Tibetan, and Chinese rugs.

Another widely used botanical motif is the many-seeded pomegranate, a symbol for fertility appearing most frequently on East Turkestan and Far Eastern rugs.

CLOUD BANDS

The cloud-band motif, which appears in both border and field designs, entered the West via Chinese artisans brought to Samarkand in the early 15th century by its Mongol conquerors. From there, it spread to adjacent areas and was soon taken up by Persian artists, whose versions include one that has an arguably *mihrab*-like shape.

Cloud bands are found in Persian, Turkish, Caucasian, Beshir Turkoman, and, of course, Central and Far Eastern Asian weavings.

HUMAN AND ANIMAL FIGURES

Strictly interpreted, the sayings attributed to Mohammed, the Prophet of Islam, in the *hadith* forbid the representation of human figures; in practice, some Muslim societies observe this stricture, and others disregard it. As a general rule, figural motifs are much less common on Turkish and Afghan rugs than on those from other rug-weaving areas. An interesting exception is a small contemporary rug I own of village origin that features a portrait of Turkey's revered father figure, Kemal Ataturk, rendered in the dashed-off style of a pen and ink sketch.

Figures in the realistic round are uncommon everywhere except on pictorial rugs. More usual are cartoon-like or stick figures, and their cheerful appearance helter-skelter in a village rug's field, along with the domestic animals who share their lives, can be counted upon to evoke a smile on a rug collector's face and a covetous wish in his or her heart.

Realistic animals appeared on early classical Persian and Indian carpets and still do on city workshop rugs; on collectible village rugs they are reduced largely to blocky stylizations, stick figures, or abstractions. In fact, except for flowers and trees, which are readily incorporated into a design structure, realistic representations are poor choices for knotted-pile and flat-woven rugs. Textiles are associated with pattern, not pictures; therefore, the more stylized and the more subordinate to the pattern a pictorial motif can be, the better.

Wild animals commonly appearing on oriental pile weavings include lions, an ancient symbol of courage and strength appearing in various guises on rugs of all Persian tribal groups, and tigers—or rather the skins

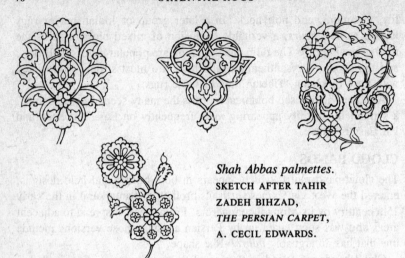

Shah Abbas palmettes.
SKETCH AFTER TAHIR
ZADEH BIHZAD,
THE PERSIAN CARPET,
A. CECIL EDWARDS.

Cloud bands. (a) Classical version used as a field motif; (b) compressed version seen in borders.

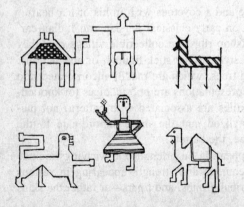

Human and animal figures are often seen on village and tribal rugs.

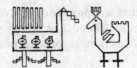

*Birds appear in a variety
of highly stylized forms,
hinting of mythic significance.*

of tigers—on some very early Turkish rugs and on the later Tibetan rugs
with which they are currently most associated. The game animal most
frequently represented is the antelope, which on the classical Persian and
Indian rugs known as "hunting rugs" was portrayed in mortal struggle
with a predator.

Camels and horses are popular motifs in all weaving areas, as are
birds, which frequently appear in highly stylized forms hinting of mythic
significance. The double-headed horned creatures in Turkoman guls are
interpreted by some scholars as crested birds. Birds in a more recognizable form, but still far from realistic, are seen on Turkoman camel trappings, Baluch rugs and bags, and Persian and Turkish village rugs, among
others. The large, realistic parrots seen on some late-19th-century workshop rugs would seem to lack any significance, including artistic.

A wholly mythic creature is the dragon, whose flamboyant picturiza-
tion on early Caucasian carpets caused its name to be associated with
those rugs as well as with a wide group of pile and flat-woven rugs made
since that are considered to have dragon-inspired figures. It is a motif
thought to have descended variously from the Chinese winged dragon
symbols introduced to Central Asia along trade routes and ancient local
myths in which heaven and earth were represented by a bird and serpent.

The Chinese had a design vocabulary all their own, which, although
it influenced Western design, was not until much later itself affected by
Western notions. The Chinese motifs representing philosophic abstractions and intellectual accomplishments have no counterparts in other rug-
producing cultures; the use of animals as symbols for desirable qualities

like strength and purity is, however, universal. Included in the Chinese repertoire, in addition to dragons, were the *feng huan*, a rooster-like bird that in combination with a dragon symbolizes peace and prosperity. (In the West, interestingly, the same combination, known as the dragon and phoenix motif, represents conflict.) Bats are symbols for happiness and good luck; cranes, for longevity; deer, for well-being; paired fish, for abundance, prosperity, or fertility. The fierce-looking temple guardians known as fo-dogs and the kylin, a wondrous stag-like animal with flaming tail and shoulders and a dragon's head adorned with a single horn are symbolic of a long and noble life.

GEOMETRIC MOTIFS

If a rug is coarsely Turkish-knotted and produced by a village or tribal weaver from designs absorbed in childhood, the design is much more likely to be geometric than one woven from supplied cartoons in an urban workshop.

As stated earlier, there also seems to be a further, culturally determined division: curvilinear designs are in general associated with Persian-influenced weaving, geometrics with the Turkic tradition. Whether this does, in fact, constitute a fundamental difference is as yet imperfectly understood by scholarly investigators trying to weave coherent theories from a tangle of conflicting ethnic, anthropologic, religious, and aesthetic considerations. All one can say for sure, according to art historian E. H. Gombrich, is that "nothing comes from nothing."

Many of the geometric designs seen on 19th-century rugs can be traced back to floral origins, as exemplified by border motifs, the majority of which were clearly derived from flower, vine, and leaf prototypes. On Turkish rugs, we often see quite realistic tulips and carnations, beloved by Ottoman textile and tile designers, used as both border and field motifs. In short, when it comes to oriental rug design, there are no absolutes.

Examples of early and extremely influential Turkish geometric rug designs are the small and large Holbeins, including their many variations, and a hooked figure used universally but referred to in its Turkish guise as the Memling gul (see Gul, below). Such designs have since been tagged with the names of the 15th-century artists who used the rugs bearing these bold patterns as colorful accents in their paintings.

Geometrically patterned rugs invariably conform to one of the six formats described earlier in this chapter, although ready assignment can sometimes be hindered by an ineptly woven version of a symmetrical design or motifs inserted chock-a-block to fill otherwise empty spaces.

Other motifs associated with the Turkish design tradition and employed elsewhere by weavers with Turkic roots include the following:

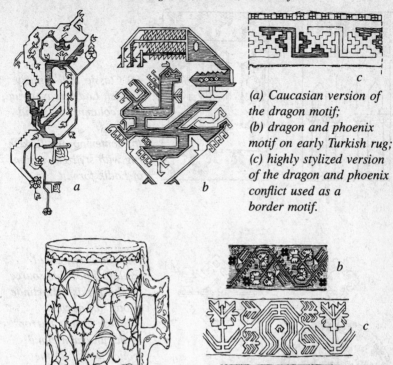

(a) Caucasian version of the dragon motif;
(b) dragon and phoenix motif on early Turkish rug;
(c) highly stylized version of the dragon and phoenix conflict used as a border motif.

(a) Ottoman carnation-decorated Iznik tankard, mid-16th century;
(b) carnation cluster border motif; (c) carnation and tulip border repeat; (d) carnation flower-based border motif.

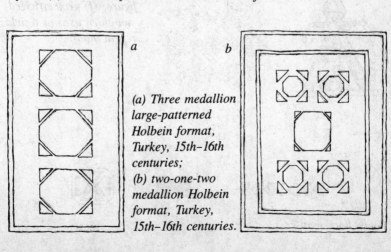

(a) Three medallion large-patterned Holbein format, Turkey, 15th–16th centuries;
(b) two-one-two medallion Holbein format, Turkey, 15th–16th centuries.

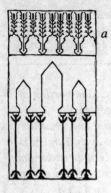 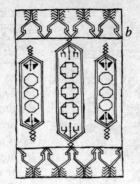

(a) Classic 18th-century Turkish Ladik prayer rug with columns and band of tulips;
(b) contemporary Turkish rug with stylized version of Ladik format.

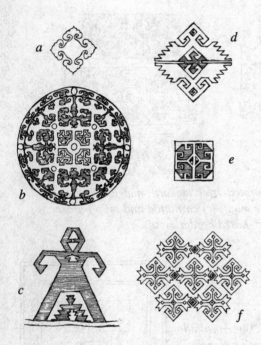

(a) Yun-chien cloud collar, a possible source of the Turkish elibelinde motif; (b) ancient Chinese bronze mirror with yun-chien cloud collar motif; (c) the elibelinde "hands-on-hips" motif; (d) another elibelinde figure seen on Turkish kilims; (e) geometricized yun-chien/elibelinde figure; (f) geometricized yun-chien used as a field repeat motif.

Ram's horn motifs.

Elibelinde
Said to be a symbol of fertility, the motif known as *elibelinde*, which means woman-with-hands-on-hips, is a very old one with many variations.

Ram's Horn
A male fertility symbol, also with many variations, is used as both a field motif—usually as part of a larger design unit—and a border element.

Star
Stars, indicating a wish for happiness, are used both boxed and unboxed, either as a repeat or in combination with other motifs.

Memling Gul
Gul (see below) is a term normally applied to the large tribal emblems on Turkoman rugs; the Memling Gul is a hooked, stepped, Turkoman-

Soumak bag face with Memling gul used as central ornament. PHOTO COURTESY OF CHRISTIE'S EAST.

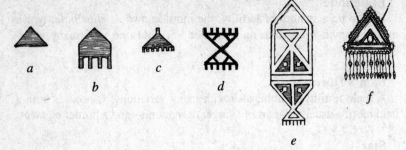

*(a–d) Amulet motifs; (e) stylized prayer rug
lamp; (f) Turkoman necklace pendant.*

gul-like figure seen on village and tribal rugs throughout the Middle
Eastern rug-producing region. The name it is known by in the West is
that of the 15th-century Flemish painter, Hans Memling, whose com-
positions frequently incorporated rugs with this design.

Amulets

The term *amulet* seems to have become the fail-safe label to apply to
geometric figures whose roots and significance as woven motifs have
become hopelessly confused in a snarl of conflicting interpretations. One
minor example is an hourglass-shaped figure with toothed, comblike
ends—sometimes a major element in a field design, sometimes a filler
motif—known variously as a bridal comb, a stylization of a mosque lan-
tern, a piece of jewelry (a type of which it does indeed resemble), and
an hourglass meant to remind the faithful of the ephemeral nature of
earthly life.

In sum, motifs referred to in the literature as amulets may in fact serve
a specific magical purpose (i.e., warding off the evil eye) or may simply
be figures whose origins and significance, if any, are uncertain.

Gul

Gul is a Persian word for flower applied to the motifs, primarily octagons of varying proportions, that ornament in a repeat pattern the woven products of the rugs and trappings made by fierce nomadic Turkoman
tribes who wandered westward from their homeland in remote Asian
steppes about 2,000 years ago. Descendants of those tribes—the Tekke,
Yomud, Salor, Ersari, etc.—today inhabit sections of northeastern Iran,
Turkmenistan in the USSR, northern Afghanistan and, as a result of the
late hostilities there, refugee camps in Pakistan, where they continue to
weave traditional rugs.

Scholars trace the generally lobed shape of the primary guls to a Chinese design known as the cloud collar, a symbol for the gateway to paradise introduced through Central Asia along the same route as the cloud band discussed earlier.

The large primary guls identified with the various tribes were knotted as tribal-specific symbols only into rugs, although they were sometimes used decoratively on bags made by other tribes, such as the Salor gul seen on late, elaborately skirted Tekke bags. Secondary guls, of lesser tribal significance, could be used on a variety of tribal weavings. On rugs, these minor guls were placed on the field at the point at which lines would intersect if drawn diagonally through the centers of the major figures in adjacent rows.

It is not possible to present here more than a sampling of Turkoman motifs, so I urge readers whose eyes linger longest on these wonderful red weavings to acquire one or more of the authoritative books listed in the Bibliography. Very high prices are routinely paid for the oldest and rarest examples; also-rans, no matter how decorative, do not count for much among the cognoscenti and therefore make a reasonably priced area for beginners to explore.

Tekke

The Tekke tribal gul is always quartered by dark lines intersecting at right angles. There are two secondary guls, and although (2) is less common it is not indicative of greater age.

Yomud

The Yomud used three primary guls, only one of which, the elaborate *kepse* gul, considered by some authorities to be a floral abstraction, is tribal-specific; it is, however, not quartered like the other two, the *dyrnak* and the animal-ornamented *tauk-nuska*. The use of secondary guls is inconstant, and there is no consistency of type when they are employed. The Yomud tribal output of weaving was, and still is, very large. Anything of a practical nature that could be woven was, and a wide variety of motifs were used for ornamentation.

Ersari

The Ersari were the largest of the Turkoman tribes and the readiest to adopt designs from other sources. For example, although they have a tribal-specific gul, the *gulli-gul*, which contains stemmed cloverleaf-like designs in each quarter, a common border design is a *boteh*-based meander. The Ersari weaving repertoire also includes variations on the Mina-Khani, cloud bands, Zil-i-Sultan, and the *boteh* used as a field design.

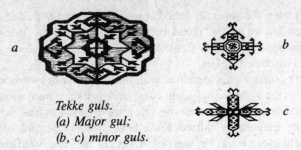

Tekke guls.
(a) Major gul;
(b, c) minor guls.

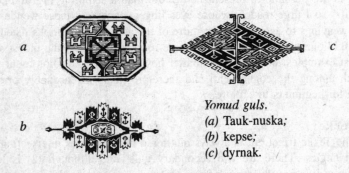

Yomud guls.
(a) Tauk-nuska;
(b) kepse;
(c) dyrnak.

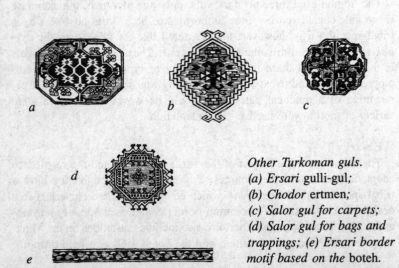

Other Turkoman guls.
(a) Ersari gulli-gul;
(b) Chodor ertmen;
(c) Salor gul for carpets;
(d) Salor gul for bags and
trappings; (e) Ersari border
motif based on the boteh.

Chodor

The primary Chodor gul, the *ertmen*, is a lozenge-shaped, stepped gul containing stylized flowers and enclosed in a delicate lattice starred with florettes. This group also used the animal-figured *tauk-nuska* gul (see Yomud above) on rugs.

Salor

This tribal gul is quartered and contains within each quarter three stemmed clover-like figures and a stylized animal figure. The secondary octagonal figure used in conjunction with it in the typically elegantly spaced Salor format is much smaller and simpler. Another large, crenellated gul appears only on weavings other than rugs.

Weavings that can be unequivocally identified with the Salors are rare; other types that escape easy attribution and for that reason not discussed here are Saryk, Arabatchi, and Kizil Ayak.

MAJOR BORDER MOTIFS

The great majority of designs used for main borders in the oriental rug-weaving cultures are floral-based, with the exception of some figures primarily associated with Turkoman rugs and a Turkish border design group derived from Arabic script and used occasionally by Caucasian weavers. Even a design like the Yomud Turkoman "boat border," at first glance seeming wholly rectilinear, can be traced back through successive stages of stylization to flowering vine and palmette antecedents.

Flowering Vine and Palmette. This classic Persian format appears in many variations. Among them are those illustrated here.

Blossom Repeats. Blossoms used in both realistic and stylized forms include carnations, tulips, garden balsam, narcissus, and, in Far Eastern rugs, lotus and peonies.

Ram's Horn. This motif, used over a wide area, is a very old Turkic symbol, appearing in a variety of guises from a simple hooked "Y" used in minor borders to more complex hooked figures seen in the borders and fields of Turkoman, Turkish, and Kurdish village and tribal rugs. The ends of the hooks are sometimes elaborated into a crested shape some scholars identify as birds.

Ashik. This steeply stepped ornament used by many Turkoman tribes, primarily in borders but also as a field design, is considered variously to be a sylized rosette or bird with spread wings. *Ashik*-like motifs are also seen on Turkish rugs.

Kufic Variations. These are geometric main border designs based on a very old rectilinear Arabic script known as Kufic.

Yomud rug with so-called boat border. PHOTO COURTESY OF GROGAN & COMPANY.

Left: *stylizations of palmette and flowering vine border motif including (c) Yomud "boat" and (d) 20th-century Soviet version, with tanks and airplanes.* Right: *three classical flowering vine and palmette borders.*

Floral motifs used in borders. (a–e) Flowering vine and leaf variations; (f) tulip and serrated leaf, known as "cup and leaf." (g) Four flower and leaf stylizations; (h) Turkoman "curled leaf" motif; (i) Caucasian flower and leaf stylization; (j) four stages of a Turkish floral geometricization.

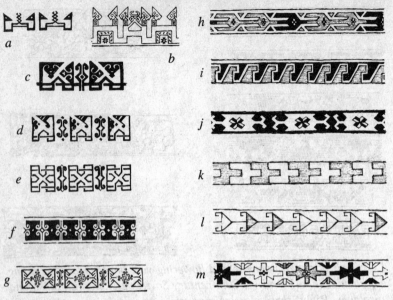

Left: *Kufic border motif variations.* (a, b) Turkey, 13th century; (c, d, e) Turkey, 16th century; (f) Turkey, 19th century; (g) Caucasus, 19th century. Right: *other geometric motifs include the six pictured here.* (h) *"Tuning fork" repeat, Turkoman;* (i) *"running dog," universal;* (j) *aina-kochak, Turkoman;* (k) *universal;* (l) *ram's horn, universal;* (m) *a variant of the stepped Ashik figure, Turkoman.*

Other Geometric Motifs

The geometric border motifs pictured here are commonly seen: three are identified with Turkoman weavings; the other three are universally used.

Cloud Bands. The Chinese cloud band discussed in connection with field motifs was also a popular border motif, often used in a humped version like a looped ribbon bow.

Trefoil. Thought to be derived from the lotus blossom, this very old three-lobed reciprocal figure is widely used in both major and minor borders.

MINOR BORDER MOTIFS

Floral and leaf forms on minor borders are typically highly convention-alized, even on workshop rugs. However, although a sort of generic rosette is the rule, a realistic pink carnation motif is often seen in the minor borders of some low-piled rugs woven in northeastern Caucasian districts.

Three versions of the reciprocal trefoil motif.

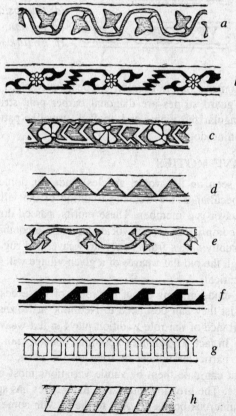

A sampling of minor border motifs. (a, b) Persian. (c, d, e) Caucasian. (f, g, h) Turkoman.

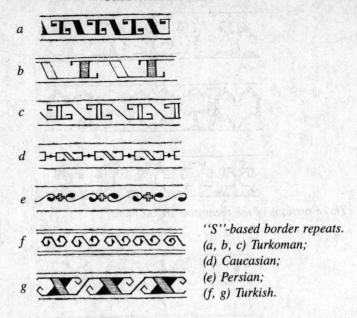

"S"-based border repeats.
(a, b, c) Turkoman;
(d) Caucasian;
(e) Persian;
(f, g) Turkish.

Among the many simple geometric repeats universally used for minor borders and guard stripes are diagonal barber pole stripes, reciprocal sawtooths, angularized vines, and hooked, wavelike patterns frequently labeled "running dog" or "latch hook."

FLAT-WEAVE MOTIFS

The designs seen on flat-woven articles made for domestic use are in most cases peculiar to the weaving tradition of the village or tribe of which the weaver is a member. These motifs, passed down through the generations, comprise an artistic vocabulary whose combination into woven phrases subtly varies from weaver to weaver and rug to rug; accordingly, although the old flat weaves of a given village will be similar, they are never identical.

Collectors enjoy arguing about the roots of these designs—some researchers insist they can be traced to Neolithic art forms—but all agree on the importance of the role tradition plays in flat-weave design, especially kilims. In fact, knowledgeable kilim collectors not only can assign a piece to a particular village or tribe on the basis of its design and coloration but can date them by subtle variations most of us would fail even to notice. The growing interest in flat weaves has sparked the publication of numerous books devoted to them, with some limited to specific types and weaving areas. You will find recommended titles in the annotated booklist in the Resource Guide.

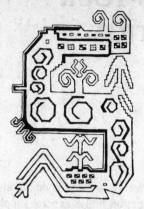 

Dragon-based figures seen on flat-woven Caucasian silehs.

Flat-weave formats tend to be dominated by repeat geometric patterns in horizontal, vertical, or diagonal rows. Banding is much more common than on pile rugs, and the size of individual design units often approach the monumental, especially on very old Turkish kilims.

Although curvilinear patterning is certainly possible, as evidenced by floral 16th-century Persian and Ottoman kilims and 19th-century Persian Senneh and Bidjar kilims, it is uncommon.

Stylized figures of animals and birds are frequently depicted on mixed-technique bags and other domestic articles. The brocaded plain-weave covers known in the trade as *vernehs*, on which camels and horses parade row upon row, are particularly popular with collectors of "folky" weavings. Another sought-after type, the Caucasian soumak flat weave known as a *sileh*, features large S-shaped compartmented figures said to be derived from the dragons on much earlier knotted rugs, which, depending on the age and type, they more or less resemble.

Collectors, with the exception of those drawn to austerity, are generally attracted by animal figures on a village or tribal weaving, a fact lost on neither dealers nor auctioneers. All other factors being equal, dragons, camels, or crested birds can be expected to exact a premium roughly proportionate to their visual appeal.

For More Information

I know of no books devoted entirely to oriental rug motifs, but many of those in the annotated book list in the Resource Guide, particularly P. R. J. Ford's *The Oriental Carpet*, provide useful information. *Hali* and *Oriental Rug Review* frequently publish articles on the sources and variations of a single motif; reasonably detailed indexes of both publications are now available.

BEGINNING YOUR COLLECTION

BEFORE YOU START

When it comes to acquiring rugs, the interests of collectors do not always coincide with those of the dealers and auction house experts supplying their needs. This is hardly surprising. Nevertheless, the advice given me for beginning collectors by knowledgeable representatives of all three groups can be distilled into one well-worn phrase: look before you leap.

If you intend to buy no more than two or three good old rugs to enhance the interior decor of your home, you need not look very far. The color, type, and size of rugs employed primarily as furnishing accessories usually complement what is already in place. One would not, for example, expect to see a silk and metallic-thread *souf* Kashan in a remodeled New England barn or a coarse, long-piled Turkish bedding rug in a Louis IX drawing room. But although an existing decorating scheme may limit one's choice, it in no way makes it less deserving of serious consideration.

At the very least, a thorough reading of the two books discussed below and visits to museum collections in your area should precede investigations of dealer stocks and auction house offerings. As your eyes become accustomed to rugs with unfamiliar patterns and palettes, you might find yourself drawn to something quite different from what you originally had in mind, like the Tabriz remembered from your grandparents' house or the mellow Heriz seen at a friend's. If the visual pleasure you experience is strong enough, you may soon find yourself seeking out more of the same, and even though floor covering remains the primary purpose of the rugs you eventually purchase, the first step up the collecting ladder has been taken.

The cornerstone of any budding collector's reference library should be the two titles heading the recommended reading list of everyone I interviewed: Murray L. Eiland's *Oriental Rugs*, third (or latest) edition, and *Oriental Carpets* by Jon Thompson. (Ordering information for publications recommended in this chapter will be found in the annotated book list in the Resource Guide.)

Dr. Eiland has traveled often and widely in the rug-producing areas. He believes in drawing his conclusions from personal experience and study, and his thorough, hands-on knowledge of rugs is straightforwardly communicated in this reliable, information-packed, conventionally organized collector's guide to 19th- and early-20th-century Persian, Caucasian, Turkoman, and Turkish rugs. Although short on historical background information and woefully below par as far as color plates are concerned—there are many useful black and whites, however—its virtues far outweigh its shortcomings.

Jon Thompson's *Oriental Carpets* has been described by one internationally respected scholar as "the best-written, best-researched . . . best illustrated general book on oriental carpets available." It has also proved to be a trend-setter in terms of organization of the material, differing from all that preceded it by discussing carpets not in the usual country-of-origin context but in terms of technical achievement. In other words, rather than grouping rugs geographically as Persian, Caucasian, Turkish, and Turkoman, he has defined four new categories based on weaving skills, which in fact closely parallel the interests of most collectors. They are tribal weaving, cottage industry rugs, workshop or town carpets, and court carpets. For the beginner seeking to define his or her own rug interest, Jon Thompson's sumptuously illustrated book is without question the place to start.

CHOOSING AN AREA OF CONCENTRATION

Let us assume you have read Eiland and Thompson and have visited one or more of the rug collections listed in the back of this book. Let us assume further that you have not become discouraged by your realization of how large and complex the collecting field you have chosen is. You could, at this point, go one of two ways: adopt the one-of-this, one-of-that, assorted cookie approach or continue looking and reading until you find yourself being consistently drawn to one type of rug or weaving above all others. It could be the color or the feel of the wool; it could be the technical excellence of the weaving; it could even be the challenge posed by uncertain attributions. Whatever it is, wait for that mental click that brings your predilection, probably already recognized at gut level, into sharp focus.

Mind you, there is nothing *wrong* about wanting to own examples of a variety of rugs; in fact, most collectors do, including Wilton Mason of North Carolina, who wrote me, "I will probably never own any of the classic rugs that look so lovely in the glossy books, but this [realization] has had a liberating effect. Within what I can afford, I now buy only the rugs that move me, that bring comfort and joy through their intrinsic beauty and uniqueness, whatever their type.''

Wilton Mason, however, is blessed with an unusually discerning eye. On average, unless one has a great deal of time to devote to one's collecting, it is very difficult to learn enough about all classes of rugs not only to unerringly choose good typical examples but to spy out the shining lights, the unique, out-of-the-ordinary rugs that challenge comfortable assumptions.

A CASE HISTORY

Let's suppose you have decided to focus on the bold, colorful rugs of the southern Caucasus. These cottage industry rugs, woven in long-established patterns for almost two centuries, are a good choice for beginners. Thanks to their enduring popularity, there is a large, well-documented and -illustrated body of literature about them; it is relatively easy to distinguish one from another; and attractive examples are not hard to come by. The downside of popularity is that stellar examples, even those with ''problems,'' command six-figure prices from the international trade. The cost factor is further exacerbated when collectors who haven't taken the time to educate themselves unjustly inflate prices by paying up to $25,000 for mediocre rugs in mint condition, having mistaken flash for substance.

Every dealer has at least one story to tell about proudly displayed collections of garish, mechanically designed turn-of-the-century Caucasian rugs with nothing to remark kindly about except condition. This could never be said about the rugs selected by Rosalie Rudnick, a Boston-based collector who, admittedly knowing nothing at the start, ten years ago began the slow, painful, yet gratifying process of self-education that has allowed her to acquire from dealers, at auction and by trading with other collectors, a distinguished group of Caucasian rugs, almost all of which predate 1850. Condition does not control her decisions. Having seen the wonders a skilled hand can work on a worn rug with an inspired design and wonderful color, Ms. Rudnick has gone most collectors one better by taking lessons from the best restorer of village and tribal rugs in New York City. She is now able to restore her own rugs with a near-professional level of skill.

Few have that degree of dedication to collecting; most of us hope for shortcuts. There are none. It is only by looking at, comparing, touching—in short, by *studying*—many, many rugs, both in and out of our area of specialization, and by asking the right questions of knowledgeable scholars, dealers, and collectors that we may hope always to be able to tell good rugs from bad ones and, eventually, the best from the good.

That's where looking before you leap comes in again. Early in my collecting career, which by chance began in the great rug boom of the late 1970s, I was like a kitten in a swarm of butterflies, wanting everything that caught my fancy. Lacking the authoritative books and periodicals available today to guide my education, as well as a mentor to counsel restraint, I made mistake after impulsive mistake. Once I knew enough to be embarrassed by my ill-chosen excesses, I couldn't shed them fast enough, but it was an expensive lesson even in that rising market.

New York collector DeWitt Mallary, who specializes in Turkoman and Baluch tribal weavings, advises the beginner to resist "buying to buy." Wells Klein, an enthusiast of Caucasian rugs, says collectors should guard against allowing the desire for a particular type of rug to override their aesthetic judgment. "Don't be desperate," he says, "another, better rug will come along." Both caution beginners about setting collecting goals beyond their financial reach. Collectors will always make mistakes—it's part of the learning process—but fewer will be made if most buying is postponed until after an area of specialization is chosen and study undertaken.

Collectors who lack easy access to museum collections and major auction house previews should consider buying the catalogs of the annual exhibitions of rugs held during the last decade by Eberhart Herrmann, a German dealer generally credited with the most discerning eye in the world rug trade. These are primarily picture books—the commentary will be of little use unless you read German—but what pictures! What rugs! In conjunction with the Eiland and Thompson books mentioned above, they provide an unparalleled visual index of collector aspirations.

Two other indispensable library acquisitions are the periodicals *Hali* and *Oriental Rug Review*, which between them cover the rug world at home and abroad, including previews and reports of auctions and news of dealer and museum exhibitions. Both are published in generally excellent color, and the advertisements, unlike those in most periodicals, provide additional useful information about current offerings on the market.

APPROACHING THE STARTING GATE

As was remarked earlier in connection with Jon Thompson's book, *Oriental Carpets*, collectors tend to specialize within categories defined roughly by the intent of the weaver and the circumstances in which the weaving is done. In the pages that follow, all collectible weavings have been assigned to one of five categories of weaving skills, within which they are further grouped geographically, starting with Turkey and proceeding east to China.

The ability to identify rugs with reasonable certainty is not easily acquired; fortunately, the illustrated, annotated catalogs of the major auction houses provide identification for us. They are not always right, as dealers and experienced collectors are quick to point out, but they are more apt to be so than the average collector. Auctioneers encountered down the scale, from smaller regional houses to country barns, either depend on a local dealer for attributions or supply nothing but the size and an implied caveat. Dealers in new orientals may know less about old rugs than a well-read novice.

Thus set adrift, as it were, beginning collectors are often reduced to attempting rug identification on the basis of design. If the rug is a traditional type, of respectable age, and if one is content to have a general rather than specific identification, the odds for making a reasonably good guess are in your favor. Late-19th- and early-20th-century rugs whose designs were dictated by commercial interests are another matter altogether. European companies like Ziegler, The Persian Carpet Company (PETAG), and Oriental Carpet Manufacturers, Ltd. (OCM)—the last organized production in Turkey and India as well as Persia—supplied their weavers with wool, dyes, and designs and sparked the great oriental rug revival at the turn of the century. The results can be seen in dealer stocks and auction rooms today. However, the designs given the weavers were not necessarily indigenous, and it was under OCM aegis that the washing of rugs with chemicals to produce instant mellowness was institutionalized, although rarely taken to such extremes as the "Golden Afghans" popular in the 1960s.

Further complicating the problems of identification is the fact that even isolated village and tribal weavers, unaffected by wide-ranging entrepreneurs, were sometimes influenced by patterns seen on rugs brought to market by weavers from other areas. Because of the ease of imitating or adapting surface designs, authorities agree that the most reliable way to assign a rug to an already defined weaving group is through a close examination of the weave pattern visible on the back. These weaving techniques, absorbed by children as they work at the loom alongside their mothers, emerge through the weavers' fingers in a linked series of habitual motions strongly resistant to change.

The weave characteristic telling the most about which weaving group is likely to have produced a rug is the weft: the color and spin of the material of which it is composed, the thickness and firmness of the ply, how many times and with what degree of tension it passes between the knots, and how firmly it is beaten down against them.

The knot, too, is a distinguishing feature—not only the kind of knot used, but the spin and thickness of the knot wool and the tightness with which it is looped around the warps. To determine whether a knot is symmetrical (Turkish; Ghiordes) or asymmetrical (Persian; Senneh) the rug should be "broken open" by folding it back parallel to a line of wefting. If the horizontal bridge of the revealed knots covers both warp threads, with the pile ends coming up between them, the knotting is symmetrical; if one of the warps can be seen *between* the emerging ends of the pile it is asymmetrical (for details see the chapter on rug structure).

Finally, the back may be relatively flat in appearance or slightly or markedly ribbed due to the depression—more accurately, displacement—of alternate warp threads. Other useful clues are the edge and end finishes—assuming they are original—the colors used in the pile design; the handle—the rug's relative firmness or floppiness—and the appearance and length of the pile wool.

Committing a dozen or more weave patterns to memory is one thing; applying that knowledge amid the distractions of a crowded auction preview is quite another. The differences between classes of weavings are often subtle, the variations sometimes encountered within them even more so. Although specialization is the best means of containing confusion, for those unwilling to curb their rug curiosity, the Neff and Maggs dictionary listed among the annotated books in the back of this book may prove useful as long as the reservations noted are taken to heart. It's out of print now, but specialty book dealers can usually supply a copy.

What if the rug one wishes to identify eludes ready assignment? Pinning down an ambiguous weave pattern to a specific time and place is an exacting yet enthralling challenge for many scholars and collectors. Dealers often consider the process more exasperating than anything else, but since large sums of money can be riding on the outcome, they too are often drawn into the controversy.

Friends are made and lost in wrangles over provenance. According to Joseph Alsop in *The Rare Art Traditions*, "in all forms of collecting, the collector's category is always controlling since all collectors require their prizes to belong to the correct category . . . [which] is another way of saying that the object collected is what it is claimed to be and not something else."

Since rug weavers seldom kept records of their work, many firmly held opinions about rug provenance are necessarily subjective: Enthusiasts are given to constructing elaborate theories based on flimsy evidence involving dyestuffs listed on ancient bills of lading, imperfectly translated journals written by travelers of uncertain reliability, and fragments of Neolithic art reported but never verified.

In recent years, however, oriental rug studies have become more rigorous, with graduate-level degrees being awarded. As a result, a generally accepted body of knowledge is fast taking shape, and thanks to its publication in a veritable torrent of books and the periodicals mentioned above, a novice has a much better chance of making accurate identifications today than as few as 15 years ago.

GET READY, GET SET . . . CONDITION

The factors that most affect dealer pricing and auction estimates are age and condition. The ability to accurately estimate the age of a rug, like an eye for natural versus synthetic dyes, comes only with experience. Chemical washing and hard usage can produce a mellow antique look, and a smoothly worn back, which occurs naturally over many years of use, can be artificially achieved with a blowtorch and elbow grease. Deliberate fakery is uncommon but becomes a possibility whenever prices soar to tempting highs. Some of the classical carpets collectors vied for early in this century were later judged counterfeit; today new flat-woven bags woven with old materials are reaping the rewards of the collector demand for tribal artifacts. An antique rug in mint condition is rare enough to demand confirmation as such by a qualified expert.

Determining a rug's condition, however, requires no more than a close and careful examination of the features discussed below. This can be accomplished by the rankest of beginners and had better be, unless one has no concern for one's pocketbook or the possibility of eventual resale.

Pile worn evenly low, which can enhance the clarity of the design of finely knotted carpets, will affect value less than uneven wear. If wear is so pronounced as to require repiling for a rug to become serviceable for normal floor use, its price should either reflect its damaged condition or, if a dealer rug, include the cost of repair.

A rug reduced from its original size, whether to fit a particular space or eliminate damaged areas, should be priced less than a similar unaltered rug, even if the new dimensions suit the place you have in mind for it. Look for missing borders and truncated designs, but be warned: reductions can be accomplished so cleverly they may be almost impossible for an untutored eye to detect.

Other common problems affecting a rug's value are:

1. Rebound or added edges, particularly if the original weft wrappings have been cut.
2. Damaged or missing fringes or plain-woven skirts.
3. Wear creases.
4. Holes.
5. Stains.
6. Unsightly repairs.

7. Bleeding or strident synthetic dyes and washed-out colors, whether synthetic or vegetable.

8. Painting to disguise exposed foundations or conceal faded, bleeding, or harsh colors.

9. Dry rot in cotton foundations.

10. Glued-on backings.

11. Ripples and uneven dimensions, although the latter, if moderate, is tolerated in tribal rugs.

Taking all of the above into account, before making a final judgment you should be sure what your primary interest is in acquiring a particular rug. The need for a purely decorative furnishing rug to be in as near original condition as possible is much less compelling than it is for a collectible weaving. One might well prefer a Heriz carpet purchased for a dining room to have tightly rebound edges even if the color and texture bear no relation to the original. A Baluch tribal rug, however, will lose some value if edges that should be overwrapped in goat hair have been reworked with new wool, no matter how careful the workmanship or exact the color match.

Speaking of color, the character, application and balance of color in rugs, qualities often underappreciated by beginners, are, in combination, more important than physical condition to many collectors and specialty dealers. In fact, one well-known dealer, when asked what qualities he looks for in a rug, routinely answers, "Three: color, color, and color." A faded rug may suit your decorative scheme, but it should be priced for less than a like piece with clear, rich colors. Similarly, although good chrome dyes are acceptable in decorative rugs, vegetable-derived colors are preferred in collectible old rugs; to the purist even a trace of a synthetic dye is anathema.

ABOUT THE PRICES

The following listings of the pile and flat-woven rugs and other articles available in today's market are intended to be no more than an overview. All were sold at auction.

I have not included a range of dealer prices along with the auction house estimates. All dealers in old rugs are affected by the auction process to one degree or another: as a source of stock, as a means of selling locally acquired rugs of world-class quality or of disposing of long unsold stock, and as a guide to what's currently hot, what appears to have fallen out of favor, and the average prices realized for both. But unless

the factors determining dealers' prices are carefully spelled out—
assuming I knew what all of them were—they can be misleading.

Some dealers in old rugs will, if they acquire a rug at a good price,
pass on part of their savings to the buyer; others mark all rugs at what
they consider the going price to provide a cushion for rugs they may be
unable to sell for enough to cover their cost. Pricing also depends on
how easily an old rug can be replaced in a dealer's stock by one of
reasonably similar age and quality. And finally, even a dealer able to
flintily resist the hardest-nosed bargainer will sometimes give a price
break to a novice who takes his or her fancy.

The auction arena is a public marketplace supplying not so much a
baseline of prices as a level playing ground. Oriental rugs do not attract
the high-flying investors who pushed the fine arts market to such absurd
heights. In fact, in December 1990, just after the bottom fell out of the
art market, Sotheby's held a rug sale more successful than any held there
in recent years, selling almost 90 percent of the lots offered, some at
more than double the high estimates. On average, however, rug collectors are the Scrooges of the collecting world: buyers of fine art appear
to pride themselves on how much they pay; rug buyers, on how little.
Accordingly, they tend to strongly resist house-hyped estimates.

Rugs offered at auction must sell within minutes of their appearance
on the block. Since an unsold rug exacts a handling charge, it is in the
consignor's interest to agree to a realistic range of estimates and reserve
figure below which it will not be sold. According to Jo Kris, the head of
the rug department at Skinner's in Massachusetts, realism usually pre-
vails, collectors' grumbles to the contrary.

Auctiongoers intending to bid are required to register and are assigned
numbers. In New York State auctioneers must by law indicate the failure
of a lot to sell; elsewhere, lots that fail to reach the reserve price are
often "knocked down" to numbers the auction house has assigned to
itself. When lots whose final bid is below the low estimate are consistently awarded to the same two or three numbers, it can be assumed
these are the house numbers for that sale. Buyers interested in rugs that
fail to sell during the auction can sometimes arrange to purchase them
postsale at attractive prices.

As you read through the following pages, be wary of drawing hasty
conclusions if a pictured rug appears similar to one seen at a dealer's
shop priced below or for more than twice the realized auction price.
Beginners are often hard put to distinguish a new, chemically washed,
vegetable-dyed Anatolian village rug from its 19th-century prototype, but
a dealer will justly tag such pieces with very different prices. Even if the
rugs compared *are* similar, price alone should not determine whether
you buy at auction or from a dealer.

Buying at auction is well suited to decisive, cool-headed types who know exactly what they're about—no returns, remember? But many collectors, including the six very sophisticated collectors, of diverse interests, whom I interviewed, prefer the flexibility inherent in buying from sympathetic dealers. At this point, however, it is important to mention how the collecting of rugs differs from other kinds of art collecting and how this difference affects the attitudes of collectors vis-à-vis the marketplace.

Rugs, unlike other art objects, appeal to the tactile sense as well as the visual, and the handle of a rug provides experienced collectors with an important clue to its probable origin. Short of renting a warehouse, however, rug dealers are unable to display their wares as dealers in porcelain, fine art, and even furniture can.

The collector, not trusting the dealer to always know what might catch his fancy, would, ideally, like to see every rug in stock. "How can I tell what I want," he says, "until I see what you have?" But most of the dealers I interviewed are not thrilled, understandably, by the prospect of spending two or three hours with collectors more interested in indulging their passion for looking at rugs than in buying one, reducing the dealer's gallery to a shambles in the process.

Dealers in small tribal pieces—The Hazara Gallery and Adraskand in California come to mind—can usually afford to allow collectors to browse through their stock, but large decorative rugs are heavy and awkward to roll out and roll up again, and area rugs, stacked in piles of 30 or more, require many to be lifted and moved to extract the one or two that catch a collector's eye. In short, we have here a classic conflict of interest. Auction buying will never, *should* never, replace the rewarding relationship many collectors have with dealers, but at auction previews we can look and touch to our heart's content, providing ourselves with both pleasure and instruction at the same time.

The prices that follow were realized for oriental rugs and other weavings selected from a total of about 6,500 sold at auction from April 1989 through January 1991 by the major houses in New York, the Boston area, and California. All prices include the buyer's premium, it having become customary not only to charge the consignors commission rates based on the amount lots sell for—the higher the hammer price, the lower the rate—but to add a flat 10 percent of a winning bid to the buyer's invoice.

The listings begin with classical carpets and early tribal rugs, proceed through later tribal weavings, rustic loom production, and flat weaves, and conclude with commercial workshop rugs. Readers should bear in mind that although no foreign auction results are included here, the oriental rug market is an international one. Prices in the United States are affected by worldwide demand, by changing tastes in rugs, and by the fluctuation of the dollar on the world exchange. In other words, the prices listed here are temporary guides, not gospel.

Remember, too, that when a winning bid soars well beyond the high estimate, it can indicate either that (1) the auction house experts undervalued the merits of that particular rug, or (2) the high bidder, for whatever reason—ego, ignorance, home decor needs—was willing to pay an inflated price to get it.

CLASSICAL CARPETS AND TRIBAL WEAVINGS, 1500–1800

To connoisseurs of Eastern rugs, quibbles about the distinction between fine and decorative arts are rendered irrelevant by the design, beauty, and historical interest of great early carpets, but the fact of the matter is that first-rate examples of the rugs woven in the court-sponsored workshops of the Safavid, Ottoman, Mughal, and Mamluk dynasties can be acquired for less than a third-rate painting.

Because of the scarcity of fine classical carpets and early tribal weavings, dealer stock is very limited and their prices determined by other than purely market forces. Dealers more likely than others to have such pieces are noted in the resource listings; but for the most part, they are consigned from distinguished collections or as deacquisitions from museum holdings to whichever of the major auction houses offers the best terms and widest presale publicity.

A fairly representative selection of early examples of wide-ranging quality was sold at auction in the last two years, with several new price records established. Some of the Turkoman weavings may date to as late as the first quarter of the 19th century, but in the context of tribal weaving—which was long undervalued and for the most part wore out in daily use—this is considered very old.

When reading the accompanying descriptions please bear in mind that because of their extreme rarity, the condition of very old carpets and tribal artifacts affects prices differently from rugs woven in the later 19th and early 20th centuries.

TURKISH CARPETS

Small Medallion Ushak Rug (1575–1625, 3′3″ ×5′). A rare and desirable very old rug with exceptional color and drawing, particularly the red ground's graceful spandrels and the cloud bands on the blue main border. Wool pile on wool foundation. Good condition for age.

This rug, though included in a general sale at a regional New England auction house, attracted the notice of specialist dealers and brought a record price for the type. .... Est. $12,000/15,000; sold for $59,400

Oushak Saph Fragment (18th century, 12′6″×7′4″). A saph is a carpet with a multiple series of prayer arches, for use either in a mosque to accommodate a number of worshippers or, according to another theory, as a mosque wall decoration. This fragmented saph has five niches; the group to which it belongs has seven or nine. Each niche has a decorative representation of footmarks and hanging lamps on an otherwise plain red ground. The field surrounding the niches and the wide border are richly decorated with floral motifs. Wool coarsely knotted on a wool foundation. Wear, major restorations, and reweaves. ....
...............................Sold just above the low estimate of $6,000 for $6,500

"Lotto" Oushak Rug (1650–1700, 5′10″×3′6″). This group of distinctive rugs is known by the name of the Italian artist, Lorenzo Lotto (1480–1556), in whose paintings early examples appeared as decorative elements. This late, off-center piece with its typical gold arabesques on red ground, is bordered in stylized flowering vines and rosettes on blue. It retains most of its original flat-woven ends and boasts better-than-average condition. Wool coarsely knotted on a wool foundation. ....Sold just below the low estimate of $20,000 for $19,800

*"Lotto" Oushak rug, Western Anatolia, 1650–1700, 5′10″ × 3′6″,
$19,800.* PHOTO COURTESY OF CHRISTIE'S EAST.

West Anatolian Rug (c. 1700, 6′5″×3′8″). This very rare rug is a variant of a geometrical type known as "Holbein," after Hans Holbein the Younger in whose 16th-century paintings earlier examples were represented. The camel-hair ground contains one large central medallion in rich blue and madder red flanked at either end with two smaller, similar octagons, the whole bordered with stylized rosettes on red. Wool coarsely knotted on wool foundation. Shows wear, reweaves, and repiling. (See color insert) .. Sold between the high and low estimates for $44,000

Ladik Prayer Rug (c. 1800, 6′1″×3′9″). The crowding of the design elements indicate a late version of this format: serrated-leaf and amulet motifs on blue above an unornamented madder-red *mihrab* with the tulips typical of this design inverted below on red. Blue primary border with floral motifs, enclosed by meandering-vine minor borders. Wool pile knotted symmetrically on wool foundation; density not known but typically of moderate coarseness. Good color. Some wear, repairs, reweaves; repiling and loss to end guard borders. ....
....Est. $8,000/10,000; sold for $8,800

Ladik prayer rug, Central Anatolia, c. 1800, 6′1″ × 3′9″, $8,800.
PHOTO COURTESY OF CHRISTIE'S EAST.

"Transylvanian" West Anatolian Prayer Rug (c. 1750, 5'8"×4'7"). A lamp representing the light of God hangs within a madder-red, columned *mihrab* flanked by tendril-filled spandrels. Good color and drawing. Restorations throughout. Knotted symmetrically on wool foundation, approximately 100 per sq. in. .... Est. $2,000/2,500; sold for $6,050

"Transylvanian" West Anatolian Rug (late 17th century, 4'8"×4'). Tomato red ground of the *mihrab* is topped by red spandrels decorated with stiff floral motifs, the whole enclosed by a bold, poorly resolved cartouche border. Wool pile, approx. 100 knots per sq. in. on wool foundation. Extensive wear, re-weaves, and other repairs. .... Sold between high and low estimates for $6,600

Oushak Carpet Fragment, West Anatolia (17th century, 9'1"×2'). These so-called bird rugs, in which the figures are actually stylizations of leaf motifs, are popular with collectors of classical carpets despite a rather drab appearance, compounded in this case by poor condition. Coarsely knotted in wool, 64 symmetrical knots per sq. in. on a wool foundation, this neatly bound strip is edged with a nice bit of cloud-band border. ...... Est. $2,000–3,000; sold for $8,250

Ghiordes Prayer Rug (c. 1800, 5'7"×4'1"). This refined prayer rug is typical of a class very popular with collectors earlier in this century, later widely and badly imitated. The rich blue field of the *mihrab* is set off by stylized red and blue leaf and floral motifs in the beige-grounded spandrels, end panels, and main border. Wool pile symmetrically knotted on wool foundation, typically 100–150 knots per sq. in. Evenly worn; repairs. ..... Est. $2,500/3,500; sold for $3,850

Ghiordes prayer rug, Western Anatolia, c. 1800, 5'7" × 4'1", $3,850. PHOTO COURTESY OF CHRISTIE'S EAST.

Central Anatolian Prayer Rug (c. 1800, 5'3" ×4'1"). Madder-red stepped *mihrab* edged by green latch hooks. Stylized branched flowers decorate green spandrel; vivid blue diamond-decorated inner border; burnt orange main border with pendant blossom repeat. Approx. 100 symmetrical knots per sq. in. on wool foundation. Corroded browns; losses to kilim ends. ....
....Est. $35,000/45,000; sold for $37,400

Konya Long Rug (c. 1800, 12'9" ×5'5"). Linked ram's-horn devices surround two bold eight-point star medallions—one red, one purple—within a stylized leaf meander border. Very coarsely and symmetrically knotted on a wool foundation. Vivid vegetable colors. Extreme wear; large reweave. ....
....Est. $5,000/10,000; sold for $6,600

CAUCASIAN CARPETS

Star Kazak, Southwest Caucasus (late 18th century, 8'2" ×5'10"). An early, very important example of a Caucasian village rug design much coveted by collectors, it brought a record price at Sotheby's in 1990. Noteworthy for its precise drawing and the vivid, saturated colors of its bold, geometricized, floral-derived figures sparkling against a cream ground. Typically, the lustrous wool pile is relatively coarsely knotted on a wool foundation, 64 symmetrical knots per sq. in. Partial side borders; reweave; patches; repairs. ....
.... Est. $225,000/ 275,000; sold for $286,000

Kuba Corridor Carpet, East Caucasus (18th century, 19'8" ×8'). A late, crowded version of a classic Caucasian pattern known as Afshan. Wool pile symmetrically knotted, 81 knots per sq. in. on a wool foundation. Lively coloration; reweaves, repairs, repiling, and rebound selvages. ....
....Est. $15,000/20,000; sold for $27,500

Kuba Runner (18th century, 3'10" × 14'). Striking large-scaled red, gold, blue, and purple shield designs on corroded brown ground enlivened with rosettes, surrounded by "S" border on ivory. Extensive wear; clumsy repiling; backed. ....
....Est. $3,000/4,000; sold for $9,000

PERSIAN CARPETS

Garden Carpet Fragment, Northwest Persia (17th (?) century, 7'10" ×6'9"). Yellow ground with alternating compartments of trees and palmettes centering on a gold octagonal swan-filled pond from which radiate garden-edged waterways contained within a wide navy blue primary border with realistic birds and trees. Wool pile, knot count unknown, probably 85 to 100 knots per sq. in. on cotton foundation. Extensive wear; repairs, patches. ....
.... Est. $15,000/20,000; sold for $55,000

"Vase" Carpet Fragment, Central Persia (1575–1625, 1'6" ×1'2", together with 18th-century Northwest Persian fragment of much lesser interest). This worn "vase" fragment includes a section of a polychrome floral trellis on an ochre field bordered by a mid-blue rosette and blossom border. The knot density of the wool pile averages 200–225 knots per sq. in. A technical feature of vase rugs of interest to scholars and advanced collectors is that they have double cotton warps, lying on two levels. .... Sold at estimated low of $800

Garden carpet fragment, Northwest Persia, 17th century, 7'10" × 6'9", $55,000. PHOTO COURTESY OF CHRISTIE'S EAST.

"Vase" carpet, Central Persia, early 17th century, 25'3" × 8'9", $82,500. PHOTO COURTESY OF CHRISTIE'S EAST.

"Vase" Carpet, Central Persia (early 17th century, 25′3″×8′9″). One of a pair with a famous Berlin rug destroyed during World War II, this rare two-plane, leaflet-lattice carpet with palmettes and numerous small blossoms on a red-bordered blue ground was deaccessioned by the Baltimore Museum of Art. Structure similar to above fragment. Shows considerable wear, reweaves, repairs, breaks in rebound selvage. .... Est. $60,000/80,000; sold for $82,500

Slit Tapestry Silk Kilim (probably Kashan, 16th century, 5′7″×4′3″). Most figural weavings leave a lot to be desired, artistically speaking. This striking exception vividly depicts a poignant scene in the Persian legend of Leila and Mejnoon. Despite wear, ragged ends, and holes, this exquisitely colored, very old rarity brought a record price at Christie's in 1990. ....
.... Est. $100,000/150,000; sold for $440,000

Northwest Persian Long Rug (18th century, 15′11″×6′9″). This boldly handsome carpet, averaging 64 asymmetrical wool knots per sq. in. on a cotton foundation, represents a rustic version of the designs and scale of earlier Persian court carpets. Outstanding use of color. Outer borders missing; some repiling.
.... Est. $25,000/30,000; sold for $30,800

"Polonaise" Carpet, Central Persia (1700–1750, 6′8″×4′8″). One of 230 examples known to exist, the term "Polonaise" arises from the mislabeling as Polish a similar carpet shown at the 1878 Paris International Exhibition. Variously attributed to Isphahan and Kashan, the design is derived from earlier Persian carpets and typically asymmetrically knotted in silk and gold/silver-wrapped silk threads on a cotton foundation with an average density of 224 knots per sq. in.

The luscious colors—salmon pinks, aquamarine greens, and azure blues—in this remarkably preserved example deacquisitioned by the Getty Museum contributed to its record-breaking price for the class in 1990 at Sotheby's.
.... Est. $70,000/100,000; sold for $440,000

Isfahan Carpets, Central Persia (17th century, 13′8″×5′10″). Two splendid and very similar carpets consigned by the Getty Museum to Sotheby's in 1990, both with rich raspberry fields decorated with intertwining layers of vinery punctuated by palmettes, lancet leaves, and blossom heads. Wool pile of about 170 asymmetrical knots per sq. in. on a cotton foundation. Both in generally good condition; both missing minor guard borders at ends; minor border repiling.
.... Est. $30,000/40,000; $20,000/25,000; sold for $121,000/$82,500

Silk Rug, Central Persia (1650–1700, 7′6″×5′6″). This small, lush rug is a type considered a precursor to the "Polonaise" group. The two-plane system of elegantly drawn arabesques and sinuous vinery are of a honey-toned coloration, sparingly accented by spots of stronger color. Knotted very finely in silk, 900 symmetrical knots per sq. in. on a silk foundation, and in generally good condition. .... Est. $125,000/175,000; sold for $506,000

Persian Vase Carpet (c. 1800, 15′10″×9′). A red ground covered by well-spaced palmettes and rosettes within a delicate lattice of flowering vines in blues, gold, ivory, saffron, rose, and green. Two vases with flowering branches stand at either end of the field, the flowers in the top vase obscured by grinning skull over which hangs a curved sword in scabbard. The symbolism of this odd memento mori is unknown. A beige primary border of palmettes, rosettes, flower clusters, and vines is enclosed by floral guards. ....
.... Est. $15,000/20,000; sold for $23,100

"Polonaise" carpet, Central Persia, 1700–1750, 6' 8" × 4' 8", $440,000. PHOTO © 1991 SOTHEBY'S, INC.

Salor Turkoman door rug, Central Turkestan, c. 1800, 6' 1" × 4' 2", $94,600. PHOTO COURTESY OF CHRISTIE'S EAST.

TURKOMAN TRIBAL CARPETS AND WEAVINGS

Salor Turkoman Engsi, Central Turkestan (c. 1800, 6′1″×4′2″). This extremely rare Salor door hanging is knotted asymmetrically in wool, with some silk, on a wool foundation, knot density unknown. The ground is brick red; other colors include dark and medium blues, wine red, yellow, ivory, apricot, blue green, brown. Note the parade of quadrapeds across the lower panel. Shows some wear, patch, breaks, and loss to end borders. ....
.... Est. $20,000/25,000; sold for $94,600

Salor Wedding Trapping, Central Turkestan (c. 1800, 7′4″×2′6″). The grand scale and fine, velvety weave of this unrivaled trapping suggests it was woven by a bride-to-be to adorn the litter in which she rode to her wedding. Wool and silk knotted asymmetrically, 260 to the sq. in. on a wool foundation. Colors in addition to the rich, deep red field include dark blue, ivory, dark violet, yellow, and cochineal. Silk areas oxidized; ends incomplete. ....
.... Est. $75,000/100,000; sold for $148,500

Salor Bag Face, Central Turkestan (c. 1800, 3′11″×1′1″). A classic example of Salor weaving but not as rare as the preceding lot. Blues, fuschias, ivory, and brown on a deep red field. Approximately 200 asymmetrical wool knots per sq. in. on a wool foundation. Wear; repaired slits; losses to sides.
.... Est. $10,000/15,000; sold for $12,650

Salor Main Carpet, Central Turkestan (c. 1800, 10′2″×7′6″). A fine example of the elegant spacing and precise drawing of guls that make Salor weavings the stars of the Turkoman group. The somber color range of this piece includes ivory, green, coral, raspberry, and several blues on a dark red ground. Averages 150 asymmetrical wool knots per sq. in. on a wool foundation. Overall wear, holes, fraying, rewoven areas, reselvaged, one kilim end replaced. ....
.... Est. $10,000/14,000; sold for $18,700

Tekke Bird Asmalyk, West Turkestan (c. 1800, 4′6″×2′10″). This camel trapping is one of 14 known of this design and one of only three retaining the original side and bottom finishes. Asymmetrically knotted in wool, averaging 250 per sq. in. on a wool foundation. Ivory, blues, browns on a liver-red field. Very good condition. .... Est. $40,000/60,000; sold for $115,500

Tekke Animal–Tree Asmalyk, West Turkestan (c. 1800, 4′8″×2′10″). The tenth known example of another rare group, the well-balanced grid design is finely knotted asymmetrically in wool, 350 knots per sq. in. on a wool foundation. Ivory, dark blue, rust, and dark brown on a deep red field. Very good condition; slight mothing; minor repair. ....
.... Est. $30,000/50,000; sold for $44,000

Yomud Asmalyk, West Turkestan (c. 1800, 3′11″×2′8″). Stylized shrubs in dark blue, aubergine, brown, and brick red decorate the honey-colored field of this extremely rare type of camel trapping, one of two known. Wool knotted asymmetrically on a wool foundation, density not known. Slight wear, stains and mothing; sides reduced. .... Est. $50,000/60,000; sold for $55,000

Yomud Main Carpet, West Turkestan (c. 1800, 9′9″×5′). This multiple-gul carpet is a veritable sampler of Yomud designs, whose patterns are the boldest and most colorful of the Turkoman groups, in this case blues, rich green, gold,

Yomud asmalyk, *West Turkestan, c. 1800, 3' 11" × 2' 8", $55,000.*
PHOTO COURTESY OF CHRISTIE'S EAST.

Yomud carpet, West Turkestan,
c. 1800, 9'9" × 5', $18,700.
PHOTO COURTESY OF SKINNER, INC.

brown, and ivory on a madder red field. Wool knotted asymmetrically on a wool foundation, density not known. Visible wear, hole, minor patches and repairs.
....Est. 12,000/15,000; sold for $18,700

Yomud Okbash, West Turkestan (c. 1800, 1′11″ × 1′5″). These pieces, when joined along one side and at the apex of the triangular tabs, were supposedly used to cover during transport the ends of strut poles used in the construction of yurts. This densely plush example, finely knotted asymmetrically in lustrous wool, 200 per sq. in. on a wool foundation, has brilliant blues, madder red, brown, black, and camel on a deep red ground. Rebound sides; one obvious rewoven area. .... Est. $25,000/30,000; sold for $27,500

INDIAN CARPETS

Mughal Carpet Fragments (17th century, each 4′ × 1′). Two pieces featuring richly colored naturalistic flowering plants on deep blue ground. Wool pile, averaging 259 knots per sq. in. on cotton and silk foundation. Losses to pile, other minor damage, bound on all sides and nicely mounted. ....
.... Each est. $3,500/4,500; each sold for $4,500

Indo-Herat Carpet (mid-17th century, 19′7″ × 15′4″). Palmettes and lancelike leaves on raspberry ground; wide dark blue border with palmettes and flowers. Wool pile, knot count not known, on cotton foundation. Pieced together, tinted, rewoven areas. .... Sold for the low estimate of $25,000

Mughal Floral Carpet, Northwest India (c. 1650, 9′10″ × 15′). This Getty Museum deacquisition has six rows of closely spaced flowering plants, including lilies, asters, and roses, which also adorn the blue primary border enclosed by ivory-grounded minor borders with flowering vine meander. The raspberry field is typical of old Indian carpets; other colors are rose, gold, several blues, greens, salmon, ivory, and black. Knotted asymmetrically in wool, averaging 180 per sq. in. on a cotton foundation. Corroded browns; eight holes in field; moth damage in borders; slits in both end borders. (See color insert) ....
....Est. $60,000/90,000; sold for $253,000

Mughal Shaped Carpets, Lahore, Northwest India (c. 1650, 14′8″ × 8′11″). This pair, also deacquisitioned by the Getty Museum and sold at Sotheby's in 1990, have the naturalistic floral patterning often seen on classical Indian carpets. Knotted asymmetrically in fine lustrous wool, averaging 200 per sq. in. on a cotton and silk foundation. Blues, plum, mauve, greens, yellow, camel, rose, ivory, browns on a raspberry ground. Moth damage; slits. ....
.... Each est. $125,000/175,000; each sold for $297,000

EAST TURKESTAN CARPETS

Khotan Long Rug (c. 1800, 9′4″ × 4′10″). Although coarsely knotted, this rug has a refined appearance. Repeat figures in blue on red; the popular trefoil border motif is red on blue. Asymmetrical wool knots 42 per sq. in. on a cotton foundation. Areas of restoration. ....Est. $10,000/12,000; sold for $20,900

Khotan long rug, East Turkestan, c. 1800, 12′7″ × 6′2″, $48,000.
PHOTO COURTESY OF CHRISTIE'S EAST.

Chinese rug, 18th century, 6′5″ × 4′5″, $29,700. PHOTO COURTESY
OF CHRISTIE'S EAST.

Khotan Long Rug (c. 1800, 12′7″×6′2″). Warm, glowing colors distinguish this outstanding rosette-adorned blue-fielded example bordered with a Far Eastern–flavored *Yun-Tsai T'ou* motif on gold. Coarsely knotted asymmetrically in wool on a cotton foundation. Shows some wear, moth damage, and a reweave. .... Est. $30,000/40,000; sold for $48,000

Yarkand Long Rug (c. 1800. 12′4″×5′11″). The explosive effect of the copper red field and its three elegantly drawn blue medallions juxtaposed with the monumental spring green trefoil border would be hard to equal. Structure typically wool coarsely knotted asymmetrically on cotton warps with wool wefts. Generally good condition; a few small reweaves. (See color insert) ....
.... Offered in 1990 by Christie's; sold for $143,000

CHINESE CARPETS

Chinese Dragon Carpet Fragment, Ming Dynasty (16th century, 2′9″×2′5″). Fragmentary stylized clouds and blue flames issuing from portion of ivory-scaled dragon on taffy field. Wool coarsely knotted on cotton foundation. Corroded browns, repair, bound on all sides. ....Sold for the low estimate of $4,000

Kansu Rug, West China (c. 1800, 9′×6′). The design layout is that of an East Turkestan rug, but the stylized butterflies and floral forms are Kansu. Coral, beige, azure blue, ivory, rose, and mahogany on a warm brick red field. Very coarsely knotted in wool, 25 asymmetrical knots per sq. in. on a wool foundation. Good condition; some repiled corroded browns. ....
.... Est. $10,000/12,000; sold for $12,100

Ninghsia Saddle Rug (c. 1800, approx. 4′6″×2′3″). Two pairs of dragons cavort on an indigo ground under puffy, stylized clouds enclosed in a wide border, all in faded shades of yellow, tan, gray, and brown wool knotted asymmetrically, about 70 per sq. in. on a cotton foundation. Outer border corroded; losses to pile; small holes. .... Est. $2,500/3,500; sold for $22,000

Chinese Runner (c. 1800, 15′×2′6″). Stylized cloud forms float the length of this piece in rich, warm browns, blues, and tans. Wool knotted asymmetrically, about 55 per sq. in. on a cotton foundation. Some corrosion of honey-colored field, otherwise good condition with plushy handle. ....
.... Est. $10,000/12,000; sold for $23,100

Ninghsia Carpet (18th century, 13′8″×6′3″). Although very coarsely knotted—25–30 per sq. in. on a cotton foundation—the lanolin-rich wool, together with clear mellow colors, provides a rug of luxurious elegance. Golds, blues, browns, and honey are used in the artfully balanced tile repeat of the field, the flowering vine inner border, and fretwork outer band. Generally good condition, with small rewoven area and corroded browns. ....
.... Est. $40,000/60,000; sold for $82,500

Qianlong (?) Rug (18th century, 4′5″×6′5″). The oldest known example with the Eight Horses of Mu Wang, according to the *Hali* auction report, and a playful lot they are, too. Camel ground with motifs in soft golds, blues, and tans within dark blue guards and graceful flowering vine main border. Superb wool knotted coarsely and asymmetrically on cotton foundation. Wear; losses to pile. ....
.... Est. $2,000/3,000; sold for $29,700

TRIBAL WEAVINGS, 1800–1925

Although many tribal weavings are flat-woven, only knotted-pile articles are included under this heading. Flat weaves, whose collectors tend to concentrate on them exclusively, are dealt with separately.

As a class, tribal weavings have the distinctive, strongly traditional character associated with kinship groups and closely knit isolated communities that have developed over time a tribal-like culture. Some were woven for sale or barter; most were made for personal domestic use. Among the pieces listed here are examples from the Central Asian Turkoman tribes of Afghanistan and Turkestan, now northeast Iran and Soviet Turkmenistan and Uzbekistan; the Baluch in northeast Persia and western Afghanistan; the Yürüks in eastern Turkey; and several Persian groups, including Kurds, Shahsavan, Lurs, Qashqai, Bakhtiyari, and Afshars.

Today few tribes are wholly nomadic. Many live in villages during the winter, taking their flocks to pasture in the highlands in summer. In eastern Turkey, I have seen these groups "going to the *yayla*," their faces alight with pleasurable anticipation. And they still weave. True, much of the present-day output is garishly colored with synthetic dyes, but occasionally a weaver's creative response to his or her environment vividly surmounts the shoddiness of the materials. Prime examples are the little mats embellished with tanks, grenades, helicopters, and Kalishnikov rifles that were woven during the USSR–Afghanistan conflict.

Collectors of tribal weavings accept the fact that because the looms used are both primitive and transportable (see chapter on rug structure), minor distortions are unavoidable. They see them as a sign of authenticity rather than poor workmanship. You might not want a deformed rug for furnishing purposes, but in January 1990 a notably skewed Star Kazak sold at Sotheby's to Eberhart Herrmann, the premier European dealer in world-class rugs, for $286,000.

TURKISH

According to Werner Brüggemann and Harald Böhmer, authors of the prize-winning book *Rugs of the Peasants and Nomads of Anatolia*, "the nomadic life style can still be found among the Kurds of East and South-

east Anatolia and among the Yürüks (including the Yüncü) who have left
the plateaus of Central Anatolia and have moved to the Taurus [Toros]
mountains and surrounding plains.''

The majority of the items made by the Taurus Yürüks, a Turkoman-
related people, are flat-woven. The Kurds, on the other hand, weave
small rugs—prayer formats are common—and large, boldly patterned
runners, both employing distinctive shades of orange-red and violet-
shaded brown. Like Baluch work, Turkish Kurdish rugs were undervalued in the past. They are not commonly seen in the market; when they
are, they are apt to be badly worn or are late examples disfigured by
poor-quality synthetic dyes. No good examples were sold at auction in
the past two years.

Kutahya Yürük Yatak, West Anatolia (c. 1875, 6′6″ × 5′6″). Square formats,
a pile of peltlike shagginess and rudimentary, bold repeat patterns are characteristic of these so-called bedding rugs. This yatak has four rows of three Memling guls flanked by star and diamond fillers on a rose red ground. Simple
polygons ornament two borders of equal size, one rose red, the other gold. Wear;
holes; selvage damage. .... Est. $1,500/2,000; sold for $3,960

Melas Bag Face, Southwest Anatolia (c. 1850, 1′10″ × 1′7″). Turkish bags
and bag faces are rarely seen on the market except for garish, synthetically dyed
late examples. This simply patterned early example with clear vegetable dyes is,
therefore, very much a collector's item. Shows wear and damage to side finishes.
.... Est. $2,000/$3,000; sold for $2,420

Yüncü Rug (c. 1875, 6′9″ × 5′9″). On a blue-latch-hooked red ground, a
diamond-shaped armed and arrowheaded ivory-latch-hooked red medallion
flanked top and bottom by two pairs of gabled arches ornamented with latch
hooks, geometric figures and rosettes within a blue and ivory vine meander
together with boxed stars on the red main border. Shows even wear; reweave;
repiling. .... Est. $5,000/7,000; sold for $4,950

PERSIAN

QASHQAI

Although the rugs in this group can be ascribed to various subtribes in
the Qashqai Confederacy of southwest Iran, for simplicity's sake I have
chosen to follow the auction house policy of grouping them together.
The Qashqai are accomplished weavers, favoring rather densely patterned rugs distinguished by a wide range of jewel-like colors. There is
considerable variation in weaving structures within this group; generally,
however, the older the piece, the more likely it is for the warps and wefts
to be wool.

Melas bag face, Southwest Anatolia, c. 1850, 1' 10" × 1' 7", $2,420. PHOTO COURTESY OF GROGAN & COMPANY.

Yüncü rug, West Anatolia, c. 1875, 6' 9" × 5' 9", $4,950. PHOTO COURTESY OF CHRISTIE'S EAST.

Rug (c. 1885, 7′6″ ×4′8″). Three red and ivory stepped diamonds on an abrashed royal blue cartouche-shaped field within red spandrels, all ornamented with the Herati motif. Ivory palmette and leaf primary border; two floral guards. Good condition. .... Est. $1,000/1,500; sold for $2,090

Scatter Rug (c. 1885, 5′2″ ×3′2″). Small blue, camel, and jade rectilinear medallion off-centered on a hexagonal madder red field within triangular camel spandrels sprinkled with *boteh* and rosettes. Floral meander borders; brocaded kilim ends. Minor wear and moth damage. Est. $1,200/1,500; sold for $2,475

Rug (c. 1885, 8′2″ ×4′2″). Three connected ivory medallions bearing typical Qashqai four-armed figure in red on midnight blue field within elongated and saw-toothed ivory spandrels, all densely patterned with animal, geometric, and leaf motifs in red, yellow, blue, and brown. Three floral borders of nearly equal width; checkerboard ends. Good condition. ....
.... Est. $3,500/4,500; sold for $4,400

Rug (c. 1885, 6′2″ ×4′2″). Format similar to preceding rug but with a very different, dressier look: ivory poled medallions on a deep blue ground with diagonal rows of tiny *botehs* in gold and red. The narrow, sawtooth elongations of the ivory spandrels contain a stylized, rectilinear bouquet-like motif. Seven narrow guards bearing geometric repeats; checkerboard ends terminating in striped kilim skirts. Good condition. ...... Est. $6,000/8,000; sold for $10,450

Rug (c. 1885, 6′5″ ×4′5″). Three medallions, one red, two ivory, with Qashqai four-armed figure on midnight blue field patterned with striking diagonal rows of flower clusters. No spandrels. Primary red border with formal palmette and curved leaf repeat; geometric guards. Ragged selvage, otherwise good. ....
.... Est. $4,000/6,000; sold for $7,425

Qashqai rug, Southwest Persia,
c. 1885, 8′2″ × 4′2″, $4,400.
PHOTO COURTESY OF SKINNER, INC.

Rug (c. 1900, 6′10″×5′7″). A variety of colorful geometric figures crowd a blue field accented with a diagonal ivory stylized-leaf motif often seen on Qashqai work. The primary border is also typically Qashqai: latch-hooked guls alternating with a pole-connected, double-ended ram's-horn motif. Shows some wear. .... Est. $2,500/3,000; sold for $3,850

Scatter Rug (c. 1885, 5′×3′9″). The field consists of narrow flower- and leaf-decorated rows in roof-peak-like diagonals upon which, in each corner, is imposed a small square containing a floral *boteh*. Floral guards surround a gold primary border with the same latch-hooked gul and ram's-horn motif described above. Brocaded kilim skirts. Extraordinary color and wool. A few small restorations. .... Est. $15,000/25,000; sold for $18,700

Bag Faces (c. 1900, each 2′×2′). Midnight blue field contains central hooked medallion and a variety of animal and geometric motifs, with Memling guls in each corner and a stylized leaf-and-vine motif on an ivory border. Vegetable dyes in reds, blues, green, and gold. Mint condition. .... Est. $3,000/4,000; sold for $3,300

KHAMSEH

The Khamseh confederation of five southwestern tribes lies to the west of the Qashqai Confederacy. According to one expert, the reds and blues of Khamseh rugs are unusually intense and a sprightly bird motif, known as the *morgh*, or chicken design, is characteristic of the group.

Rug (c. 1910, 6′6″×5′2″). Dark red diamond medallion inset with an ivory-lobed gul-like figure enclosed by diagonal rows of blue, gold, and jade blossoms. Similar ivory guls decorate the corners of the dark blue field upon which the medallion blossoms are repeated. Three meander guards. Small patch, otherwise good condition. .... Est. $1,500/2,000; sold for $1,760

AFSHAR

The inclusion of Afshar work among tribal weavings is complicated by the fact that many rugs made by Afshar weavers are in fact village workshop rugs, often of large size, influenced by designs originating in Kerman, south of which many Afsharis settled in the 19th century.

One curious but seldom mentioned characteristic of Afshar rugs is their tendency to approach the square. Many have decorative flat-woven ends; their wefts, usually double, are dyed orange, and alternate warps are depressed so as to produce a greater or lesser degree of ribbing on the back. Tribal Afshar weaving is knotted symmetrically; Afshar village workshop rugs usually have asymmetrical knots.

Rug (c. 1885, 5′9″×3′6″). On an ivory ground, two rows of very large red and dark blue *botehs* containing three smaller *botehs*, a striking motif known as "mother and child." The dark blue primary border has a simplified palmette, rosette, and vine repeat; the two guards are floral meanders. Damaged selvages; sewn tear. .... Est. $1,500/2,000; sold for $3,080

Afshar rug, South Persia, c. 1885, 5'9" × 3'6", $3,080. PHOTO COURTESY OF SKINNER, INC.

Rug (c. 1885, 5'4" ×4'7"). A traditional Afshar design consisting of a stepped red medallion centered with a leaf-jagged light blue diamond, on a dark blue rectangle within a more broadly stepped red rectangle—upon which, in this example, small animals perch—set within a light blue field filled with very small gold and red *botehs*. Shows wear. .... Est. $2,000/3,000; sold for $6,050

Bag Face (c. 1885, 1'6" ×1'). Midnight blue field covered with red and green ram's-horn devices and stylized leaves within a red star medallion border. Glossy wool; good condition. .... Est. $1,800/2,200; sold for $1,980

OTHER PERSIAN TRIBAL RUGS

Luri Rug (c. 1900, 7'6" ×4'8").Characteristic Luri pattern of stylized cypress trees and plant motifs in red, blue, gold, and jade within a sawtooth hexagonal red lattice on a midnight blue ground. Three borders: one ivory, two red with stylized plants. Shows slight wear. .... Est. $1,200/1,500; sold for $1,760

Fars Lion Rug (c. 1900, 7'2" ×5'2"). A polychrome leashed lion with a surprised expression crouches within a red flower-bordered rectangle within a gold hexagon decorated with potted plants upon which birds perch; flower stalks with a single perching bird fill the green spandrels. The blue-grounded multicolored ram's-horn primary border has barber-pole guards. Slight wear and moth damage. (See color insert) .... Est. $2,500/3,500; sold for $4,180

Luri rug, Southwest Persia, c. 1900, 7′6″ × 4′8″, $1,760. PHOTO COURTESY OF SKINNER, INC.

West Persian Tribal Long Rug (c. 1850, 10′10″×5′4″). A classic pattern of three Harshang medallions flanked by Afshan-type flowers primitively rendered in ivory, dark blue, and red on a honey field sprinkled with colorful geometric motifs and animal stick figures, within a bold reciprocal madder red and ivory reciprocal trefoil border. Corroded browns; rewoven areas; missing end guards. .... Est. $5,000/7,000; sold for $5,500

South Persian Saddle Rug (c. 1900, 2′10″×3′6″). A central floral column decorates a midnight blue field patterned with ivory dots and edged with ivory bowlike motifs and enclosed by floral guards, all in shades of blue, tan, and rust red. Partial ends, otherwise good condition. .... Est. $3,500/4,500; sold for $3,850

Northwest Persia, Shahsavan Long Rug (c. 1875, 9′8″×4′). Three boxed four-poled medallions of a type seen on early Shahsavan bag faces are placed one above the other on a dark blue sawtooth-bordered reserve. The red main border with hooked diamonds is flanked by an ivory inner border with animal and checkerboard motifs and an outer rust border with a dark brown reciprocal trefoil. Richly colored in green, reds, dark and medium blue, coral, orange, ivory gold, and aubergine. Slight loss to one end, otherwise good condition. .. .. Est. $4,000/6,000; sold for $3,025

KURDISH

Kurdish groups, both weaving and nonweaving, live throughout the large area in northwest Iran known as Kurdistan, to the south in the vicinity of Kermanshah, and in the northeast above Khorasan. Some of the most famous old Persian rug names, like Senneh and Bidjar, belong to the distinctive products of long-settled Kurdish weavers.

The assignment of tribal Kurdish rugs to particular groups has just begun, but in general we are speaking of lustrous all-wool small or runner-size rugs, often heavy and shaggy, with edges double-overcast in dark brown wool. The tribal variety is typically somewhat misshapen but hard-wearing and boldly colored with rectilinear versions of a variety of medallion designs. A common bag face pattern is composed of poly-chrome interlocking diamonds.

Quchan Tribal Rug, Northeast Persia (c. 1885, 7′9″ × 5′5″). Two dark blue rectangular medallions with six gabled and square projections on an abrashed rust field together with Memling guls and small geometric filler motifs, enclosed by a barber-pole guard, an ivory main border with a repeat cross motif and one human figure. The gold outer border has a polychrome geometric repeat. Striped kilim ends. Good condition. .... Est. $3,000/3,500; sold for $4,400

Small Runner, Northwest Persia (c. 1885, 6′9″ × 3′4″). Horizontal bands with zigzags of stylized flowering vines in red, dark and medium blue, gold, and blue-green within a gold border of stylized leaves and rosettes and two floral guards. Rebound edges; patch. .... Est. $1,800/2,200; sold for $1,760

Pair of Bags, Northwest Persia (c. 1885, each 3′3″ × 2′6″). Memling gul on a dark blue hexagon on madder red field flanked with a variety of animals and amulet motifs. Polychrome stylized leaf and flower border within ivory floral guards. Original loops and bindings; striped kilim backs. Good condition. .... Est. $3,500/4,500; sold for $3,850

Long Rug, West Persia (c. 1900, 10′9″ × 3′6″). Seven polychrome latch-hooked hexagons on an abrashed brown ground edged with bold, colorfully banded sawtooth projections within a polychrome diagonally striped main border and meander guards. Cotton warp; vegetable dyes. Good condition. .... Est. $4,000/6,000; sold for $4,950

BALUCH (Baluchi, Balouch, Beluch)

The tribal assignment of the rugs known generically as Baluch (the term Baluchi refers properly to the language, not the people) presents many of the same difficulties as Kurdish weavings. Northeast Persia and west-ern Afghanistan was home to the nomadic Baluch and related tribes for whom, when they settled in villages there, weaving became a source of income.

The classic Baluch rug is knotted asymmetrically of wonderfully silky wool in shades of red and blue and touches of white on a wool foundation with brown goat-hair edge finishes. On old examples, decorative flat-woven ends are seen more often than not. Camel's hair is often used for

Baluch bag face, Northeast Persia, c. 1885, 3' × 2'5", $5,500.
PHOTO COURTESY OF SKINNER, INC.

the ground of prayer rugs. A number of other tribal groups tend to be herded under the Baluch umbrella, and although their rugs often have format and pattern similarities, the structure and coloration can be quite different. The weaving of the nomadic Baluch in Baluchistan, a province of present-day Pakistan, is limited to flat weaves that are virtually unknown in the American market.

Bag Face, Northeast Persia (c.1885, 3'×2'5"). On a midnight blue field, a red-rosette-decorated brown lattice centered with glowing red Turkoman-influenced latch-hooked figures known as *aina-kochak*. Stepped polygons ornament the red main border enclosed in narrow ivory diamond guards. Corroded browns; small repairs. Achieved record price at Skinner's for Baluch bag face.
.... Est. $1,000/1,200; sold for $5,500

Bag Face, West Turkestan (c. 1900, 2'8"×2'6"). Striking gul-like medallion in ivory, blue, and red on rust rectangle on a red field bearing a repeat of stars in diamonds, within a floral repeat blue border edged with white zigzags. Very good condition; one minor reweave. .... Est. $1,500/1,800; sold for $2,475

Baluch prayer rug, Northeast Persia, c. 1885, 5′1″ × 3′1″ $2,860. PHOTO COURTESY OF SKINNER, INC.

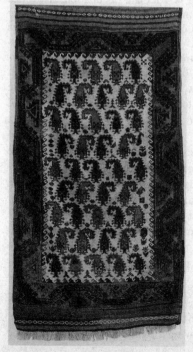

Baluch rug, Northeast Persia, c. 1885, 5′ × 2′11″, $2,420. PHOTO COURTESY OF CHRISTIE'S EAST.

Prayer Rug, Northeast Persia (c. 1885, 5′1″×3′1″). Classic, beautifully spaced example of tree-of-life format: a rusty rose and dark blue tree on camel ground with rusty rose curled-leaf border on blue and another border with blue and ivory geometric repeats on rusty rose. Brocaded kilim ends. Very good condition. .... Est. $1,200/1,500; sold for $2,860

Scatter Rug, Northeast Persia (c. 1885, 5′×2′11″). Rows of rectilinear *botehs* and filler motifs in rose red and dark and medium blues on an ivory ground edged with polychrome latch hooks. A brown stylized leaf-and-vine motif known as the Turkoman line is used in the wide, rose red border. Silky wool; brocaded striped kilim skirts. Rebound edges; slight wear. ....
.... Est. $2,500/3,000; sold for $2,420

Bird Bag Face, Northeast Persia (c. 1875, 2′7″×2′2″). Three bands of stylized red and brown birds parade across a midnight blue ground. One bird is ivory; smaller quadrapeds march along the bottom edge. Ivory border with stylized serrated leaf-and-flower motif is enclosed by several narrow, geometric guards. Superior version of pattern popular with collectors. Slight wear; patch. .... Est. $1,800/2,200; sold for $2,640

Tile Pattern Rug, Northeast Persia (c. 1875, 6′5″×3′6″). The *aina-kochak* pattern within a red lattice on a blue ground, the use of color creating diagonal rows. Two ivory guards frame an ivory-flowered *mina khani*, vine and palmette main border repeat on a red ground. Chevron kilim skirts with brocaded ends. Shows some wear. .... Est. $3,000/3,500; sold for $3,850

TURKOMAN

Among the Turkoman tribes, weaving is a female occupation that relies on the weaver's ability to recall from memory the knotting sequence required to translate their sometimes elaborate tribal patterns into rugs and domestic trappings. Comparisons are often drawn between Turkoman motifs and those on very old Turkish carpets, which is hardly surprising given the tribes' Turkic origin on far Asian steppes. Despite their similarities of origin and culture, however, the weaving done by the tribes differs significantly from one to another in structure, form, and coloration, although to the uninitiated they may seem en masse to be a veritable sea of red.

It is virtually impossible to attach exact dates to Turkoman rugs made before 1880, when synthetic dyes began to be used by Turkoman weavers. No records were kept, and the designs changed very slowly over a long period of time. For that reason ranking Turkoman weavings in order of age and tribal type depends almost entirely on a determination of the natural dyestuffs and color-affecting mordants used by the various tribal groups and the gradual alterations in the forms and arrangements of the traditional motifs. (See the chapter on sizes, formats, and motifs for further information)

Tekke

The acclaimed red Bokhara is the trade name for Tekke tribal rugs, the best known of the Turkoman weavings. Synthetic dyes played havoc here as elsewhere in the late 19th century, but the best Tekke rugs and bags boast a glowing madder red and velvety handle. The colors used are reds varying from ruby to liver, blues, ivory, green, brown, and some yellow; occasionally cochineal-dyed silk is used for special details. The asymmetrical knotting is the finest of the Turkoman group; the foundation is wool; the back is flat, and the pile is low.

Main Carpet (c. 1875, 9′10″×6′2″). Excellent finely woven example of classic Tekke format: four rows of ivory and mahogany-red quartered guls are interconnected by narrow blue lines on a glowing, madder red ground within a primary border of floral octagons and a variety of geometric motifs. Wide striped pile skirts; narrow fringed ivory kilims. Very good condition. (See color insert) ....Est. $6,000/9,000; sold for $12,100

Tent Band (c. 1850, 43′6″×1′). Traditional red and blue pile ornamentation on an ivory flat-woven band. Minor repairs and patches; selvage wear. .... Est. $3,000/5,000; sold for $9,350

Bag Face (c. 1850, 3′7″×1′6″). Six apricot, blue, jade, and ivory main guls and blue, red, and ivory secondary guls are well spaced on a plum brown field within a geometric border. Even wear; sides reduced. .... Est. $1,000/1,500; sold for $2,970

Tekke Turkoman tent band, West Turkestan, c. 1850, 43′6″ × 1′,
$9,350. PHOTO COURTESY OF SKINNER, INC.

Tent Door Rug (c. 1850, 5′1″×3′4″). Velvety, brick red ground with an ivory-outlined, three-section panel of horizontal rows of horned, Y-shaped motifs bordered by wide bands of stylized, leafed flower stalks. The outer red border bears an ivory key-fret motif; the plum pile skirts are ornamented with symmetrically arranged stylized flowers. Shows wear and moth damage; repairs; reduced top border. .... Est. $2,000/3,000; sold for $2,860

Small Bag Face (c. 1885, 2′4″×1′). Densely knotted mahogany red ground has three rows of four ivory *aina-kochak* figures set in quartered blue and light magenta rectangles with white cotton and cochineal-dyed silk highlights. The primary border is of ivory and blue diamond-shaped figures within two narrow geometric guards. Slight wear, corroded silk. ....
....Est. $1,400/1,800; sold for $1,210

Large-Pile and Flat-woven Bag (c. 1875, 4′×2′10″). Tightly flat-woven claret ground with velvety pile stripes in varying widths finely knotted with a variety of well-drawn dark blue, red, and ivory geometric motifs. The white cotton skirt is ornamented with red, blue, and russet stylized trees-of-life. Magenta and yellow silk highlights. Repair in skirt. ...... Est. $3,500/4,500; sold for $6,050

Yomud (Yomut)

Yomud weaving displays a greater variety of motifs and bolder coloration than other tribal work, and since it is also one of the largest and most diverse groups, a wider choice of their old and antique rugs, bags, animal trappings, etc., is usually available on the market. Early Yomud work may have either symmetric or asymmetric knots, sometimes both, on a wool foundation; the density is finer than the robust look of the

Yomud Turkoman bag face, West Turkestan, c. 1885, 3′9″ × 2′7″, $1,760. PHOTO COURTESY OF CHRISTIE'S EAST.

firm-handled pieces would lead one to expect. The Yomud red varies from brick to brown to a distinctive purple-brown. White, yellow, turquoise, green, brown, and a range of blues were generously used.

Kepse Gul Carpet (c. 1875, 9′5″×5′9″). A classic, well-spaced kepse-gul pattern in color-determined diagonals with no minor guls on a mahogany ground within a primary border of vine meanders and curled leaves on ivory with red diamond-figured guards. Rows of stylized flowers decorate the full skirts. Vegetable dyes in red, dark and medium blue, gold, mahogany. Some stains and moth damage. .... Est. $10,000/15,000; sold for $18,700

Camel Trapping (c. 1875, 4′×2′4″). Five vertical poled tree motifs in shades of jade, blue, rust, gold, and brown within an ivory ram's-horn border. A common design, finely woven. Good condition. ... Est. $2,500/3,000; sold for $3,300

Bag Face (c. 1885, 3′9″×2′7″). Classic example with rich dark mahogany ground and three rows of three well-spaced, ivory-highlighted guls flanked by a minor ornament composed of boxed stars enclosed by an ivory main border with cross-motif repeat within red running-dog guards. Dark blue chevron banding along top edge; the deep skirt is unornamented. Brick red, mahogany, salmon, dark blue, and ivory. Shows slight wear. ... Est. $2,000/3,000; sold for $1,760

Carpet (c. 1875, 8′9″×4′9″). Three vertical rows of 12 quartered ivory and red *tauk nauska* guls on a mahogany ground, with latch-hooked, diamond-shaped minor guls highlighted with cornflower blue and forest green. The ivory main border has a red, blue, gold, and mahogany curled-leaf-and-vine meander along the sides and *ashik* motifs in the same colors top and bottom. The guards have polychrome diagonal motifs; the deep pile skirts are patterned with rows of stylized serrated leaves. Slight wear and moth damage, corner reweave. ....
.... Est. $3,500/4,500; sold for $4,400

Mat (c. 1875, 1′10″×1′7″). Densely woven and plushy, rust brown ground covered with stylized floral figures in color-determined, nicely spaced diagonals within geometric main border and barber-pole guards. Ivory, light red, dark blue, and teal. Good condition. .... Est. $2,500/3,000; sold for $2,860

Camel Trapping (c. 1885, 3′10″×2′4″). The ivory field of this showy example has a red, mahogany, and dark blue serrated lattice pierced by tuning-fork-ornamented poles bearing symmetrical figures that are centered within each lattice-formed space. Red *ashik* and ivory and gold ram's-horn devices ornament the dark blue primary border enclosed by ivory guards with a mahogany running-dog motif. Original polychrome tassels suspend from the sides and bottom edge. Good condition. (See color insert) .... Est. $3,000/5,000; sold for $7,700

Salor

The Salor is the oldest and most respected of the Turkoman tribes; the ornamentation of its weaving is refined, elegantly spaced, and beautifully drawn. Although a wide range of colors was used in combination with the dominant clear red, Salor weavers employed them with much less abandon than did the Yomud. The finest pieces often include areas of cochineal-dyed silk. Salor goods are knotted asymmetrically on a wool foundation almost as finely as Tekke work; the back has a ribbed look due to the strong depression of alternate warps.

Salor Turkoman bag face fragment, Central Turkestan, c. 1820, 2'1"
× 2', $5,225. PHOTO © 1991 SOTHEBY'S, INC.

Large Bag Face (c. 1850, 4'6"×2'10"). Very finely woven cranberry ground
on which major and minor Salor guls in mahogany, ivory, midnight blue, and
aubergine are spaced with characteristic elegance. The mahogany *aina-kochak*
main border is guarded by narrow S-stripes. Stylized dark blue and mahogany
trees decorate the skirt. Magenta silk highlights. Nicks, stain, repairs on ends;
one corner rewoven. ....Est. $10,000/15,000; sold for $33,000

Bag-face Fragment (c. 1820, 2'1"×2'). The saturated crimson color and extraordinary luminosity of its finely woven velvety pile distinguish this fragment,
which displays one of the three turreted octagonal guls and one of two pairs of
the stepped grids peculiar to this pattern, with details highlighted by magenta
silk. An ivory-centered geometric dark blue figure ornaments the crimson main
border guarded with a narrow, dark blue S-band. The skirt has diagonal rows of
stylized flowering plants in dark blue, mid-blue, and ivory. ....
.... Est. $3,000/5,000; sold for $5,225

Ersari

The sturdy red rugs with the large so-called elephant's-foot gul are
known in the trade as Afghan rugs and are woven by the Ersari, the
largest of the Turkoman tribes, who have settled for the most part in
Afghanistan. Although the classic brown-red ''Afghan'' is a coarsely

knotted workhorse rug characterized by huge, closely spaced guls, the Beshir, a settled subtribe, weave rugs of considerably more sophistication, which may be found in the rustic rug category.

The red ground of old Ersari work is warm and clear; blues, turquoise, coral orange, brown, white, and yellow complete the color range. The hard-wearing pile is knotted asymmetrically on a wool foundation; dark brown goat hair is used for the side finishes. Maroon-red used as a ground color is an indicator of post–World War II manufacture.

Ersari Rug, Afghanistan (c. 1870, 7′11″ ×6′2″). A warm, brick red ground with three rows of six very large gulli-guls with minor blue-outlined octagonal guls and some scattered geometric fillers. The primary border has *ashik* figures within connected squares enclosed by a sawtooth edge border. Red, dark and medium blue, gold, and ivory. Shows wear; repiled areas, reduced end guard borders. .... Est. $5,000/7,000; sold for $4,620

Tent Door Surround (c. 1885, 4′4″×2′2″). The curled-leaf design usually seen in Turkoman borders is used here in the narrow ivory field in navy, light blue, rust red, and gold, bordered with a variety of geometric motifs. A trapping infrequently seen but not a prime example. Good condition. ....
.... Est. $1,500/1,800; sold for $1,650

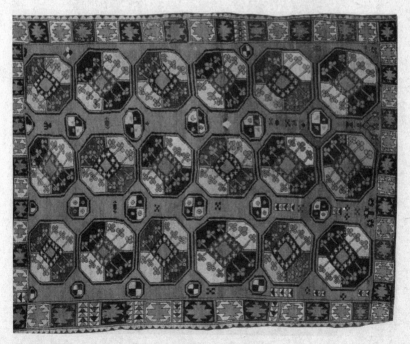

Ersari Turkoman carpet, Afghanistan, c. 1870, 7′11″ × 6′2″, $4,620. PHOTO COURTESY OF CHRISTIE'S EAST.

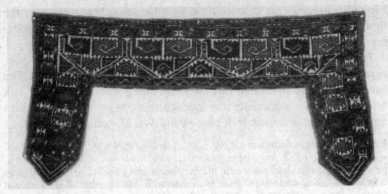

*Ersari Turkoman tent door surround, Central Turkestan, c. 1885, 4'4"
× 2'2", $1,650.* PHOTO COURTESY OF SKINNER, INC.

*Ersari Turkoman tent door rug, Central Turkestan, c. 1875, 7' × 5',
$4,200.* PHOTO COURTESY OF CHRISTIE'S EAST.

Tent Door Rug (c. 1875, 7′ ×5′). Warm brick ground with two arched panels, one above the other, flanked with so-called candelabra motifs contained by a cross-centered geometric border with an outer border of reciprocal latch hooks, all in dark and medium blues, red, ivory, and touches of gold. An olive-brown skirt ornamented with stylized flowering shrubs is edged with a wide striped kilim. Good condition. .... Est. $4,000/6,000; sold for $4,200

Note: In 1990–91, nine additional antique Ersari *engsi* from this same well-known collection, all of similar age and condition, were sold at auction. Estimate range: $3,000/10,000; average, $5,800. Sale price range: $4,620/$13,200; average, $5,800.

Beshir Rug, West Turkestan (c. 1860, 5′9″ ×4′8″). A striking design, much less complex than those seen on most Beshir weavings, indicates, along with its smaller size, a tribal origin for this rug. On a red ground, eight horizontal rows of well-spaced, blue-sawtoothed, gold and brown-figured red *botehs* are arrayed in an endless repeat, together with a scattering of star motifs. The linked ivory hexagons on the red main border house *aina-kochak* figures within dark blue, red, and yellow barber-pole stripes. .... Est. $3,000/4,000; sold for $12,100

Beshir Turkoman rug, Central Turkestan, c. 1860, 5′9″ × 4′8″, $12,100. PHOTO COURTESY OF SKINNER, INC.

*Chodor Turkoman bag face, Central Turkestan, c. 1885, 5'3" ×
1'7", $3,080.* PHOTO COURTESY OF CHRISTIE'S EAST.

*Chodor Turkoman tent door rug, Central Turkestan, c. 1860, 5' × 4',
$4,950.* PHOTO COURTESY OF CHRISTIE'S EAST.

Chodor

Very old Chodor pieces have a characteristic purple-brown ground color and a distinctive main gul. The wool warps are dark brown; the knots, asymmetrical; and the wefts either wool or cotton. The density is moderately fine. Other colors used are clear red, salmon, dark brown, blues, green, yellow, and white. Old Chodor work is not as commonly available as Ersari, Tekke, and Yomud.

Medium Bag Face (c. 1885, 5′3″ × 1′7″). Three interconnecting stepped guls in mahogany, ivory, and light brick red with dark blue, blue-green, and red fields, gold floral motifs within a primary border of geometric repeats surrounded by a plain mahogany outer band. Shows some wear. ....
.... Est. $3,000/4,000; sold for $3,080

Main Carpet (c. 1885, 13′2″ × 7′9″). Brownish red ground with endless repeat of red and ivory stepped guls within an ivory lattice ornamented with rosettes. Ivory side borders with leaf and meandering vine motif; top and bottom with diamond and vine repeat. The deep skirts have a chevron design composed of red, mahogany, and ivory *ashik* motifs. Slight wear, selvage repairs, reweaves. .... Est. $6,000/9,000; sold for $6,050

Tent Door Rug (c. 1860, 5′ × 4′). Endless repeat of vertical rows of connected diamonds with blue, red, or plum central figures on an ivory ground punctuated with red and blue geometric figures, all within two borders of equal width: one red, one ivory, both with curled-leaf repeat. Plum skirt has nine stylized trees-of-life. Shows wear; reweaves, repairs. ..... Est. $4,000/6,000; sold for $4,950

Other Turkoman Weavings

Kizil Ayak Area Rug (c. 1875, 6′6″ × 3′9″). Mahogany ground with endless repeat of hooked, ivory-trimmed arch devices in dark blue alternating with red, centered with stylized gold and dark blue shrubs, and bordered with a geometric endless repeat with tuning-fork and barber-pole guards. The striped kilim ends are reduced. Some wear. .... Est. $6,000/9,000; sold for $8,800

Arabatchi Large Bag Face (c. 1875, 5′4″ × 2′9″). Mahogany ground with magenta-centered ivory and red-quartered guls with intricately detailed green-outlined minor guls within geometric repeat borders. The pile skirt is ornamented with a row of ivory, dark blue, and red flowers. Cotton and silk highlights. Shows some wear; skirt reduced. ....
.... Est. $9,000/12,000; sold for $12,100

Rare Turkoman Trapping or Bag Face (c. 1850, 4′5″ × 2′11″). Rows of elegant claret, ivory, and dark blue diamonds on a dark mahogany ground; the minor gul, an *aina-kochak* variant, is ornamented with tiny claret animal figures. Red, dark blue, and ivory geometric border and guards. Sides, ends, and corners somewhat worse for wear. .... Est. $8,000/12,000; sold for $49,500

RUSTIC RUGS, 1800–1900

The vast majority of rugs of collectible interest fall into this category, but the assignment of particular rugs to it is accompanied by a good bit of collector push and pull.

The patterns of commercial carpets, adapted from traditional designs by professional artists, may or may not have anything in common with the traditions of the weavers employed to produce them. Conversely, the forms seen on tribal rugs were chosen from a reservoir of motifs that evolved within a kinship unit and passed through the generations from mother to daughter.

The best commercial carpets, substantial numbers of which were made on village looms, are both skillfully woven and highly decorative; so too are the finest tribal weavings, which in addition have been accorded the status of icons. This being the case, it is hardly surprising that honest rustic rugs of respectable age are increasingly being borne up on the wings of collector—and dealer—wishful thinking into the rarefied realm of tribal art. However, although the weavers of these rugs were indeed in many cases settled members of formerly nomadic tribes, design purity on a village level is always threatened with dilution by "foreign" influences, perhaps introduced via intertribal marriages, perhaps seen and admired on market days on products from other villages.

Commercial carpets are contract-woven for profit; the old rustic rugs being collected today were—although made in a domestic setting and certainly used there—also a significant source of family income. Originality was neither expected nor rewarded, but few weavers could resist enlivening the traditional patterns with personal touches: an unusual juxtaposition of colors, a borrowed field motif adapted for a border repeat, or a traditional medallion skewed in an untraditional way. Whatever it might be, it allowed the weaver of a completed rug the satisfaction of saying, if only to herself: *this is mine.*

Toward the end of the 19th century the demands of merchants for designs of proven salability tended to discourage woven expressions of creative play; accordingly, rugs of that era whose color and choice and spacing of motifs are deemed superior to an otherwise look-alike crowd are sometimes claimed to be dowry pieces, the prideful weaving of which was never affected by economic considerations. Romantic notions of this sort abound in the rug world and in fact are sometimes justified, but budding collectors would be well advised to keep several grains of salt always at the ready.

Please bear in mind as you read through these listings that some collectors value condition much more highly than others do. Put another way, although a wonderful rug in wonderful condition invariably commands a high price, a good rug in wonderful condition often sells for more than a wonderful rug in fair condition.

TURKISH RUGS

Collectors accustomed to the coloration of Persian and Turkoman rugs are sometimes slow to cultivate a taste for Turkish village rugs, but once acquired it often takes over.

Except for Yağcibedir and some Bergama rugs limited to an almost exclusive use of red, dark blue, and white, Turkish rug colors are generally as vivid as those seen on Caucasians, but the palette is quite different. The reds are hotter—except for an exception mentioned later—and the greens more springlike. Salmon and bright copper are favored over mahogany and plum; the lighter shades of blue are used more often than the dark shades, and Turkish dyers excel at purple-toned colors ranging from aubergine to a clear, limpid lavender. Late-19th-century examples often have a blue-toned cochineal red—rugs made in Kirşehir, for example—of a brighter shade than that found in Persian Kermans.

As one proceeds from west to east in Turkey, the colors take on a browner tone, perhaps because of the greater abundance of brown-fleeced sheep in the flocks kept by the seminomadic Kurdish peoples who inhabit those wilder regions. According to Werner Brüggemann and Harald Böhmer, authors of *Rugs of the Peasants and Nomads of Anatolia*, "All Anatolian rugs show red and blue . . . [but] as far as surface area is concerned, yellow is the outstanding colour in Central Anatolia." They go on to say that only half of the East Anatolian rugs they surveyed contained all three primary colors, and not one of them contained all three of the secondary colors: violet, green, and orange. In West Anatolia, on the other hand, "10% . . . contain all three secondary colours, whereas this figure is 60% for Central Anatolia."

The typical honest, sturdy Turkish village rug is symmetrically knotted on a wool foundation with a density that rarely exceeds 60 knots per square inch. The edges consist of from two to four bundles of warps secured and protected by an overcasting with the weft threads alone or strengthened by a second overcasting with a yarn that may or may not match the weft. The plain-woven band used as an end finish is usually red and itself ends in a simple fringe. It may be ornamented with motifs meant to identify the weaver or to ward off the evil eye or both.

In this section we will be looking at a selection of rustic rugs made in western and central Turkey. In recent years, good examples have begun to command prices worthy of their untutored charm and graphic power. If I lived in a far northern clime deprived of winter sunlight, I would save my pennies to buy one if only to remind me of the colors of summer during the long drear days of winter.

Turkish prayer rug, Bergama area, c. 1885, 4′9″ × 4′1″, $10,450.
PHOTO COURTESY OF CHRISTIE'S EAST.

BERGAMA

Weaving has been carried on here near the Aegean Sea for centuries, and rugs made in the 19th and early 20th centuries have much in common with earlier prototypes. The larger and more colorful rugs woven in the nearby stone villages of the Yuntdag and near Ayvacik are often labeled by the trade and auction houses as Bergama, although they are quite different in both look and handle. A weaving cooperative begun ten years ago to reintroduce the use of vegetable dyes and hand-spun wool has sparked a revival of quality weaving in the entire area. Some of these projects are described in the chapter on contemporary collectibles.

Rug (c. 1850, 9′5″×7″). Thus unusually well-balanced rectilinear stylization of a classical double-niche Oushak design features a medium blue double-ended medallion ornamented with smaller medallions and geometric figures in dark blue, red, apricot, and ivory on a red field within U-shaped arches bearing similar decoration. The white-dotted red spandrels have a variety of boxed stars and floral sprays. The pale gold main border has a squared-leaf repeat and S-figured gold guards. Corroded browns, patched corner. ....
.... Est. $12,000/15,000; sold for $11,000

Rug (c. 1850, 6′6″×5′2″). Another classical Turkish design, the two-one-two Holbein, featuring in this example a blue-grounded, multibordered medallion with geometric patterning and floral corner figures in red, flanked by two pairs of red rosette-centered gul-like hexagons, all on a red ground with boxed-star fillers. The dark blue boxed-star and ram's-horn main border has ivory and gold guards with stylized floral meanders. The wide plain-woven blue skirt is striped with red. Shows wear; several noticeable patches. ....
.... Est. $6,000/8,000; sold for $5,225

Rug (c. 1875, 7′6″×6′1″). A stepped light-blue diamond medallion has a hooked, vinelike frame on a rich red field flanked by rectilinear, ivory-hooked, abrashed blue spandrels ornamented with large geometric motifs in gold, ivory, apricot, and red. Geometrically figured gold guards enclose a red main border of hooked ivory medallions alternating with figured ivory hexagons within a tracery of blue. Around the edge is a dark blue sawtooth repeat on red. ....
.... Est. $6,000/9,000; sold for $6,050

Prayer Rug (c. 1885, 4′9″×4′1″). The plain, rich red, stepped *mihrab* has a border of inward-facing blue and gold rosettes and ivory spandrels with black and red tendrils enclosed within three decorative borders, with gold, brown, red, and ivory floral stylizations on vivid blue. The wide and striking main gold border has a red, blue, and ivory rosette repeat alternating with rows of red and blue florettes, enclosed by red and blue barber-pole stripes. The outer blue borders have red, yellow, and blue repeats of flower and vine figures. Shows very slight wear. ....Est. $4,000/6,000; sold for $10,450

Rug (c. 1850, 7′4″×5′4″). Derived from an 18th-century model, a vertical pair of large ivory-grounded, latch-hooked octagons containing smaller octagons with eight straight-edged raylike arms almost fill the soft red field enclosed by a main border of rectangle-connected diamonds within two S-figure guards. Shows wear. ....Est. $1,500/2,000; sold for $2,750

Dimirci prayer rug, West Anatolia, c. 1885, 4'7" × 4', $1,210.
PHOTO COURTESY OF CHRISTIE'S EAST.

DIMIRCI

Often tagged as Kulas, these flower-ornamented rugs have a unique construction in which alternate rows may be single- or double-wefted. The
pretty, rather loosely drawn dark-fielded prayer rug described below is
representative of the production, which ceased in the early part of this
century. The Kula prayer rugs that were once very popular with collectors also have columnar floral elements, but the coloration is more subdued and the design more detailed and formal in appearance.

Prayer Rug (c. 1885, 4'7" ×4'). The chocolate brown field contains a vase
with a billowing bouquet of flowers within a keyhole-shaped floral meander border flanked by floral-ornamented camel spandrels. The pale green primary border has a flowing repeat of blossom heads and florettes enclosed by stylized
vine-and-flower meanders on red. Shows some wear. ....
....Est. $2,000/3,000; sold for $1,210

KONYA

The 13th-century Seljuk rugs found in the Central Anatolian Konya
mosques suggest a weaving tradition of greater antiquity than that of any
other area in Turkey. For that reason, perhaps, the Konya name is a

conveniently prestigious one to attach to old rugs made in nearby towns as well. The prayer rug format is often seen; green and gold are used with mellow reds to great effect. Boldly patterned runners were also made in this area, as were pile pillow covers known as *yastiks*, which, when removed from their backing, are used as decorative mats. The row of roofed boxes known as *lappets*, commonly seen along the ends of *yastiks*, were meant to indicate the thickness of the pillow within; similar rows at the ends of some Turkish rugs are purely ornamental.

Yastik (c. 1885, 3′3″ ×2′). The ivory cartouche has a star-centered, pendanted, brick red medallion. A flowering plant ornaments each of the dark blue spandrels, and interconnecting jagged-edged, geometric-figured ivory medallions are repeated on the wide rose border. The mahogany pile skirts have ivory lappets containing floral quatrefoils. Shows slight wear; holes, small repairs. .... Est. $1,800/2,200; sold for $4,620

Rug (c. 1885, 5′9″ ×4′2″). A gold cruciform-figured red diamond is centered on an ivory rosette and carnation-edged green stepped medallion on a red ground with leaf and boxed-rosette ornamentation. Polychrome flowerheads are repeated around a green primary border guarded by ivory rosette and red floral-and-vine meander minor borders. Good condition. Est. $9,000/12,000; sold for $8,800

Yastik, Konya area, c. 1885, 3′3″ × 2′, $4,620. PHOTO COURTESY OF CHRISTIE'S EAST.

Konya rug, Central Anatolia, c. 1885, 5'9" × 4'2", $8,800. PHOTO
COURTESY OF CHRISTIE'S EAST.

Prayer Rug (c. 1875, 4'7" ×3'10"). Two pairs of narrow ivory columns on a
triple-arched red field lead to a green rhomboidal prayer niche on red. The very
wide gold border has bold stylized flowerheads in red, dark blue, brown, and
purple within S-figured and rosette-ornamented guards. Shows wear; repiling,
replaced selvage. .... Est. $4,000/6,000; sold for $4,950

Rug (c. 1880, 6'8" ×5'). This damaged plushy rug has an aubergine ground
with a dense allover pattern of boldly drawn rosettes and palmettes and other
floral figures in vivid shades of red, green, blue, gold, brown, and ivory flanked
by an interconnected blue ram's-horn repeat on the main red border and two star-
flower repeats on the ivory and gold guards. Shows wear; reduced and patched
end borders, corrosion. ....Est. $900/1,200; sold for $1,760

Prayer Rug (c. 1870, 4'3" ×4'). A red cruciform figure extends from the lightly
flower-strewn red field into an abrashed green niche ornamented with red and
ivory rosettes. Memling guls are repeated in red, aubergine, dark blue, and green
on a dark gold main border enclosed by dark blue and ivory guards with rosette
repeats. Corroded brown; small repair in one border. ....
....Est. $12,000/15,000; sold for $13,200

Yastik (c. 1860, 3'9" ×2'1"). The rust ground has an allover well-spaced repeat of stylized serrated palmettes in dark blue and green alternating with cruciform latch-hook figures within a diagonally barred border. The ivory pile skirts have dark blue lappets bearing simplified palmette-like figures. Shows some wear; patch, slight loss to ends. .... Est. $600/900; sold for $1,430

MAKRI

The Makri rug of Southwestern Anatolia has a distinctive prayer rug format consisting usually of two vertical panels with contrasting colors and differing filler motifs bordered by a highly stylized rectilinear meandering vine. Blues, earthy reds, and bright yellows and greens were used to color the lustrous wool.

Prayer Rug (c. 1875, 6'×3'9"). Below a carnation-banded niche, one half of the typically divided field is red, with rayed octagons; the other half is dark blue with carnation clusters within a stylized flower, leaf, and vine meander on gold and interconnected diamonds on ivory. Even wear, small hole, dog-eared corner, corroded browns. .... Est. $1,500/1,800; sold for $1,870

Rug (c. 1910, 4'4" ×6'2"). The gold field has two long cartouches: one is royal blue with a vertical column of floral figures; the other, rust with blooming flower stalks. The mustard inner border has a serrated leaf-and-flower meander and the outer main border has a simple vine meander on ivory. Even wear; slight selvage damage. .... Est. $1,200/1,800; sold for $1,760

LADIK

Another well-known village prayer rug format is associated with the town of Ladik in Central Anatolia north of Konya. These rather long and narrow small rugs with their distinguishing row of stiffly erect tulips have been made since at least the 18th century. On early examples a panel of tulips crosses above the *mihrab* and spandrels; on later rugs the tulips bloom upside down in a panel crossing below the niche. The fields of early Ladiks are apt to be an unornamented rich, glowing red. Later, filler motifs were added to fields, spandrels, and cross-panels, and the well-spaced early rosette-and-vine borders became squashed and poorly resolved at the corners.

Prayer Rug (c. 1875, 6'7"×3'9"). The band of upside-down tulips below the prayer niche indicates a rather late date. The field ornamentation is confined to a pair of small rosettes and lamp in the *mihrab* of an otherwise open red ground, and the jade spandrels have stylized floral motifs. The primary abrashed medium-blue border has a rosette- and stylized-tulip repeat; the two dark blue guards have vine meanders. Corroded browns, some repiled moth damage, one partial end border. .... Est. $5,000/7,000; sold for $5,500

MELAS

The rugs associated with this Aegean town have a prayer rug format featuring a rather narrow *mihrab*, usually red, with a broad diamond

Melas prayer rug, Western Anatolia, c. 1880, 5'1" × 3'8", $3,850.
PHOTO COURTESY OF CHRISTIE'S EAST.

head nipped in at the neck. Palmettes decorate ivory spandrels, and the broad gold borders bear stylized palmettes together with leaf and flower figures. Good examples sparkle with well-balanced color.

Prayer Rug (c. 1880, 5'1"×3'8"). The rosette-and-amulet-decorated red field with typical nipped-in *mihrab* leads to an ivory prayer niche ornamented with chevron rows of stylized flower motifs, all bordered by a polychrome rosette repeat on green. The wide gold primary border has rosette-centered stars in brown, rust, ivory, green, red, and medium blue; four additional borders in red and brown have a variety of meanders and star figures, and the outer ivory border has a lively repeat of polychrome octagons. Shows very slight wear. ....
.... Est. $4,000/6,000; sold for $3,850

Prayer Rug (c. 1885, 5'×3'5"). Same format as the preceding rug but with a smaller prayer cartouche enclosed by a stylized leaf repeat. The very wide peach border has a loosely flowing palmette, rosette, and flowering vine ornamentation in shades of gold, ivory, and aubergine enclosed by an ivory border with polychrome octagons. Small areas of wear; edge fraying, edge gouge. ....
.... Est. $1,500/2,000; sold for $1,540

Rug (c. 1885, 5'8" ×4'4"). A frequently seen Melas design featuring carnations is exemplified by this piece with vertical ivory, rust, and saffron bands of carnations and vinery flanked by narrower stripes of *botehs* within a chevron-figured guard. The main rust border has a variation of the field band's vine meander; the outer aubergine border has a stylized flowerhead repeat. Corroded browns. .... Est. $4,000/6,000; sold for $4,675

OUSHAK

Many of the classical Turkish rugs are said to have been made on Oushak looms, including the so-called Transylvanian designs and the elegant star and medallion carpets. Although it is doubtful that all of the rugs thus attributed could have been woven in this one western Anatolian town, weaving has been an established industry in Oushak for hundreds of years. By the end of the 19th century, however, the Oushak production had degenerated into coarse, synthetically dyed, low-end commercial goods. A pleasing exception was offered at auction in early 1991.

Oushak rug, Western Anatolia, c. 1880, 7'6" × 4'11", $6,600.
PHOTO COURTESY OF CHRISTIE'S EAST.

Rug (c. 1880, 7′6″ ×4′11″). A small four-lobed pale green medallion ornamented with stylized red figures and bordered and pendanted in royal blue sits upon a rich, madder red field otherwise plain save for two trios of small blue, cream, and gold characters flanking the medallion. The gold main border carries a loose rosette and flowering-vine repeat in red, pale green, royal blue, and purple flanked by light green and royal blue minor borders with floral meanders and two gold guards with polychrome X-repeats. Even wear; reduced side guards, replaced selvage. .... Est. $3,000/4,000; sold for $6,600

OTHER TURKISH RUGS

Three examples unattributed to specific weaving villages are worthy of mention here:

Central Anatolian Rug (c. 1900, dimensions not given). This scatter-size rug has a series of six stepped *mihrabs* in shades of dark rust, spring green, and brown surrounded by a hooked repeat around the edge of the rich coral ground, all within an ivory border with boxed geometric repeats. Very good condition. .... Est. $1,500/2,500; sold for $5,390

East Anatolian Runner (c. 1880, 10′ ×4′2″). Five compartments in rust red and medium blue alternate stepped diamonds with stepped-hexagon medallions, both types containing geometric figures in apricot, medium blue, ivory, and rust red. The compartments are bordered with S-figures and ram's-horn repeats on ivory, all enclosed by a wide main apricot border with a highly stylized palmette and leaf meander and an outer narrow zigzag guard in blue, brown, rust red, and ivory. Areas of wear; repairs, one rewoven end border. .... Est. $3,500/4,500; sold for $5,280

East Anatolian Rug (c. 1860, 7′3″ ×3′11″). This two-one-two design variation has a dark brown ground with symmetrically spaced geometric fillers in an ivory-edged, slate blue and ivory geometric-figured octagonal, dark red, pendanted medallion with, in this case, four pairs of smaller flanking medallions: the upper and lower pairs are star-filled ivory squares; the middle pair are gold arrow-headed rectangles. The ivory main border has a connected-diamond repeat and a pair of blue, red, and ivory zigzag guards. Good condition. .... Est. $6,000/8,000; sold for $6,600

CAUCASIAN RUGS

The scatter, prayer, and area rugs made in the Caucasus in the 19th and early 20th centuries have an enduring appeal. Although woven largely for export sale, their striking designs and vivid coloration symbolize for many collectors mythic origins rooted in semibarbarism. The truth is a good deal less extravagant. Most Caucasian patterns have links to Persian, Turkoman, and Far Eastern designs, as typified by those seen in the monumental 17th- and 18th-century Caucasian carpets whose size stamps them as workshop productions.

Caucasian rugs have no need of romantic notions to bolster their vitality, and vegetable colors need not be brewed in mountain fastnesses to be beautiful. They are generally divided into two main classes. The first, exemplified by South Caucasian Kazaks, Gendjes, and Moghans, is a symmetrically and coarsely knotted wool fabric with a medium to long pile. Large-scale motifs dominate relatively open fields, which allow blocks of color to be boldly juxtaposed. The second group, exemplified by Eastern Caucasian Shirvans and the Northeastern Kubas, has densely packed short pile, also symmetrically knotted; finely spun yarns; and fields covered more often than not with elaborate small-scale ornamentation. Think of the first type as firecrackers; the second, sparklers.

The place names attached by the trade to the various types of Caucasian rugs don't have a great deal to do with where they were actually made, but this is not a forum suitable for pursuing the subject. Should you decide to collect within this group, reports on the ongoing research concerning Caucasian attributions will be found in *Hali* and *Oriental Rug Review*. Here, the rugs will be listed under the names familiar to most dealers, auction houses, and collectors and under which they are indexed in most currently available books. One caution: Because Caucasian designs are so distinctive, it is tempting to assign rugs an attribution on the basis of their design alone; as always, however, structure is the final arbiter.

Bordjalou Kazak, South Caucasus, c. 1875, 6' 7" × 4' 7", $4,620.
PHOTO COURTESY OF CHRISTIE'S EAST.

LONG-PILED, COARSELY KNOTTED CAUCASIANS

Kazak

Bordjalou, Borjalu. Vertically arranged, latch-hooked medallions usually dominate the fields of these long-piled, almost shaggy rugs, in which a lavish use of ivory sets off the vivid reds, blues, and golds. Latch-hooked figures are also used in the wide primary borders. Other Bordjalou field designs are often accompanied by a main border bearing a reciprocal trefoil motif in ivory and brown.

Rug (c. 1875, 6′7″ × 4′7″). A classic Bordjalou format with an infinite repeat featuring three large latch-hooked diamonds in red, gold, rust, medium and dark blue, and ivory on a dark blue ground within a primary ivory border with polychrome latch-hooked devices. The two guard borders have reciprocal trefoil repeats and are edged with ivory and red barber-pole stripes. Missing one-half of guard border at one end. .... Est. $5,000/7,000; sold for $4,620

Rug (c. 1885, 8′5″ × 4′6″). A royal blue pendanted medallion on a red ground flanked above and below by two pairs of facing fantailed birds above a trio of geometric-figured cartouches and accompanied by a variety of small geometric fillers within a reciprocal trefoil primary border and two running-dog guards. Very good condition. ....Est. $7,000/9,000; sold for $11,000

Eagle, Sunburst, Chelaberd Karabagh. Two, sometimes three very large and striking medallions derived from an early Persian floral-based palmette motif dominate this design, which was mentioned in a 1907

Eagle Kazak (Karabagh), South Caucasus, c. 1875, 6′9″ × 4′5″, $6,600. PHOTO COURTESY OF GROGAN & COMPANY.

OCM catalog as a ''variety of modern rug . . . being made by Tartars in the province of Kazak.'' The ground color is usually red, occasionally blue. The medallions are knotted in ivory, golds, greens, reds, and blue. (See Karabagh)

Rug (c. 1875, 6'9" ×4'5"). Two flower-ornamented sunburst medallions in ivory, medium and dark blue, gold, dark brown, and red on a madder red ground with a scattering of small geometric fillers within a primary border with stylized flower-and-vine meander on ivory and two guards with black sawtooth repeats on blue. Shows wear; repairs. .... Est. $6,000/8,000; sold for $6,600

Rug (c. 1885, 9'4" ×4'3"). On a red ground, three sunburst medallions in ivory, dark and medium blue, and red, with floral elements in gold, ivory, red, blue, and apricot, are flanked by boxed stylized floral elements. The ivory primary border with stylized leaf-and-flower meander is enclosed by barber-pole-edged blue and red zigzag guards. Good condition. ....
.... Est. $4,000/6,000; sold for $5,500

Fachralo. Precisely drawn gabled medallions are used either singly or in pairs as the major focus or as part of a more complex field format.

Long Rug (c. 1885, 6'6" ×3'2"). On a madder red ground are four gabled and rather simplified Fachralo medallions in green and blue with latch-hooked inner devices and flanked with polychrome checkerboarded diamonds. A bold and highly stylized red, green, gold, and blue leaf-and-vine meander dominates the ivory main border enclosed by blue guards sawtoothed in brown and edged with red and ivory barber-pole stripes. .... Est. $7,000/9,000; sold for $7,700

Karachov, Karachopt, Karachopf. This format of one large central rectilinear medallion with two pairs of similar, smaller medallions above and below is seen on early Anatolian carpets. The field's filler motifs and border designs vary from rug to rug. Collectors prize the wonderful color, balance, and texture of the best examples. Six classic examples

Fachralo Kazak, South Caucasus, c. 1885, 6'6" × 3'2", $7,700.
PHOTO COURTESY OF CHRISTIE'S EAST.

Karachov Kazak, South Caucasus, c. 1875, 5'8" × 5'2", $24,200.
PHOTO COURTESY OF CHRISTIE'S EAST.

sold during this period at prices ranging from $4,000 to $24,200 that were largely determined by condition, color and age. The full-piled superior example described below that sold for the highest price could be considered a bargain.

Rug (c. 1875, 5'8"×5'2"). A geometric-figured ivory hexagon flanked above and below by two pairs of latch-hooked, star-filled squares sits in a gold, red, and blue-dotted square on a blue-green abrashed ground within a frame of boxed double-ram's-horn figures, all in shades of red, gold, blue, ivory, brown, and purple. The rich gold primary border has a bold stylized leaf, flower, and vine meander and a pair of barber-pole-edged ivory and red reciprocal trefoil guards. Slight wear, minor repair. .... Est. $25,000/35,000; sold for $24,200

Lambalo. This design consists typically of a narrow rectangular field either plain or sparsely ornamented and with four to seven borders, one of which has a distinctive stylized red and blue flowering-vine repeat on ivory.

Rug (c. 1920, 8'5"×5'4"). The plain, dark red field with blue sawtooth edges and ivory inscription in Arabic has simple triangular blue spandrels within an inner ivory border with a red and blue flowering-vine meander, a dark red main border with rosette repeat, and three blue minor borders with red and white florettes, all edged with a red and ivory barber-pole stripe. Good condition. ...
.... Est. $2,000/3,000; sold for $2,530

Lori Pambak. A hexagon-enclosed cruciform medallion, whose horizontal members resemble tulip blossoms, is displayed in threes, twos, or singly on a field that otherwise is usually lacking in ornamentation. The proportions of the medallion differ from rug to rug: when well drawn it can be elegant; too often it is ill-defined and squat. In the past two years, nine examples of varying condition, age, and interest sold at auction at prices ranging from $5,500 to $25,300. The most interesting example, which is described below, brought the second-highest price.

Rug (c. 1880, 8′1″ ×5′11″). A blue latch-hooked ivory medallion containing a typical red and green Lori-Pambak motif is flanked above and below with large pendant-like figures containing concentric rows of blue, green, and gold latch hooks, all on a rich green-edged madder field with a variety of boxed geometric figures, rosettes, and birds in saturated hues of gold, green, blue, and ivory. The ivory primary border with highly stylized flower-and-vine meander has two royal blue guards with geometric repeats, all with red and white barber-pole stripes. Rewoven corners. .... Est. $8,000/10,000; sold for $18,700

Lori Pambak Kazak, South Caucasus, c. 1880, 8′1″ × 5′11″, $18,700. PHOTO COURTESY OF CHRISTIE'S EAST.

Pinwheel. The so-called pinwheel motif can be traced to two possible sources: one is the stylized flower-and-leaf motif seen in many variations on many rugs over the centuries; the other is a 15th-century Iznik tile design adapted as a textile pattern on early rugs. It is usually centered with a rosette of contrasting color and flanked by serrated-leaf diagonals. Prime examples like the one described below command high prices; average examples (see picture) in very good condition also do well.

Rug (c. 1885, 7′6″×6′). On a red ground a dark blue pinwheel with ivory rosette is the central figure, with six additional symmetrically spaced pinwheels flanked by four, paired, green leaf forms and eight ivory rosettes. The pinwheels are sparsely decorated with polychrome *botehs*, diamonds, and other small geometrics in green, gold, red, blue, and ivory. All figures are unusually precisely drawn. Interconnected diamonds and latch hooks are seen on an ivory primary border enclosed by red, green, and dark blue zigzag guards. Restorations, corroded browns. ....Est. $10,000/12,000; sold for $22,000

"Pinwheel" Kazak, South Caucasus, c. 1885, 8′2″ × 5′8″, $17,600.
PHOTO COURTESY OF SKINNER, INC.

Sewan. This very large shieldlike, keyhole-shaped medallion, another borrowing from the Turkic design pool, is lent delicacy in some versions by snowflake-like dots of white or gold on a red or green field.

Rug (c. 1885, 7′3″×4′10″). The large ivory-edged green and red keyhole medallion has stars, latch hooks, and numerous geometric figures in blue, green, red, gold, and ivory on a red ground, with stars and flanking stylized trees-of-life. Boxed polychrome stars ornament the primary blue border within gold flower-meander guards, all edged with red and white barber-pole stripes. Corroded browns; otherwise good condition. ....
....Est. $15,000/20,000; sold for $13,200

Shikli. A hexagonal arrowheaded medallion is centered on a somber field, usually dark blue or mahogany red; at both ends are staggered trios of stylized cypress trees. This design, which is not commonly seen, is more formal in appearance than other Kazak designs.

Long Rug (c. 1920, 11′×6′2″). A blue arrowheaded and latch-hooked hexagon on the mahogany field is flanked above and below with offset trios of cypress trees in medium and dark blue surrounded with a variety of small geometric fillers. The ivory main border has a geometric repeat and two guards with highly stylized vine-and-leaf meanders. Small hole; otherwise very good condition. .... Est. $2,000/2,500; sold for $5,225

Tree. Branched trees-of-life in blue and ivory are arranged freely on what is usually a red ground. Sometimes the trees are the major design figure; in Gendje variations they are often used to fill the space around a vertical row of medallions. Although not as colorful as most rugs in this group, good examples have the same appeal as the Kurdish willow and cypress tree carpets.

Rug (c. 1885, 7′5″×5′9″). On a dark red ground a well-spaced column of ivory, red, and blue gul-like hexagons are flanked by three pairs of branched ivory and slate blue trees surrounded by a wide variety of geometric and quadruped fillers in gold, bright blue, plum, apricot, tan, green, and ivory. The slate blue border has a stylized rosette repeat and two pairs of simple sawtooth guards. Wear creases. .... Est. $4,000/6,000; sold for $5,225

The designs seen on Kazak rugs are by no means confined to the ten named types described above. Here are a few more worthy of mention.

Scatter Rug (c. 1885, 5′5″×3′4″). An appealing stylized assortment of small and large quadrupeds and birds and one human are arrayed in informal rows on a rich royal blue field in shades of red, gold, jade, and ivory with an S-figured ivory primary border and two red and black cross-motif guards. Small hole. ....Est. $1,200/1,500; sold for $2,310

Rug (c. 1850, 6′10″×5′1″). A striking format featuring three vertical rows of large red, gold, dark blue, brown, and ivory stylized flowers on red and blue bands within a red and blue reciprocal trefoil border, an outsize leaf and flower "crab" repeat in blue, red, green, gold, and brown on the ivory main border

Kazak rug, South Caucasus, c. 1850, 6' 10" × 5' 1", $5,720. PHOTO
COURTESY OF CHRISTIE'S EAST.

and a secondary gold border with hooked blue, ivory, red, and aubergine diamonds within geometric repeats on dark blue guards. Shows wear; repiling; outer
border stripe missing, selvage replacement. ....
.... Est. $1,500/2,000; sold for $5,720

Rug (c. 1885, 7' 10" × 4' 10"). The field consists of diagonal stripes figured with
small hooked boxes in vivid shades of medium and cornflower blue, red, green,
gold, ivory, and brown within an unusual main border featuring horizontally
poled, polychrome hooked diamonds on ivory with a simple dark brown sawtooth repeat on the blue guards, all edged with gold and red barber-pole stripe.
Good condition. ....Est. $15,000/20,000; sold for $25,300

Gendje (Genje)

Gendje rugs are not easily distinguished from others of the coarsely
knotted, long-piled type on the basis of design, except for a distinctive
pattern of polychrome diagonal stripes figured with small floral designs
sometimes alternating with rows of *boteh* figures. A stylized flower, leaf,
and palmette border motif known as "crab" is frequently used to great
effect with these colorfully striped fields. Runners are commonly seen.

Rug (c. 1900, 7′5″ ×4′). The diagonal stripes that make up the field have symmetrically spaced floral figures, all in vivid yellow, jade, red, and dark blue. The wide ivory main border with a polychrome flower-and-leaf "crab" repeat is enclosed by three geometric inner borders and a running-dog outer border. Some corroded browns; otherwise good condition. ....
.... Est. $1,500/2,500; sold for $2,750

Karabagh (Qarabagh)

Karabagh rugs were made in larger sizes than most Caucasian rugs; many have obviously commercial designs, two examples of which may be found in the commercial listings. Workshop rugs are apt to have the cool red associated with cochineal-based dye; village rugs have the warmer madder red. A wide variety of designs were made, and most authorities now assign the "eagle" or "sunburst" design rugs discussed above under Kazak to Karabagh weavers. Some late Karabaghs are disfigured by garish and unstable synthetic dyes.

Rug (c. 1900, 7′10″ ×4′10″). On a rust red ground, three dark blue medallions in a variant of the Kazak pinwheel design are centered with diamond-shaped ivory rosettes and flanked by human and quadruped figures in dark blue, gold, and ivory within a primary blue border with boxed flowerheads and two ivory guards with polychrome zigzags. Shows slight wear; repairs, loss to one end guard, break at one end. .... Est. $4,000/6,000; sold for $4,950

Karabagh rug, South Caucasus, c. 1900, 7′ 10″ × 4′ 10″, $4,950.
PHOTO COURTESY OF CHRISTIE'S EAST.

Moghan

Hooked medallions of the type associated with Bordjalou rugs are also seen on Moghan pieces. The medallion format most often used by Moghan weavers, however, has Memling guls in one (rarely), two, and sometimes three vertical rows. These rugs are more finely woven than most types in this group, and the wefts are sometimes cotton. Good examples are very desirable.

Runner (c. 1860, 13′1″×3′). The dark blue ground has three long vertical rows of polychrome star-filled octagons within a red primary border of stylized rosettes and two guard borders in gold and ivory bearing rosette repeats, all edged with barber-pole stripes. Shows wear; guard border reduced on three sides; small repair. ....Est. $8,000/10,000; sold for $7,700

SHORT-PILED, FINELY KNOTTED CAUCASIANS

Daghestan

This name is often applied to a type of delicately lattice-patterned Shirvan (see below) rug that usually has a white ground.

Runner (c. 1875, 8′10″×3′6″). Precisely drawn keyhole-shape connected medallions with ivory diamond-repeat borders and blue-bordered red and ivory octagons on a warm red ground with a variety of geometric fillers and stylized quadrupeds. The ivory main border has a stylized rosette repeat and polychrome diagonally barred guards, all edged with red and blue barber-pole stripes. Repairs, reweaves. ....Est. $6,000/8,000; sold for $6,050

Daghestan prayer rug, Northeastern Caucasus, c. 1850, 4′6″ × 3′2″, $6,050. PHOTO COURTESY OF CHRISTIE'S EAST.

West Anatolian rug, c. 1700,
6′5″ × 3′8″, $44,000.
PHOTO COURTESY OF
CHRISTIE'S EAST.

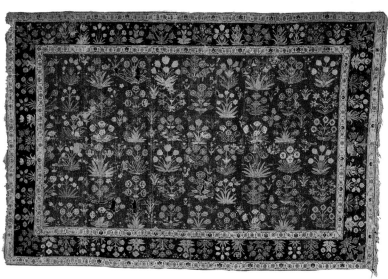

Mughal floral carpet, Northwest India, c. 1650, 9′10″ × 15′,
$253,000. PHOTO © 1991 SOTHEBY'S, INC.

Yarkand long rug, East Turkestan, c. 1800, 12'4" × 5'11", $143,000. PHOTO COURTESY OF CHRISTIE'S EAST.

Tekke Turkoman carpet, West Turkestan, c. 1875, 9'10" × 6'2", $12,100. PHOTO COURTESY OF CHRISTIE'S EAST.

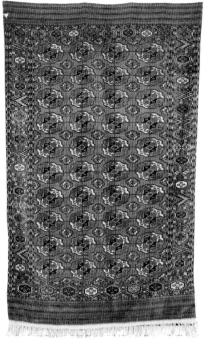

Caucasian Verneh horse blanket, c. 1875, 8' 8" × 4' 9", $27,500. PHOTO © 1991 SOTHEBY'S, INC.

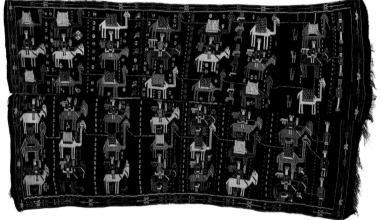

Yomut Turkoman asmalyk, West Turkestan, c. 1885, 3' 10" × 2' 4", $7,700 PHOTO COURTESY OF CHRISTIE'S EAST.

Shahsavan Soumak bags, Northwest Persia, c. 1900, 4' 4" × 1' 11", $23,100. PHOTO © 1991 SOTHEBY'S, INC.

West Anatolian rug, Canakkale area, c. 1885, 7′5″ × 5′4″, $6,050.
PHOTO © 1991 SOTHEBY'S, INC.

Karagashli rug, Northeast Caucasus, c. 1885, 6′9″ × 3′9″, $19,800.
PHOTO © 1991 SOTHEBY'S, INC.

Fars lion rug, Southwest Persia, c. 1900, 7′2″ × 5′2″, $4,180. PHOTO COURTESY OF CHRISTIE'S EAST.

Qashqai rug, Southwest Persia, c. 1885, 6′10″ × 4′9″, $18,700. PHOTO COURTESY OF CHRISTIE'S EAST.

Northwest Persian carpet,
c. 1885, 9′ 10″ × 9′ 4″,
$56,100. PHOTO © 1991
SOTHEBY'S, INC.

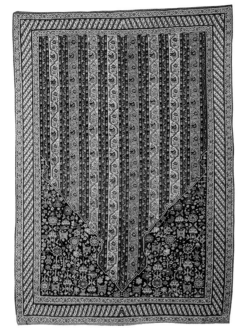

Senneh prayer kilim,
Northwest Persia, c. 1880,
6′ 2″ × 4′ 7″, $28,600.
PHOTO COURTESY OF
CHRISTIE'S EAST.

Bidjar kilim, Northwest Persia, dated 1863, 5′4″ × 3′, $14,500. PHOTO COURTESY OF SKINNER, INC.

Dragon Sileh carpet, Caucasus, c. 1885, 9′5″ × 7′, $15,400. PHOTO COURTESY OF CHRISTIE'S EAST.

Sarouk carpet, Western Persia, c. 1875, 9′ 11″ × 6′ 9″, $12,100. PHOTO COURTESY OF CHRISTIE'S EAST.

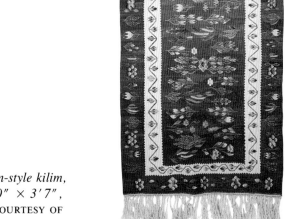

Turkish Romanian-style kilim, Izmir, 1989, 5′ 10″ × 3′ 7″, $1,200. PHOTO COURTESY OF WOVEN LEGENDS.

Prayer Rug (c. 1850, 4′6″×3′2″). A variety of polychrome flowers within a dark blue serrated-leaf lattice on an ivory ground below a dark blue arch with shieldlike device and ivory spandrels containing a variety of amulet motifs, all within a medium blue and brown reciprocal trefoil repeat. The primary border has a stylized-leaf repeat on red within dark blue minor guards bearing a repeated cross motif and numerous narrow geometric stripes. Shows wear; breaks; loss to ends; replaced selvages; repiling. .... Est. $6,000/8,000; sold for $6,050

Kuba

A variety of old rugs produced in the Kuba district in the Northeastern Caucasus not only have a similar structure but were made by weaving groups whose identity is in many cases conjectural. The better-known trade names, which are associated largely with particular designs, are Konagend, Perepedil, Seychour, Chichi, and Karagashli. It is hoped that rug researchers will in time be able to supply collectors with the hard information needed for proper attributions.

The Kuba's knot density falls into a range like that of the Shirvans, but unlike them the wool warps are more or less depressed. The wefts are more likely to be wool than cotton; the edges are double-corded and often overcast in blue or white. The end finish usually consists of a narrow strip of flat weave followed by multiple rows of tightly knotted or braided warps.

Runner (c. 1875, 8′8″×3′5″). The narrow abrashed royal blue ground has an interconnected series of geometric forms and stylized palmettes accompanied by symmetrically spaced small geometric fillers and quadrupeds, all in vivid shades of red, gold, green, ivory, and warm brown within a leaf-and-cup repeat on an ivory primary border enclosed by stylized polychrome rosettes on red minor borders and reciprocal trefoil guards. Shows slight wear. ....
.... Est. $4,000/6,000; sold for $8,800

Rug (Karagashli District) (c. 1885, 6′9″×3′9″). Three striking interconnected ivory-rayed, flower-ornamented hexagons with red and ivory Harshang-like pendants on a midnight blue ground together with ivory snowflake forms, Talish rosettes—all in vivid shades of red, green, gold, royal and light blue, and brown within a gold primary border with overlapping hooked triangle forms. The minor borders have rosette repeats guarded by narrow red and ivory geometric-figured stripes. Multiknotted warp fringe on blue plain weave at upper end; blue plain-weave band at lower. Some corroded browns; one side has nick. (See color insert) .... Est. $14,000/18,000; sold for $19,800

Rug (Konagend District) (c. 1885, 5′×3′9″). A large keyhole-shape garden plan bordered with latch-hook motifs on ivory has a pale blue fantailed bird in a flower-ornamented central square, all in soft shades of red, gold, yellow, medium blue, and ivory within an ivory primary border with flower-and-leaf "crab" repeat and black minor borders with typical Caucasian carnation repeat. Good condition. .... Est. $5,000/6,000; sold for $5,500

Prayer Rug (c. 1885, 5′×3′3″). A column of four Memling guls extends into the *mihrab* from the abrashed cornflower blue field filled with geometrics, stylized male figures, and amulets. A detached red prayer arch is flanked with a variety of floral and geometric figures, all within an ivory main border with a stylized dragon-motif repeat and two minor borders. Corroded browns ....
.... Est. $2,500/3,000; sold for $2,420

Rug (c. 1885, 5′7″×3′5″). A bold pattern known as Bidjov, consisting of ascending angular palmettes in three chevron-like rows on a dark brown field with flanking Afshan blossoms and stylized vinery, all in shades of yellow, jade blue, deep rose, pink, medium blue, and ivory within a complex running-dog border in blue and ivory edged with plain stripes. Good condition. ....
.... Est. $2,500/3,500; sold for $6,600

Rug (Seychour, Seichur District) (c. 1860, 4′11″×3′2″). Very decorative example of a large X-shaped exuberantly floral medallion that in later versions becomes stiffly rectilinear. On an ivory ground decorated with flowering leafy vines and curvilinear spandrels, a palmette-pendanted pair of medallions flank a flower-encircled rosette, all in vivid shades of red, rose, rich green, cornflower and medium blue, brown, ivory, and black within a rose and blue carnation repeat on red and a complex ivory and blue running-dog border sometimes seen on other Caucasian rugs (see preceding Bidjov rug) but associated most strongly with Seychour weavings. Closely knotted ivory warps. Good condition. ....
.... Est. $10,000/15,000; sold for $12,100

Shirvan

As a class, the Shirvans are relatively finely knotted, with a count ranging from 90 to about 200. Wefts are wool in early pieces, but cotton was being used by the turn of the century, and a narrow double-corded edging finished in white cotton is typical of late-19th- and early-20th-century examples. The colors are very good but less boldly used than those on long-piled Caucasians.

The format popularly associated with this group has a vertical row of lozenge-shaped medallions on a field liberally supplied with geometric filler motifs and, to a lesser extent, stylized animals. Many other designs are also seen: allover repeats, compartmented florals, vertical or diagonal stripes bearing floral or geometric motifs, Mina Khani florals, etc. A densely ornamented type featuring facing pairs of flamboyantly tailed birds is known as Akstafa; the Marasali subgroup employs a distinctive *boteh* variation on the field and a highly stylized *boteh*-like form in the primary border. The dark blue–fielded Marasali prayer rugs are particularly popular with collectors.

Long Rug (c. 1875, 8′10″×3′7″). On a dark blue ground are eight latch-hooked diamonds together with small geometric fillers and paired quadrupeds in quiet shades of red, blue, gray-green, gold, ivory, and brown, within a striking primary border of reciprocal arrowheads in ivory and red on blue, red and blue minor borders with geometric repeats, and six narrow decorative guards. Slight wear. .... Est. $5,000/7,000; sold for $6,380

Long Rug (Akstafa type) (c. 1875, 8'10"×3'7"). Three gabled, ivory-bordered, and latch-hooked medallions on a dark blue ground with facing pairs of flamboyantly fantailed birds, all in subdued shades of soft red, blue-green, gold, medium blue, and olive together with a variety of polychrome geometric fillers within an overlapping hooked-triangle repeat on ivory and two narrow S-figured guards in red and blue. Shows slight wear; repaired selvage. ....
.... Est. $2,500/3,500; sold for $3,300

Prayer Rug (Marasali type) (c. 1885, 4'9"×3'4"). Four rows of flaming polychrome *botehs* on an abrashed midnight blue ground topped by a row of grimacing warriors whose leader stands in the *mihrab* surrounded by geometric devices and amulets. The ivory prayer arch is flanked by flaming *botehs* and more small fillers, all within a gold border bearing the chevron-striped stylized birds characteristic of Marasali rugs. The red guard borders have a star repeat. Shows wear; repairs, rebound selvages. .... Est. $1,000/1,500; sold for $1,540

Shirvan Marasali prayer rug, East Caucasus, c. 1885, 4'9" × 3'4", $1,540. PHOTO COURTESY OF SKINNER, INC.

Shirvan long rug, East Caucasus, c. 1885, 8′6″ × 3′7″, $5,225.
PHOTO COURTESY OF SKINNER, INC.

Long Rug (c. 1885, 8′6″×3′7″). A stylized variant of the floral Afshan motif derived from early Caucasian blossom carpets together with stepped hexagons and diamond medallions on a dark blue ground densely covered with a variety of small geometric fillers, all in shades of red, sky blue, orange, gold, blue-green, and ivory. The dark blue-green border has a Kufic repeat; a typically Caucasian leafed-carnation repeat is seen on the dark blue guards. Shows even wear. .... Est. $5,000/6,000; sold for $5,225

Talish

The Talish weavers live in villages near the Caspian Sea and the city of Lenkoran, the name given to a type of rug, usually a runner, that according to one authority is the product of Talish weavers. The Lenkoran design is dominated by large clunky medallions that resemble sea turtles more than the palmettes from which they were probably derived.

The typical Talish rug is a long, narrow rug of great elegance with a red or dark blue field that is either entirely open or displays two or three judiciously placed, precisely drawn rosettes. Fields with more ornamentation are occasionally seen. The inner border is often a delicately drawn reciprocal arrowhead motif; the primary border, usually white, alternates rosettes of the type used in the field with squares made up of four smaller and more highly stylized rosettes. Wefts are wool in the oldest examples; in later rugs, cotton.

Long Rug (c. 1875, 7′3″×3′8″). The gold reciprocal trefoil-bordered midnight blue ground displays a row of three floral devices in ivory, red, and royal blue, one horned animal and a handful of other small devices within an ivory main border with a repeat of typically finely detailed rosettes alternating with boxed-star quartets, guarded by a boxed-star repeat on red, all in shades of red, gold, three blues, and ivory. The outer blue and black reciprocal trefoil border is edged in red and blue stripes. Repairs. .... Est. $8,000/10,000; sold for $15,400

Left: *Talish long rug, East Caucasus, c. 1875, 7′3″ × 3′8″,* $15,400. PHOTO COURTESY OF CHRISTIE'S EAST. Right: *Talish long rug, Lenkoran district, c. 1885, 8′6″ × 3′11″, $11,000.* PHOTO COURTESY OF CHRISTIE'S EAST.

Long Rug (Lenkoran District) (c. 1885, 8′6″×3′11″). On a dark brown ground, three well-drawn Lenkoran medallions separated by red-armed royal blue rectangles and surrounded by well-spaced geometric figures, all in shades of red, gold, royal blue, forest green, mahogany, and ivory within a finely detailed reciprocal trefoil repeat on a narrow primary border within two pairs of very narrow guards. Good condition. ... Est. $10,000/12,000; sold for $11,000

PERSIAN RUGS

Some names familiar to you may not be included in the following listings. This could be because as a class the rugs bearing these names lack sufficiently distinctive designs and coloration to be classed as collectible, because examples of good quality were not offered at auction during the two years under consideration, or because they are listed in another category.

AFSHAR

Perhaps the reason Afshar rugs have taken so long to catch on as collectibles is the confusing variety of design influences seen in their weavings. Some Afshars live in northeastern Iran near Meshed, others near Bidjar, and a large number live south of Kerman. In short, it's hard to collect something one can't easily define. But even though the designs of some old Afshar rugs were obviously influenced by contemporaneous commercial Kerman rugs, a distinctive group of rustic Afshars has begun to establish itself in the collectors' hall of fame.

Afshars woven in a rustic setting have an all-wool foundation on which the lustrous pile yarns may be knotted either symmetrically or asymmetrically. According to dealer-scholar James Opie, the former is associated with the tribal work discussed in the tribal weavings listings, the latter with the village rugs listed below. The wefts are usually dyed orange; double wefting is the rule, and the warps are noticeably depressed. Afshar rugs frequently have highly decorative flat-woven end finishes; the side finishes vary, often displaying barber-pole overcastings in two or more colors.

Rug (c.1885, 5′×4′2″). Two ivory diamond-shaped medallions on a dark blue ground within a distinctive red crenellated and stepped large cartouche on a royal blue ground filled with polychrome geometric fillers. A stylized flowering-shrub-figured border is contained by polychrome diagonally striped guards. Good condition. .... Est. $2,000/3,000; sold for $1,870

Rug (c. 1885, 4′9″×3′8″). Tiny stylized flowers are repeated along the field-filling chevron stripes in dark and royal blue, red, gold, rust, ivory, and jade, all within seven narrow, geometrically figured border stripes and a main border of a floral meander on dark blue. Shows area of wear. ....
.... Est. $1,500/1,800; sold for $1,870

Carpet (c.1900, 12′×6′9″). A navy blue pendanted cartouche with serrated edge contains 12 latch-hooked diamond figures in blue, rust, and ivory with a multitude of polychrome *botehs*, all on a rust ground, which is similarly *boteh*-populated, within a rust, zigzag vine-and-flower main border and two narrow ivory meander-figured guards. Shows wear, including crease wear; damaged selvage. .... Est. $5,500/6,500; sold for $5,500

Rug (c. 1875, 6′×4′7″). A Kerman-influenced, navy blue, lobed and pendanted medallion containing palmettes and rosettes in red, gold, medium blue, ivory, rose, and jade on a floral-decorated ivory ground with red spandrels enclosing stylized vines bearing white flowers. All surrounded by a floral meander on navy blue; two ivory stylized meander guards and a palmette, vine, and rosette main border on medium blue. Loss to ends; otherwise good. ....
.... Est. $6,000/8,000; sold for $7,700

Afshar rug, South Persia, c. 1875, 6' × 4'7", $7,700. PHOTO
COURTESY OF CHRISTIE'S EAST.

Rug (c. 1875, 5'4" ×4'1"). The navy blue rectangular field is closely filled
with rows of elaborately floral-decorated *botehs*, enclosed by a rather odd stylized floral repeat on a wide yellow main border with five additional floral
meander-figured guards. Brilliant vegetable colors in red, blues, yellow, gold,
jade, aubergine, and ivory. Shows repairs; corrosion. ....
.... Est. $3,500/4,500; sold for $4,400

BAKHTIARI

According to C. E. Edwards, the author of *The Persian Carpet*, the area
and room-size rugs known in the trade as Bakhtiari were not woven by
members of the tribe of that name. Rather, they were made in villages
in the Chahar Mahal area east and south of Isfahan. Old examples were
symmetrically knotted of good lustrous wool on a wool foundation.

Rug (c. 1885, 7'2" ×4'8"). Compartmented garden designs are a particular
favorite of Bakhtiari weavers. This example has three columns of eight squares
filled with alternating flowering tree and shrub motifs in vivid shades of dark
and royal blue, red, gold, and blue-green, enclosed by a wide gold border with
a palmette, rosette, and leaf repeat. Even wear; loss to one end. ....
.... Est. $1,500/2,000; sold for $2,090

Bakhtiari rug, Northwest Persia, c. 1885, 7'2" × 4'8", $2,090.
PHOTO COURTESY OF SKINNER, INC.

BAKSHAISH (BAKSHAYESH)

Rustic in look as well as production, these symmetrically and rather coarsely knotted all-wool rugs are similar to others made in the Heriz area and enjoy the same popularity with collectors and decorators. A frequently seen pattern is a stylized animal-pelt-like medallion on an open field ornamented with sinuous pink figures, probably derived from the cloud-band motif. The corner joinings of the bold patterns on the characteristically wide main borders are invariably poorly resolved. A camel-color outer edge is common.

Scatter Rug (c. 1885, 4'11"×3'10"). An element of the Bid Majnun design, incorporating a central tree-of-life on a camel ground flanked by blue and coral weeping willows and cypress trees. Serrated-leaf and rosette motifs are repeated on the coral main border; the guards have a floral meander on blue. Ends missing; minor repairs. .... Est. $1,200/1,500; sold for $2,200

Rug (c. 1885, 6'×4'5"). An ivory, rectilinear, pink-pendanted medallion filled with palmette, floral, and star figures within a rose-stepped and blue-bordered medallion on a camel ground. Blue spandrels are ornamented with a variety of palmette, floral, and star motifs. Enclosed in a narrow ivory, red, and brown reciprocal trefoil border and a wide red main border bearing stiffly stylized vine and rosette meanders. Corroded browns; new selvages; repaired slits; restorations, missing borders. .... Est. $6,000/8,000; sold for $6,600

Carpet (c. 1885, 11'2" ×8'11"). A rectilinear apricot medallion with geometric palmette and flower-inspired figures set within a larger medium blue-grounded peltlike medallion with curious, madder rose X-figured squiggles, set in turn on a camel ground ornamented with stylized stalks of flowers. The medium blue spandrels contain more of the madder rose figures in a more recognizably cloud-band configuration. Stiff stylizations of palmette leaf and flower motifs are repeated on a dark blue main border guarded by flower-and-vine meanders on mahogany, all enclosed by a plain camel band. Corroded browns. .... Est. $30,000/35,000; sold for $30,800

Note: Another "animal pelt" carpet of similar age and size but with partial end borders also was sold during this period. ....Est. $15,000/20,000; sold for $26,400

Rug (c. 1885, 7'1" ×5'10"). A red medallion with Herati motifs is set upon an arrowheaded pole with long leaf-and-flower-terminated arms extending into a honey diamond-shaped field enlivened with trios of alert quadrupeds. The saw-tooth, red-edged blue spandrels are filled with Herati motifs, enclosed by a honey main border with leaf, palmette, and vine meander, guarded by two soft red floral-meander borders and finished with a plain camel band. ....Est. $8,000/10,000; sold for $10,450

Bakshaish rug, Northwest Persia, c. 1885, 7'1" × 5'10", $10,450.
PHOTO © 1991 SOTHEBY'S, INC.

Carpet (c. 1885, 16′×12′1″). Well-drawn, beautifully spaced, large-scale end-less Herati repeat in ivory, rose, jade, three blues, apricot, gold, and ivory on a soft madder red field with numerous narrow guards and a highly stylized flower meander on a dark blue main border, all enclosed by a camel band. Repiled areas. ....Est. $25,000/30,000; sold for $34,100

Carpet (c. 1870, 9′4″×7′9″). Nine awkwardly drawn, stepped, diamond-shaped medallions in medium blue, ivory, and brown on a pendanted and stepped madder red field with numerous geometric fillers. The ivory spandrels contain red vinelike angularities; the wide medium blue border has a large-scale floral "crab" repeat in red, ivory, and brown. Very rustic in appearance. Severe erosion to the ends of the enclosing dark brown camel band; repiled areas. ....
.... Est. $20,000/25,000; sold for $22,000

Carpet (c. 1885, 13′9″×11′3″). On a pale honey field, an endless repeat of rows of stylized branched flowering plants in red, apricot, and dark blue. Two pairs of blue and apricot guards with pretty floral meanders enclose a soft red main border with a strikingly bold, highly geometricized palmette, vine, and flower meander in blue, red, apricot, and ivory. ....
....Est. $30,000/35,000; sold for $46,750

BIDJAR (BIJAR)

Old Bidjars are densely packed, well-nigh indestructible rugs knotted asymmetrically by Kurdish weavers on a wool foundation with hand-spun

Bidjar rug, Northwest Persia, c. 1885, 11′4″ × 7′9″, $14,300.
PHOTO © 1991
SOTHEBY'S, INC.

yarns dyed with beautiful vegetable colors. Collectors esteem the variety of appealing floral and tree designs seen on rustic examples and the handsome rectilinear medallion format associated with old rugs with a slablike handle. (Also see the commercial rug listings.)

Carpet (c. 1885, 11′4″×7′9″). A classic rectilinear Bidjar format featuring a palmette-pendanted, stepped, diamond-shaped, soft red medallion with an all-over repeat of floral figures in gold, blues, green, and mahogany, which in this example is in dramatic contrast to the unornamented midnight blue field. Stepped gold spandrels contain flowering plants, all within two pairs of narrow floral meander guards enclosing a red main border bearing a stylized palmette, vine, and flower meander. Good condition. ... Est. $8,000/10,000; sold for $14,300

Rug (c. 1900, 6′4″×3′8″). An abrashed dark blue pendanted medallion with palmette and rosettes is set on a red field ornamented with a handful of geometric fillers and groups of quadrupeds flanked by dark blue spandrels abloom with flowering vines, all within a narrow meander border. Two small patches; otherwise good condition. .... Est. $1,800/2,200; sold for $2,090

Carpet "Sampler" (c. 1900, 5′8″×11′). One vertical half of a large palmette-pendanted ivory medallion with graceful leaf and flowering vine ornamentation is set upon a similarly ornamented curvilinear rust cartouche with light blue floral spandrels. Rust guards with floral repeats enclose the ivory main border featuring a stylized palmette-and-leafed-vine meander. Even wear. ....
.... Est. $2,500/3,500; sold for $4,840

Carpet (c. 1875, 17′7″×10′5″). The abrashed dark blue ground is ornamented with very large rose and tan palmettes alternating with medium blue and tan arabesques enclosing smaller palmettes in tan, green, and aubergine, with numerous realistic green-stemmed sprays of ivory, blue, and rose flowers enlivening the carpet's overall air of stateliness. The wide tan palmette-and-leafy-vine meander main border is flanked by two red borders with floral meanders. Areas of wear; stains. ....Est. $3,500/4,500; sold for $14,300

Long Rug (c. 1900, 7′8″×4′6″). A cornflower blue, lobed and pendanted floral medallion is set upon a stepped coral ground decorated with stylized Herati motifs. Flowering vines fill the green-gold spandrels. Three narrow borders in medium blue and coral have flower-and-vine meanders, all enclosed by a reciprocal trefoil edge stripe. Loss to one end border; otherwise good condition. .... Est. $3,500/4,500; sold for $3,850

BALUCH (BELOUCH, BALUCHI, BELOUCHISTAN)

Rugs made by the settled Baluch weavers in the Khorasan region of northeast Persia share the rather limited palette of nomadic examples, but the weave and finish tends to be finer and the motifs are frequently village versions of classical Persian motifs like the Mina Khani, Herati, and Harshang.

The knotting is asymmetrical on a wool foundation; old rugs frequently have ornamental skirts, and the edges are invariably overcast with brown goat hair.

Baluch rug, Northeast Persia,
c. 1900, 5′4″ × 3′1″, $2,420.
PHOTO COURTESY OF CHRISTIE'S EAST.

Scatter Rug (c. 1900, 5′4″ ×3′1″). A central row of four Harshang variations in red, mahogany, dark blue, and ivory on an ivory ground flanked by symmetrically placed palmettes in the same colors and stylized flowers in royal blue. The wide red primary border has an unusually well-resolved Turkoman line in dark and royal blue, mahogany, and brown enclosed by two very narrow red and brown reciprocal trefoil repeats on ivory. Blue and red striped plain-weave bands terminate in a partially eroded ivory band with red and blue wefts in a wave pattern. Very good condition. .... Est. $1,800/2,200; sold for $2,420

HAMADAN

The weaving villages surrounding the city of Hamadan in northwest Iran have, over the years, produced vast quantities of rugs, almost all of which have only one weft passing between each row of symmetrical knots. The foundation, which was wool in older rugs, has been cotton since about World War I. Sturdy and serviceable, few are collected save for the finer-quality Malayers, which are comparable to Ferahan Sarouks (see the commercial carpets listings), and the very beautiful camel-ground carpets made in the 19th century. The latter are often mistakenly tagged as Serabs (see below), most of which were made in runner sizes.

The Hamadan area production was not only large but extremely variable. Unfortunately, all rugs made there have become unfairly burdened with the reputation of the lesser examples. I recently purchased a lovely old vegetable-dyed, village-made scatter whose glowing cypress-tree design has spurred me to seek examples of similar quality. Bearing in mind that the road less traveled is often the most rewarding, perhaps other open-minded collectors will be encouraged to do the same.

Long Rug (c. 1885, 10′ × 4′11″). Finely detailed *botehs* in closely spaced horizontal rows in an endless repeat on a dark blue field enclosed by a wide abrashed coral border with a pretty palmette, vine, and flower motif poorly resolved at the corners. Vegetable dyes in shades of blue, salmon, yellow, ivory, and olive. Even wear. .... Est. $1,500/2,500; sold for $2,420

Carpet (c. 1880, 20′7″ × 12′6″). Cataloged as a 1900 Serab, this is more likely an older type of Hamadan no longer made. This handsome glossy-piled rug has diamond medallions with red, dark blue, and green geometric figures set in a widely spaced endless repeat on a pale camel ground with a light brown allover tracery characteristic of this group. The wide cornflower blue border has a palmette, rosette, and leaf repeat in reds, tans, and blues guarded by pretty polychrome flowering vines on ivory, all enclosed in a camel band, which is missing at one end. Shows very slight wear. ....Est. $12,000/15,000; sold for $28,600

HERIZ AREA

A rectilinear medallion format is popularly associated with rugs woven in the Heriz district in a range of qualities from coarse to relatively fine, variously labeled Heriz, Gorevan, and Serapi, the latter name usually reserved for the more finely knotted examples. One expert is of the opinion that the rugs known in the trade as Bakshaish (see above) should also be included here. The older Heriz-area rugs are adaptable to a variety of settings, and their inventive variations on the medallion theme commend them to collectors seeking noncommercial-looking floor coverings.

Allover patterns are also seen—the large-scale Herati designs are particularly noteworthy—and although room-size rugs are the norm, runners and area rugs are also occasionally seen, the latter more apt to be square than rectangular. The border designs on village rugs are usually poorly resolved at the corners.

The foundations have been cotton for about the last hundred years, and the symmetrical knotting ranges from 30 per square inch to 80 in the finer grades. There are two wefts, often dyed blue, and the double selvage has a sturdy, serviceable finish.

Rug (c. 1885, 8′7″ × 6′4″). Although smaller than average, this rug commanded a carpet price for its striking combinations of a red-bordered, red leaf-filled and pendanted ivory medallion with arcs of serrated ivory leaves above and below on a floral-ornamented midnight blue field. The mahogany-edged jade floral spandrels are enclosed by an ivory border with faux calligraphy in blue and red; the red primary border has a serrated-leaf-and-palmette meander in two blues, rose, brown, and jade. The red-edged, floral-meander outer ivory border is partially missing. Good condition. .. Est. $20,000/25,000; sold for $20,900

Carpet (c. 1900, 12'×9'10"). A larger carpet similar in design to the one above but with much paler coloration. ....Est. $15,000/20,000; sold for $16,500

Rug (c. 1900, 6'7"×6'2"). The square cream field is ornamented with vivid polychrome leaf and flower figures symmetrically placed within an angular vinery centered with a large rosette. The simple and rather narrow dark blue rosette border has two red floral meander guards. Good condition. ....
....Est. $6,000/8,000; sold for $9,900

Carpet (c. 1885, 12'5"×9'10"). A monumental latch-hooked, rectilinear, and pendanted red medallion with a central royal blue diamond flanked by large ivory serrated leaves is set on an abrashed cream field with sparsely floral-figured cream spandrels. The light red main border has a stiff, rather poorly resolved palmette-and-leaf repeat in blues, reds, cream, and ivory, all enclosed by geometrically figured guards. Partial loss to one end border. ....
....Est. $25,000/35,000; sold for $41,800

Carpet (c. 1900, 14'10"×10'7"). Uncommon allover repeat of polychrome cypress trees within a vinery lattice on a cream ground enclosed by a primary camel border with a flowering vine meander and two pairs of red and dark blue guards with simple floral meanders. Partial end borders; otherwise good. ......
....Est. $15,000/20,000; sold for $26,400

Carpet (c. 1870, 10'10"×9'8"). This striking old rug has a madder red, sparsely floral-ornamented, pendanted central medallion on a plain, strongly abrashed gold to green ground with serrated-edge salmon spandrels. A narrow red primary border with a vine-and-flower meander has three narrow flower-and-vine repeats on pale gold. Shows some wear; loss to end guard borders. ....
....Est. $15,000/20,000; sold for $19,800

Carpet (c. 1900, 12'7"×8'5"). An allover pattern of large-scale, vivid-polychrome, vine-connected palmettes on a midnight blue ground within an ivory calligraphic border enclosed by a wide, abrashed green primary border bearing a palmette, flower, and vine repeat with poorly resolved corners. The two pale red guards have a simple flower-and-vine meander. ....
.... Est. $20,000/25,000; sold for $20,900

Carpet (c. 1900, 14'11"×10'). A classic format featuring a rectilinear, almost square, dark blue floral medallion with a red and ivory gul-like figure at its center. The flower-and-vine ornamented abrashed red field has gracefully stepped dark blue spandrels with a sinuous polychrome vinery. The red main border has a palmette, leaf, and vine repeat and two very narrow ivory guards with floral meanders. Partial end borders; otherwise good condition. ....
....Est. $18,000/22,000; sold for $19,800

Heriz area Runner (c. 1920, 10'6"×2'10"). A column of nine bold and geometrically figured square medallions in tan alternating with dark blue are connected by simple flowering vines on a red field, and the two navy and tan borders have diagonal leaf and flower repeats within narrow barber-pole guards. ....
....Est. $1,000/1,500; sold for $1,210

Carpet (c. 1920, 11'6"×8'8"). The Bid Majnun weeping willow design in shades of rose, medium blue, tan, and pale jade fills a rust-red field punctuated with two trios of small dark blue birds, all enclosed by a dark blue main border with a serrated-leaf-and-rosette repeat and two gold guards with floral meanders. Small areas of repair. .... Est. at $5,500/6,500; sold for $6,050

Heriz carpet, Northwest Persia, c. 1900, 14' 11" × 10', $19,800.
PHOTO © 1991 SOTHEBY'S, INC.

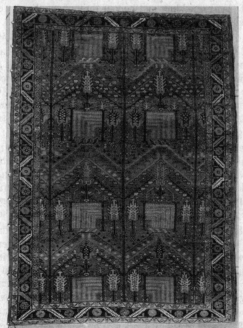

Heriz carpet, Northwest Persia, c. 1920, 11' 6" × 8' 8", $6,050.
PHOTO COURTESY OF SKINNER, INC.

The Heriz-area rugs and carpets listed below were cataloged as Serapi:

Carpet (c. 1885, 11'4"×8'4"). The ultimate decorative rug: a rose-colored lobed and pendanted medallion with symmetrically placed rosette and palmettes within a cream, flower-decorated, broadly stepped cartouche rests on a soft red ground flanked by graceful pale green spandrels ornamented with palmettes, rosettes, and blooming vines, all in soft shades of blue, gold, green, and two shades of blue with midnight blue accents. The rose primary border has a palmette, leaf, and vine repeat and is guarded by two narrow ivory bands with flower-and-vine meanders. Evenly worn. ..Est. $12,000/16,000; sold for $24,000

Rug (c. 1880, 5'7"×5'3"). The almost square, brick red field is filled with highly stylized, large-scale vine and palmette figures in salmon, mustard, jade, cream, and pale and dark blues within a wide palmette, rosette, and flowering vine repeat on a dark blue main border enclosed by narrow guards with simple floral meanders. Shows wear; eroded end borders. ....
....Est. $3,000/4,000; sold for $6,050

Carpet (c. 1880, 12'7"×9'5"). On a rust, vine-ornamented ground is a dramatic lobed and pendanted midnight blue medallion with palmettes arrayed around a rust, boxed central figure. A single large, dark blue palmette dominates each ivory spandrel, all within a rust primary border with a palmette-and-flowering-vine repeat enclosed by two narrow olive guards with floral meanders. Soft shades of tan, rose, blue, and copper throughout. Even wear; loss to end borders; reweaves and repairs; painted areas. ....
....Est. $15,000/20,000; sold for $15,400

Runner (c. 1880, 14'8"×5'7"). A long, rust red cartouche has a lobed, dark blue central medallion upon a pole ornamented with palmettes and surrounded with floral sprays and vine, leaf, and *ashik* motifs in cream, rose, blue, tan, and plum. Similar motifs fill the medium blue stepped spandrels. Floral meanders are repeated on a rust primary border and two narrower dark blue guards. Shows some wear. ....Est. $10,000/12,000; sold for $14,300

Carpet (c. 1880, 14'×9'). The flower-ornamented rust ground has a midnight blue central pendanted medallion with flamboyant leaf and rosette motifs in red, cream, and pale and dark blue. Blue-edged serrated leaves arc below each pendant, and red, tan, and blue leaves and flower stalks fill cream, blue-bordered spandrels enclosed by a wide midnight blue border with graceful palmette, rosette, and leafy vine figures and a pair of floral-meander ivory guards. Even wear; some repiling. .... Est. $20,000/25,000; sold for $22,000

Carpet (c. 1885, 10'11"×9'1"). A large quatrefoil cream medallion with central sea green lozenge and palmette-and-flower decoration centered upon a rust ground filled with generously spaced palmette, leaf, and flowering vine figures. There are no spandrels in this example. The wide abrashed green primary border has a striking version of a flower-and-vine meander border enclosed by floral-meander ivory guards. Even wear; loss to end borders; patch along one edge; stains. .... Est. $12,000/15,000; sold for $9,900

Carpet (c. 1885, 11'2"×9'2"). On a rust ground a dark blue rosette with pale coral leafy extensions is centered, together with symmetrically placed palmette and leaf motifs within connected cream spandrels with large leaf motifs. Soft shades of red, coral, three blues, brown, and olive green are used throughout. The charcoal brown primary border has a striking stylization of a common rosette, leaf, and flower meander, all enclosed by two red floral-meander guards. Shows wear; loss to ends; repair along border. .... Est. $12,000/14,000; sold for $9,350

Carpet (c. 1885, 14′4″ × 10′10″). Three graduated, stepped medallions in blue, ivory, and red, each with leaf and flower ornamentation, on an abrashed dark blue field with stylized palmettes and vines. Four realistically drawn fish in red and white flank the ends of the medallions. The wide, blue main border has a spacious flower-and-leaf meander enclosed by two pairs of floral meander guards in red and ivory. Good condition. .... Est. $16,000/18,000; sold for $19,800

KARADJA

Nearly all rugs attributed to this Tabriz-area town have a column of distinctive squared medallions. Because they are single wefted, the appearance of the back is similar to rugs made in the Hamadan district.

Runner (c. 1885, 12′2″ × 3′9″). The abrashed midnight blue field has five well-spaced typical medallions accompanied by sprays of white flowers, *botehs*, and numerous geometric motifs, all within an ivory border of floral-figured diagonal bars and a pair of red guards with flower-and-vine meanders. Shows wear; hole; repairs; loss to ends; crease wear; damaged selvage. .... Est. $2,000/3,000; sold for $1,980

KELARDASHT

Usually cataloged, as this was, as South Caucasian, old Kelardashts are actually made in "that Persian tail of the Caucasus which coils around the southern shores of the Caspian sea." The beautiful, well-made pieces of old were produced in small numbers by Kurdish weavers for domestic use. They are rarely available in this country, and when they are, few recognize them.

Small Runner (c. 1900, 8′6″ × 3′4″). A classic example displaying a column of 11 precisely drawn Memling guls in brown, ivory gold, and jade on a brick red field within a medium blue primary border with alternating geometricized flower-and-rosette motifs and a pair of ivory guards with a red trefoil repeat. Good condition. .... Est. $3,000/5,000; sold for $2,970

Kelardasht runner, Northwest Persia, c. 1900, 8′6″ × 3′4″, $2,970.
PHOTO COURTESY OF SKINNER, INC.

KURDISH

Most of the village rugs made by Kurdish weavers are associated with the towns and areas in which they were made. This small rug, cataloged simply as Kurdish, is obviously a village product; the rather dressy pattern is one seen on Bidjars in scatter and area rug sizes, which this may in fact be.

Rug (c. 1900, 5′8″×3′5″). Three tan and gold lions climb the sinuous branch of a blossoming tree with outsize, irregularly shaped leaves in shades of slate blue, rose, red-brown, and peach on a dark red field. A pair of zigzag guards enclose the wide black leaf-and-vine border in a simpler version of one seen on commercial Garus-design Bidjar carpets. Areas of wear; edges reovercast. .....
.... Est. $1,200/1,500; sold for $3,025

NORTHWEST PERSIAN

Some rugs go begging for exact attributions either because not enough is known about the weaving in the area to allow accurate assignment, or because the person doing the classification lacks sufficient information. Whatever the reason, the following rugs fall into this no-name limbo, at least for the time being.

Runner (c. 1885, 18′10″×3′4″). The modified Harshang motifs and palmettes that dominate the center of the midnight blue ground are accompanied by symmetrical repeats of rosettes, flowering plants, and fantailed pairs of birds in shades of red, blue, gold, green, brown, and plum, within a red primary border with flowering vine repeat contained by two ivory guards with leaf-and-vine meander. Slight loss to end borders; otherwise good condition. ....
.... Est. $5,000/7,000; sold for $4,400

Runner (c. 1880, 11′1″×3′7″). The navy blue ground is covered with a serrated red and ivory lattice containing floral sprays. The primary ivory border has a border of precisely drawn rosettes like those associated with Caucasian Talish rugs; the blue rosette guards are themselves contained by red and ivory barberpole stripes. Shows even wear; repairs; one end border rewoven. ....
.... Est. $2,500/3,500; sold for $3,520

Long Rug (c. 1860, 8′10″×4′8″). The damage suffered by this rug over the years hardly detracts from its spectacular qualities: set against the corroded dark brown field are nine symmetrically placed flamelike palmettes and a variety of small floral and geometric motifs, all in vivid hues of red, gold, royal blue, jade, ivory, and an aubergine of rare richness. The gold primary border of stylized brown and red vine-and-flower meander is contained by bright blue guards with a stylized flower-and-leaf repeat. Corroded browns; reduced end borders, reweaves. .... Est. $7,000/9,000; sold for $35,200

SENNEH

The finely woven, delicately patterned, and closely clipped Senneh rug is entirely unlike the sturdy fabrics produced by other Kurdish weavers, with floral and *boteh* motifs favored. Unlike most old village rugs, the foundation is cotton, with silk used for the warps of the finest pieces.

Left: *Northwest Persian long rug,
c. 1860, 8′ 10″ × 4′ 8″, $35,200.*
PHOTO COURTESY OF CHRISTIE'S
EAST. Right: *Senneh rug,
Northwest Persia, c. 1885,
7′ × 4′ 10″, $3,300.* PHOTO
COURTESY OF SKINNER, INC.

Ever popular with collectors, its peculiar structure lends the back a distinctive gritty texture even the rankest amateur can readily identify. Sennehs are almost always seen in area rug sizes.

Rug (c. 1885, 7′ ×4′ 10″). Staggered rows of large, finely detailed *botehs* in cornflower blue, red, rose, gold, and jade are set upon an ivory field swirled with flowering vines. The dark red main border has a rosette repeat and two floral-meander blue guards. Even allover wear. ....
.... Est. $1,000/1,500; sold for $3,300

Rug (c. 1900, 6′5″ ×4′5″). A red-centered, brilliant gold floral-ornamented and pendanted medallion is set on a dark blue hexagon filled with flowers and birds. Herati-like motifs are symmetrically spaced upon the red spandrels, all enclosed by an ivory main border with a rather cramped palmette, flower, and vine repeat and two narrow red floral-meander guards. Good condition. ....
.... Est. $5,000/7,000; sold for $4,400

SERAB

Sturdy camel-color grounded runners were woven in the Heriz district in a group of market towns in the vicinity of the market town of Serab.

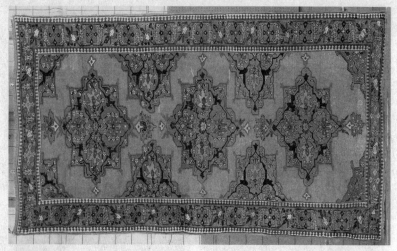

Serab long rug, Northwest Persia, c. 1900, 10′8″ × 6′3″, $5,500.
PHOTO COURTESY OF CHRISTIE'S EAST.

Typically, these rugs display elegantly drawn pole-connected medallions in madder rose, pale gold, ivory, and two or three shades of blue.

Long Rug (c. 1900, 10′8″×6′3″). The camel-color ground has a well-spaced infinite repeat of soft red flower-and-palmette-ornamented and pendanted medallions clearly inspired by the classical star design seen on antique Turkish Oushak rugs. The red border has a nicely resolved rosette, leaf, and flowering vine repeat crisply contained by the brown reciprocal trefoil repeats on the narrow ivory guards. Even wear; repiling. ..... Est. $3,500/4,500; sold for $5,500

Long Rug (c. 1885, 11′×5′2″). The abrashed camel ground has 1½ large blue-outlined cartouches, within which are diamond-shaped pendanted medallions set on a cream tracery with stylized floral ornamentation in the spandrels in dark, medium, and light blues, soft red, gold, and brown. The camel border of alternating palmettes and rosettes is guarded by narrow camel borders with a flower-and-vine meander, all within an outer camel band. Shows slight wear. ....
.... Est. $3,500/4,500; sold for $7,150

Runner (c. 1885, 11′10″×3′5″). Three poled hexagonal ivory medallions containing blue, red, and gold stylized floral figures on a camel field ornamented with polychrome *boteh* and enclosed by a green and brown reciprocal trefoil border, all within a plain camel band. Spots of wear. ....
.... Est. 1,200/1,500; sold for $2,475

SOUTHWEST PERSIAN

Some of the rugs made by the settled tribal groups of southwest Persia have been included with the tribal weavings, a few with the commercial rugs. The rugs listed below were made on rustic looms with an eye for profit but without compromising their tribal vitality. Their lively and distinctive patterning, soft lustrous wool, and vivid vegetable dyes are prized by collectors.

Khamseh Rug (c. 1875, 5′8″×4′1″). The ivory hexagonal field of this delightful rug is edged with cypress trees; a rectangular central panel presents a bucolic scene in miniature: trees, a flowering shrub, resting birds, and a facing pair of finned fish. The dark blue spandrels are filled with floral motifs, as are the three stylized borders. Shows even wear. .... Est. $3,000/4,000; sold for $3,190

Khamseh Rug (c. 1920, 6′6″×5′2″). The dark red central diamond and the corners of the dark blue field on which it sits display lobed ivory medallions containing motifs similar to the Chinese *yun-chien* motif seen in many variations on Turkish weavings. Both the red and blue fields are covered with branched flowering stalks in blue, gold, and pale jade within a primary border with leaf and flower meander on ivory and six narrower geometric-figured guards. Small patch; otherwise good condition. .... Est. $1,500/2,000; sold for $1,760

Khamseh Rug (c. 1900, 6′9″×4′10″). On a navy blue ground are repeats of a stylized version of the roses, known as *gol farang*, or foreign flower, seen in more realistic forms on Kerman and Bidjar rugs made for the European market. The floral and geometric fillers that crowd the field are vividly colored, as is the red primary border's palmette, rosette, and vine repeat. The ivory guards have a flower-and-vine meander; the ends are finished with three decorative checkerboard borders and a band of striped plain weave. Good condition. ....
.... Est. $5,000/7,000; sold for $3,850

Qashqai Rug (c. 1885, 4′8″×2′10″). This version of a classic format has a pendanted ivory medallion within which is a distinctive palmette variation often seen on rugs of this group. The midnight blue field displays the bird motif known as *morgh* and numerous polychrome flowering plants, as do the connected gold spandrels whose most prominent decoration is a flower-filled palmette-like shape in medium blue. The ivory primary border, which is enclosed by a pair of red flower-meander guards, has a simplified rosette-and-vine repeat. The ends have a narrow geometric-figured stripe. Shows small stains. ....
.... Est. $7,000/9,000; sold for $6,600

Qashqai Rug (c. 1880, 6′1″×3′8″). A finely knotted (169 per sq. in.) variation of the above pattern with three poled medallions—two ivory, one red—on an abrashed, brighter blue ground. In this example, the main border is mahogany with a flower, vine and *boteh* meander; the floral meander guards have a vivid gold ground. .... Est. $15,000/20,000; sold for $13,200

Qashqai Rug (c. 1875, 6′9″×4′3″). A column of two ivory and one dark blue diamond-shaped medallions with palmette-like figures is displayed on a brick red field containing numerous boxed cruciform motifs. Flowering plants decorate the dark blue spandrels. The wide ivory border has a bold palmette, rosette, and vine repeat guarded by two dark red floral-meander guards; the ends are finished with three decorative bands. The grayed colors diminish the attractive format's appeal and suggest a date later than cataloged. Shows some wear. ....
.... Est. $4,000/6,000; sold for $3,300

Qashqai Rug (c. 1860, 5'7" ×3'2"). Floral-figured narrow chevron stripes in red, gold, ivory, and dark and light blue fill the field of this finely woven rug with part-silk wefts. The dark blue primary border has a traditional repeat of pole-connected, latch-hooked octagons within narrow floral-meander ivory guards and a variety of narrow borders.

These fine silk-warped or wefted Qashqai rugs could have been woven either on domestic or workshop looms. A *millesfleurs* rug will be found in the commercial listing because of its technical perfection and borrowed design; this rug has been classed as a rustic product on the basis of its poorly resolved corner design. Small repair; end fraying. .... Est. $6,000/8,000; sold for $8,250

Qashqai Rug (c. 1885, 6'10" ×4'9"). On an ivory pendanted medallion a red rosette on a medium blue diamond is ringed by flowering vines in red, cream, light and medium blue, olive, aubergine, and gold, which are repeated in larger scale on the dark blue ground surrounded by connected red spandrels ornamented with cream arabesques. The flower-and-vine-meander red main border is enclosed by two pairs of floral-meander guards; the ends terminate in checkerboard bands. Shows some wear. (See color insert) .... Est. $6,000/8,000; sold for $18,700

Qashqai Rug (c. 1900, 6'10" ×3'5"). A Kerman-influenced floral design having a central ivory column of stylized leafy sprays of florettes flanked by two dark blue columns ornamented with realistic blooming plants. Rosettes decorate the primary border enclosed by a pair of rust geometric guards. The ends terminate in figured checkerboard bands. Shows repairs; breaks to ends. ....
.... Est. $1,500/2,000; sold for $1,870

Qashqai Rug (c. 1885, 6'9" ×4'1"). A ground composed of narrow vertical ivory, red, and dark blue stripes ornamented with refined floral meanders within medium blue stepped spandrels whose gold lattices enclose stylized floral motifs. The primary dark blue floral border has a pair of geometric guards; the ends terminate in figured checkerboard guards. Shows some wear; slight loss to one end border; reselvaged. .... Est. $1,500/2,000; sold for $4,400

Qashqai Rug (c. 1885, 7'6" ×4'8"). A commonly seen design displaying three latch-hooked medallions—in this example two red, one ivory—on a large abrashed royal blue hexagon. Polychrome Herati motifs ornament both the hexagon and red spandrels, all within an ivory palmette and curved-leaf repeat with floral-meander guards. Good condition. .... Est. $1,000/1,500; sold for $2,090

Shiraz Long Rug (c. 1885, 11' ×4'10"). When the origin of a rug of this group is in doubt, it is often labeled Shiraz, the market city for many weavings of the southwest area. On this rug, three ivory and two red latch-hooked diamonds containing palmette-like figures usually associated with Qashqai rugs are displayed in a column on a flower-covered dark blue field edged with red spandrels, all in soft shades of red, gold, blue, mahogany, and brown. The narrow primary border has a floral meander on ivory, and the four flower-figured guards are alternately red and blue. Corroded browns; some repiling. ....
.... Est. 7,000/9,000; sold for $9,900

Southwest Persian Corridor Rug (c. 1885, 12'11" ×7'4"). The lustrous ivory ground has an endless repeat of offset rows of blue, raspberry red, gold, and ivory shrub-filled cartouches within a dark blue sawtooth border on red, a primary raspberry red border with stylized floral motifs, and a pair of gold guards with floral meanders. Shows wear; loss to plain weave at both ends. ....
.... Est. $2,500/3,500; sold for $6,325

Left: *Qashqai rug, Southwest Persia, c. 1860, 5'7" × 3'2"*, $8,250.
Right: *Beshir Turkoman long rug, c. 1875, Central Turkestan, 10'6"
× 5'6"*, $16,500. PHOTOS COURTESY OF CHRISTIE'S EAST.

TURKESTAN

Most of the Turkoman rugs will be found in the tribal weavings listing;
however, noted rug scholar Jon Thompson has made a good case for
classifying the Ersari rugs known as Beshir, which were ''woven within
the . . . cultural sphere of Bukhara,'' as a commercial village product.
He cites their typically large sizes and use of nontribal motifs in formats
that have more in common with classical Turkish weaving than tribal
traditions.

Beshir Long Rug (c. 1875, 10'6"×5'6"). The abrashed blue ground has the
classical Turkish two-one-two arrangement of medallions, in this case octagons
of a type associated with Ersari Beshir weaving, together with rows of red serpent-
like cloud bands. The primary and secondary borders have compartmented floral
and palmette figures, respectively, in red on an abrashed blue ground separated
by narrow gold guards with geometric repeats. Slight wear, reweaves. ....
.... Est. $10,000/15,000; sold for $16,500

EAST TURKESTAN

The oasis-woven rugs of East Turkestan, which sprawls across the trade corridor linking China with western Asia and India, draw from both Far Eastern and Western design pools. The most commonly seen formats include symmetrically placed roundish medallions containing cloud-band floral figures, repeats of stylized floral and pomegranate figures, and tilelike repeats of latch-hooked gul-like figures. Favored border motifs were fret repeats, cloud-band stylizations, rosettes, reciprocal trefoils— often on a gigantic scale—and stylized flower-and-vine meanders with a distinctly Persian look. The vegetable-dyed colors are intense and tend to be warmly toned; rugs with synthetic dyes often have fields faded almost to gray from the original mauve-magenta, an early and notorious fugitive dye.

Although sumptuous silk carpets were made, the examples of interest to most collectors have cotton warps, and the wefts may be cotton or wool, sometimes both in the same rug. The edges were rather insecurely finished with a single cord bundle overcasting, which may be why so few old rugs retain their original edges. The ends may have a plain-weave band.

Khotan Corridor Carpet (c. 1850, 12′7″×6′2″). An ovoid blue medallion with rosette and six geometric figures is centered on a red ground between two stalks of stylized flowers ascending from blue vases flanked by dark blue quarter-oval spandrels. The field ornamentation also includes stylized flower and leaf forms in gold, dark and medium blue, apricot, and brown, all contained within a gold flower-and-leaf-meander main border, narrow borders with fret and chevron repeats, and an outer red band. Slight wear. ....
.... Est. $25,000/35,000; sold for $25,300

Khotan Long Rug (c. 1860, 8′2″×4′3″). Four blue medallions each with four boxed star figures on a rust red ground ornamented with boxed stars enclosed by an apricot diamond repeat on blue within a primary red border with well-spaced rosettes, all in copper, apricot, cream, salmon, white, tan, and brown. An apricot fret outer border is enclosed by a plain red band. Shows wear; restorations. .... Est. $5,000/7,000; sold for $7,150

Yarkand Long Rug (c. 1850, 10′10″×4′9″). Four medium blue ovoid medallions filled with graceful vinery and rosettes upon a brick red ground ornamented with blue pomegranates and well-spaced flowerheads in apricot, gold, blue, and rose, all within a blue fret repeat on a red primary border, a secondary curling-vine meander in gold and an outer blue-striped plain red band. Shows some wear. .... Est. $20,000/30,000; sold for $55,000

Yarkand Corridor Carpet (c. 1850, 13′8″×6′8″). Three large ovoid blue medallions filled with blossomheads and vinery are set upon a plain red ground with dark blue key-fret spandrels outlined in light blue. The two inner borders with simple geometric repeats are surrounded by a traditional *Yun Tsai T'ou* repeat in brown, two blues, gold, and apricot, all within a wide bold reciprocal trefoil repeat in bright blue, gold, and red on brown with an outer red band. Shows wear and old repair. .... Est. $40,000/60,000; sold for $27,500

Yarkand long rug, East Turkestan, c. 1850, 10′10″ × 4′9″, $55,000.
PHOTO COURTESY OF CHRISTIE'S EAST.

TIBETAN RUGS

Until about ten years ago most collectors were both uninterested in and unknowing about the plushy, lustrous, gaily colored small rugs and saddle blankets woven by Tibetan weavers. The designs are for the most part quite similar to those seen on Chinese rugs but are more exuberantly expressed in a looser, larger scale with brighter colors. One indigenous design seen in many variations incorporates a flayed tiger skin symbolizing Buddhist efforts to control man's ego-centered mind, but to Western eyes the expression knotted on the tiger's face is usually more smile-provoking than sobering.

Weaving is a craft of comparatively recent vintage in Tibet, probably done on a primitive level in scattered locations before 1800 but not on a scale large enough to be documented before that time. The oldest rugs have all-wool foundations; cotton began to be used for warps around 1900, often in combination with wool wefts. Although synthetic dyes became available in the 1870s, vegetable dyes continued to be used as well.

Old Tibetan rugs were coarsely knotted, with a distinctive looping technique, and when finished, supplied with a border of stout red cloth on all four sides. The weaver, knowing the rug would be bound in this manner, left the edges and ends rather insecurely finished.

Rug (c. 1860, 5'6" ×4'). This very old example has a rosette and circlet of blossoms at the center of a gold field ornamented with floral sprays. Flowering vines form the spandrels within a blue and cream checkerboard minor border enclosed by a gold-grounded main border with flower-filled cartouches and a variety of fret, diamond, and floral repeats in dark, medium, and light blue, cream, coral, and lavender. Shows some wear; repairs, missing selvages. ....
.... Est. $1,000/1,500; sold for $2,420

Tibetan saddle cover, c. 1920, 3' 10" × 2' 1", $550. PHOTO COURTESY OF CHRISTIE'S EAST.

Saddle Cover (c. 1920, 3′10″×2′1″). A rectangular indented-corner cover with a dark blue ground, each half showing an ivory Fo-dog, light blue cloud motif, and salmon, gold, and ivory floral sprays within a fret border and a salmon primary border with dragon and phoenix repeats in green, gold, red, ivory, and light blue. An outer dark blue border is finished with a faded red cloth binding. ....Est. $300/500; sold for $550

Saddle Cover (c. 1920, 3′10″×2′2″). Each half of the dark blue ground has a large cream, apricot, and red rosette surrounded by stylized cream florettes and floral spandrels within a copper fret border ornamented with red, cream, and green flowerheads. An outer dark blue border is finished with a red cloth binding. Good condition. ....Est. $500/700; sold for $550

Saddle Cover (c. 1920, 4′×2′). Each half of the red ground displays a crane with wings spread within a flower-ornamented stylized landscape edged in cream and blue. The rust primary border has a flowering-vine meander with cloud-form spandrels, all in shades of blue, cream, plum, black, orange, tan, gold, ivory, and jade green. The outer midnight blue border is finished with a red cloth binding. Good condition. ....Est. $500/600; sold for $1,210

CHINESE RUGS

Weaving in China is an ancient, well-documented craft. Old Chinese rugs are asymmetrically knotted, averaging 50 knots per square inch, and their warps lie in a single plane, which results in a rather loose-textured, flat-backed rug. The lanolin-rich pile of the best of the early examples has an incomparably lush handle.

Unlike most other rustic rugs, those made in China have cotton foundations: hand-spun in early examples, machine-spun after about 1850. The edges and ends, which were not as a rule very securely finished, were easily damaged, resulting in the frequent loss of adjacent pile knots. The palette of vegetable dyes was limited: indigo blues, yellow, ivory, blacks, and browns; although madder red was used, it was never to the degree seen elsewhere. Village rug designs tend to be simple blends of floral and symbolic motifs used together with medallions and tile-pattern repeats. Both floral and fret motifs are seen in borders.

Twenty years ago superb antique Chinese rugs could be bought here for comparatively little because they were little known and unappreciated, even by the trade. Today, except for the occasional unrecognized treasure spotted at a country auction or antique shop, this is no longer the case.

Rug (c. 1860, 8′3″×5′3″). Six appealing Fo-dogs in blues and tans gambol with pearls on the soft coral ground in the center of which is a sterner Fo-dog with paws atop a larger pearl. Widely spaced fish, birds, cloud bands, and assorted traditional symbols complete the ornamentation, all contained within a dark blue, cream-dotted inner border with a coral fret guard and a wide beige outer band finished in dark blue. Shows some wear. ....
....Est. $7,000/9,000; sold for $6,600

Chinese rug, c. 1860,
8'3" × 5'3", $6,600.
PHOTO COURTESY OF
CHRISTIE'S EAST.

Pillar Rug (c. 1870, 12'5"×6'4"). Designed to clothe the columns in Buddhist temples, the ornamentation of most pillar rugs includes, as this example does, a pair of large scaled dragons, monks blowing conch shells, a vase of flaming pearls, masks, hanging lamps, a variety of Buddhist motifs, and stylized wave, mountain, and cloud borders. The colors include navy and light blue, pale rose, tan, and light jade on a deep gold field. Stain; slight moth damage. ....
.... Est. $3,000/5,000; sold for $10,450

Rug (c. 1830, 6'6"×3'5"). The abrashed medium to light blue field has a central geometric figure with floral circlets accompanied by well-spaced floral sprays and large butterflies, which also serve as decorative spandrels, in shades of blue, ivory, rust, and apricot, all within a navy fretwork border on paler blue. Shows wear; fraying at ends. .... Est. $1,500/2,000; sold for $8,250

Carpet (c. 1830, 12'×11'6"). The square tan field has a central medallion with a stylized landscape encircled by cloud forms and accompanied by lotus and vine motifs and paired lotus spandrels, all in cream, gold, dark and light blue, and brown within a flower-and-vine meander on gold, a primary border with lotus and cloud-band repeat on dark blue, several narrow guards in cream, blue, and dark gold, and an outer dark blue border. Some restoration; cloth-bound sides.
.... Est. $5,000/7,000; sold for $14,850

Mat (c. 1860, 3'×3'). The taupe field displays a crane with outspread wings at the center surrounded by cloud bands, bat motifs, and flying cranes, all in shades of brown, gold, and blue within stripes of blue and cream and a royal blue outer border. Spots of wear; reweaves. .... Est. $2,000/3,000; sold for $2,640

Two Mats (c. 1860, each 1′1″ × 1′1″). Both with dark blue grounds, one displaying a stylized cream and gold crane holding a flower in its beak and with wings outspread in a circular pattern within gold spandrels and a narrow gold border. The other has a symbolic central figure encircled by flowers within butterfly spandrels, all in shades of gold, tan, cream, and light green and enclosed by a narrow gold border. Reweaves. .... Est. $250/350; sold for $1,540

Corridor Carpet (c. 1875, 17′2″ × 5′). The lustrous blue ground with three large circular floral medallions and a smaller trio of similar medallions at each end along with floral sprays and symbolic figures in cream, pale green, and light blue within a wide honey border with dark blue frets and bat motifs and pale rose and green floral traceries, all enclosed by an outer plain blue band. Shows slight wear. ....Est. 7,000/9,000; sold for $7,150

Carpet (c. 1900, 9′11″ × 7′8″). The Eight Horses of Mu Wang cavort upon a cream field within a stylized landscape of rocks, trees, and shrubbery enclosed by a fret minor border, lotus-and-vine main border and plain blue outer band. Areas of repiling. .... Est. $3,500/5,000; sold for $5,775

Chinese carpet, c. 1830, 12′ × 11′6″, $14,850. PHOTO © 1991 SOTHEBY'S, INC.

FLAT WEAVES, 1800–1900

Rug collectors attuned to the resonance of tradition are apt to be particularly attracted to flat weaves. In fact, a mystique—and ongoing controversy—has developed concerning the claimed neolithic origins of motifs seen on some very old Anatolian kilims. Neolithic or not, their slow evolution over the centuries provides the collector of these beautiful weavings a satisfying source of never-ending speculation.

Bales of rugs used to be shipped from the east wrapped in old kilims, which until recently were considered too humble to be collectible—assuming they were considered at all. Today those sadly undervalued wrappings would be reverentially hung where their exquisite colors and bold patterning could be seen to the best advantage.

Soumak rugs, whose structure is more technically demanding than that of kilims, were made in workshops in the Caucasus early on and produced there in quantity for commercial sale during the revival period. Although they lack the mythic quality of very old rustic kilims, they too are sought by collectors, who find their textured counterweave more appealing than what one aficionado, writing in *Oriental Rug Review*, referred to as "the harder, flatter kilim weaves or burr-cut stumps of yarn that constitute pile weaving." Tribal-woven soumak-faced bags—in fact,

West Anatolian kilim, c. 1875, 9'2" × 5'3", $1,980. PHOTO
COURTESY OF SKINNER, INC.

flat-woven bags of all types—remain a stunning and affordable alternative to abstract paintings despite their recent run-up in price.

Because flat weaves are not in the mainstream of oriental rug collecting, a representative selection of fine examples is usually lacking among auction offerings. In the two years examined here, there was an interesting and collection-worthy variety, but there were no noteworthy Turkoman examples and only a limited sampling of Turkish flat weaves aside from kilims. Specialty dealers (see the Resource Guide) are still the best source.

KILIMS

TURKISH

West Anatolian (c. 1875, 9′2″×5′3″). Dark blue field with column of five ivory-bordered, latch-hooked medallions with projecting arms, in red, light brown, and green-blue. Embroidered S-figures ornament the field; rows of polychrome hourglass figures march across the wide ivory end borders. Patches and small repairs. .... Est. $1,200/1,500; sold for $1,980

Central Anatolian, Konya Area (c. 1850, 6′4″×4′). Good example of the archaic *elibelinde* motif employed as an allover pattern on an ivory ground within side borders with boxed torso-like figures and end borders with stylized floral motifs, all in soft shades of red, rust, pale green, gold, purple, and two shades of blue. Restorations; very good condition. .... Dealer's rug, $5,200

Konya area kilim, Central Anatolia, c. 1850, 6′4″ × 4′, $5,200. PHOTO COURTESY OF MARIAN MILLER RUGS.

Prayer kilim, Central Anatolia, c. 1885, 5'6" × 3'7", $3,080.
PHOTO COURTESY OF CHRISTIE'S EAST.

Central Anatolian Prayer Kilim (c. 1885, 5'6"×3'7"). On a gray-green field topped with red and ivory stylized trees-of-life, a triangular rust red *mihrab* with blue and ivory tree-of-life ascends within a wide ivory border bearing stylized polychrome floral bouquets and enclosed by geometricized flower-and-vine meanders on black guards. Slight staining; some repairs. ....
.... Est. $2,500/3,500; sold for $3,080

Yüncü, West Anatolian (c. 1850, 8'4"×5'2"). Good example of distinctive type with madder red field bearing cream and midblue joined vertical bands with latched offshoots within a wavy banded border. Stains. ....
.... Est. $2,500/3,500; sold for $4,125

CAUCASIAN

Avar Runner, East Caucasus (c. 1900, 13'2"×4'6"). Dark blue ground with three characteristically elongated red Avar medallions with long, hooklike pendant projections. Two borders with attenuated, linked red S-figures enclose a wide red main border bearing crisp, widely spaced geometric figures in black, green-gold, and ivory. Mint condition. ..... Est. $2,500/2,500; sold for $2,860

Left: *Avar kilim runner, East Caucasus, c. 1900, 13'2" × 4'6", $2,860.* PHOTO COURTESY OF CHRISTIE'S EAST. Right: *Kuba kilim, Northeast Caucasus, c. 1885, 10'7" × 5'2", $1,540.* PHOTO COURTESY OF SKINNER, INC.

Kuba, Northeast Caucasus (c. 1885, 10'7"×5'2"). Six rows of large ivory and red shield medallions with projecting arms on a dark blue field with a highly stylized zigzag flower-and-vine meander in the side borders; red, gold, and green geometric figures on the ends. Worn areas, small repairs, hole. ....
.... Est. $1,500/2,500; sold for $1,540

Shirvan, East Caucasus (c. 1885, 9'4"×5'). Dark blue field densely covered with hooked diamond-shaped figures in yellow, ivory, green, brick and cherry red, and light and medium blue within a narrow ivory border with polychrome diamond repeats. Good condition, except minor end and edge wear. ....
.... Est. $1,000/2,000; sold for $1,320

Shirvan, East Caucasus (c. 1885, 9'8"×6'). Seven wide bands, alternating red and blue, three with four large, stepped hexagons, four with hooked diamonds, all figures in light blues, gold, ivory, and black. Each band bordered by a wave meander on ivory; no edge border. Two small patches; otherwise good condition. .... Est. $2,000/3,000; sold for $1,870

Left: *Shirvan kilim, East Caucasus, c. 1885, 9'8" × 6", $1,870.*
Right: *Qashqai kilim, Southwest Persia, c. 1900, 8'9" × 4'9",*
$3,575. PHOTOS COURTESY OF SKINNER, INC.

Qashqai kilim cradle, Southwest Persia, c. 1885, 4' × 3'5", $3,850.
PHOTO © 1991 SOTHEBY'S, INC.

PERSIAN—SOUTHWEST

Qashqai (c. 1900, 8'9"×4'9"). Three rows each of seven squares centered with stepped diamond figures on an abrashed ground in shades of yellow, brick red, dark blue, ivory, and gray-green all within a wide blue and brown border zigzagged with white, and outer reciprocal trefoil border. Striped kilim skirts. Good condition. .... Est. $3,000/3,500; sold for $3,575

Qashqai Cradle (c. 1885, 4'×3'3"). Polychrome-banded, stepped diamond medallion flanked by white and dark blue *aina-kochak* figures on a red ground with polychrome-banded spandrels within a gold, medallion-toothed border, and reciprocal trefoil guards. Brocaded ends finished in tassels. Very good condition. .... Est. $2,000/3,000; sold for $3,850

PERSIAN—NORTHWEST

Bidjar (dated 1863, 5'4"×3'). Two palmette-shaped midnight-blue-fielded medallions with polychrome floral motifs on a red ground with gold-edged ivory spandrels ornamented with stylized flowering vines. The polychrome diagonally barred main border has two flower-and-vine meanders. Brilliant vegetable dyes. Some wear and repair. (See color insert) .. Est. $2,500/3,500; sold for $15,950

Senneh (c. 1900, 6'3"×4'3"). Silk-warped, finely woven piece with a central lobed square medallion ornamented with flower and leaf figures, which are repeated in a pair of bouquets at either end of the midnight blue field and in the wide border. Unusual palette of red, gold, pale blue, spring green, gray-green, and beige. Very good condition. .... Est. $10,000/12,000; sold for $11,000

Senneh kilim, Northwest Persia, c. 1900, 6'3" × 4'3", $11,000. PHOTO COURTESY OF CHRISTIE'S EAST.

Senneh Prayer Kilim (c. 1880, 6'2" ×4'7"). Very fine example of floral flat weave: vertical rows of flowering meandering vines lead to midnight blue niche sprinkled with flowers. A main border of delicately rendered ivory and red diagonals is enclosed by a pair of floral guards. Gold, green, pink, red, three blues. Good condition. (See color insert) .... Est. $20,000/25,000; sold for $28,600

Senneh Prayer Kilim (c. 1900, 5'8" ×4'5"). Uncharacteristically bright and bold pattern of white and red stylized flowers in color-determined horizontal rows separated by red, green, and dark blue zigzags leading to a niche filled with polychrome diamonds on ivory, within a border of linked, gul-like hexagons. Very good condition. ....Est. $12,000/15,000; sold for $24,200

Senneh Horse Cover (c. 1900, 6'5" ×5'). Two concentric pendanted medallions—one ivory, the other red; both ornamented with stylized floral motifs—on a dark blue field densely patterned with floral and Herati motifs within a yellow floral primary border enclosed by two geometric guards. Shows slight wear. ... .Est. $2,000/3,000; sold for $4,400

Shahsavan (c. 1885, 10'3" ×5'). Three polychrome palmette medallions within dark blue diamond reserves on a cream stepped diamond field. Saturated vegetable-dye colors. Nicks on edges, holes. ....Est. $5,000/7,000; sold for $10,450

BAGS AND BAG FACES

CAUCASIAN

East Caucasian Bags (c. 1900, 3'9" ×1'8"). Pair of complete bags with narrow rust, ivory, dark and medium blue, yellow, and gray-green diagonal stripes with closely spaced hooked rectangles within a dark blue–grounded border of starred hexagons. Some stains; otherwise good condition. ....Est. $1,000/1,500; sold for $935

Shahsavan soumak bag face, Northwest Persia, c. 1850, 2' × 1'8", $9,570. PHOTO COURTESY OF SKINNER, INC.

PERSIAN

Shahsavan Soumak Bags (c. 1900, 4′4″×1′11″). Each face with a dark blue ground and red-centered, ivory-poled, turtle-shaped medallion with red, blue-figured hexagons in each corner and stylized animals and geometric motifs used as fillers. The dark blue border has a nicely spaced polychrome repeat of stars alternating with *yün-chien* motifs; red stripes zigzagged with ivory serve as guards. Vivid shades of crimson, jade, three blues, mauve, tan, coral, and brown. Silk highlights; backs have alternating stripes of brown and cornflower blue. Mint condition. (See color insert) .... Est. $7,000/10,000; sold for $23,100

Shahsavan Soumak Bag Face (c. 1850, 2′×1′8″). Classic design of red, dark blue, and ivory diagonal bands with unusually generously spaced small latch-hooked rectangles in red, gray-green, gold, blue, and ivory. Bordered by stepped diamonds within quartered rectangles, guarded in turn by a stylized wave motif in red on green. Good condition. .... Est. $1,500/2,500; sold for $9,570

Shahsavan Soumak Bag Face (c. 1875, 2′×1′8″). *Yün-chien* motif in dark blue and jade on three rows of four alternately red and ivory compartments within a gold border bearing simple star and octagon motifs. Polychrome kilim tabs along top edge. Slight reduction to one side. ....
....Est. $800/1,200; sold for $2,750

Shahsavan soumak salt bag, Northwest Persia, c. 1885, 2′1″ × 1′7″, $3,080. PHOTO © 1991 SOTHEBY'S, INC.

Shahsavan Soumak Bag Face (c. 1850, 1′9″×1′5″). Very finely woven with *yün-chien* motif in light blue and yellow on bold red medallion with four ram's-horn projections in red on ivory ground with red corner spandrels. Stars and ram's-horn hexagons alternate on dark blue border edged with geometric motifs. Slits, repairs, selvage wear. .... Est. $1,800/2,200; sold for $2,640

Shahsavan Soumak Salt Bag (c. 1885, 2′1″×1′7″). A variety of well-spaced dotted S-shaped geometric figures on broad green and red diagonal bands separated by narrower bands with simple S-repeats in black and red on ivory, mahogany on gold. Brocaded strap, cotton whites, kilim back. Very good condition. .... Est. $2,500/3,500; sold for $3,080

West Persian Kilim Salt Bag (c. 1900, 1′5″×1′). Simple chevron-striped horizontal bands edged with checkerboard stripes, all in mustard, jade, rust, red, ivory and blue. Good condition. ....Est. $200/400; sold for $495

OTHER PERSIAN EXAMPLES

Soumak Cargo Bag Side (c. 1880, 3′4″×2′3″). A wide horizontal ivory band with geometric figures ornamenting and flanking three large hexagons, flanked in turn by poled "pinwheel" motifs on ivory. Border bears simple version of curled-leaf motif. Gold, ivory, brick red, green, and blue with chocolate and red chevron-striped kilim skirt. Small repairs. .... Est. $250/350; sold for $550

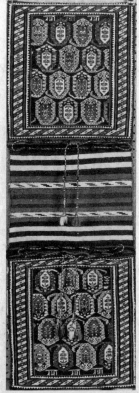

Soumak bags, Persia, dated 1885, 4′ × 1′5″, $2,090.
PHOTO COURTESY OF CHRISTIE'S EAST.

Soumak Bag (dated 1885, 4′ ×1′5″). Complete bag with four horizontal rows of polychrome floral *botehs* on midnight blue ground within ivory and white diagonally striped border with narrow ivory sawtooth guards. Blue red and ivory striped kilims; original tassels. Mint condition. ....
.... Est. $1,000/1,500; sold for $2,090

Soumak Bag Face (c. 1875, 2′ ×1′11″). On a soft red ground, a central ivory reserve with Memling gul in soft red, green, ivory, and aubergine edged with dark blue and chocolate brown. Primary ivory border with polychrome ''pin-wheel'' repeat is enclosed by a green and a dark blue guard ornamented with ivory rosettes. Green and red kilim tabs at top edge. Slight wear; kilim has repairs. .... Est. $1,500/2,000; sold for $2,420

SOUMAK RUGS—CAUCASIAN

East Caucasus (c. 1860, 5′5″ ×4′6″). Light coral field with centered gul-like medallions in a variety of sizes, together with numerous small geometric rosette, star, and other motifs in shades of yellow, jade, ivory, and dark and light blue. The wide ivory border with polychrome, closely spaced octagons is flanked with ivory double-eight figured guards, all enclosed by a running-dog outer border. Corroded browns, hole. .... Est. $1,500/2,500; sold for $8,250

Soumak rug, East Caucasus, c. 1860, 5′5″ × 4′6″, $8,250. PHOTO
COURTESY OF SKINNER, INC.

Soumak rug, East Caucasus, c. 1875, 10'4" × 7'8", $13,200. PHOTO
COURTESY OF CHRISTIE'S EAST.

East Caucasus (c. 1875, 10'4"×7'8"). On a pale ruby ground covered with
small geometric fillers is a connected row of three bold dark blue medallions,
each enclosing a cross-centered, rosette-filled octagon. The medium blue main
border has a repeat of diamonds and rectilinear flower-and-leaf meander, all
within narrow guards and running-dog outer border. Signed and dated. Near
mint. .... Est. $8,000/12,000; sold for $13,200

East Caucasus (c. 1860, 8'1"×3'4"). Unusual soumak version of a striking
pile design known as Bidjov: on a dark blue ground, a central column of bold
palmettes and stylized blossoms is flanked on each side by shield-derived figures,
all in blues, red, pink, green, gold, and ivory. Three narrow borders—two red,
one ivory—with delicately rendered flower, leaf, and vine meanders. Some restoration; corroded browns. .... Est. $6,500/8,000; sold for $10,450

Dragon Soumak, East Caucasus (early 19th century, 10'6"×6'8"). Highly
stylized dragons in ivory, dark blue, and green on a tomato red ground with
numerous other stylized figures in red, green, gold, ivory, and shades of blue.
The wide primary brown border of stepped and figured polychrome hexagons is
enclosed by rosette-starred gold guards, all within a red outer border with blue
running-dog motif. Shows wear and repairs. ....
.... Est. $12,000/15,000; sold for $13,200

Northeast Caucasus (c. 1885, 6'5" ×5'). Two indigo and one jade gul-like medallions on a warm madder red ground accompanied by geometricized floral motifs within a border of boxed stars. Good condition. ....
.... Est. $3,000/4,000; sold for $8,525

East Caucasian Long Rug (c. 1875, 8'10" ×3'8"). Ivory ground with eight star medallions within latch-hooked hexagons in dark and medium blue, red, yellow, light green, and ivory. The primary main border of a stylized flower and leaf "crab" repeat on ivory is flanked by a narrower border of rosettes on red and an outer polychrome S-border. Slight wear, some repiling. ....
.... Est. $3,000/4,000; sold for $6,500

OTHER FLAT WEAVES

Caucasian Sileh (c. 1880). These so-called dragon sileh, a soumak variant woven in two panels and sewn together after removal from the loom, are considered to have originated in the Caucasus. Two examples of similar size—8'8" ×6'1" and 9'5" ×7'—sold within five months of each other at Christie's: on a madder red ground, four rows of four large rectilinear S-figures in dark blue alternating with ivory and filled with small polychrome S-motifs. In both cases the bends of the large S are filled with hourglass-like figures, and the single narrow borders have a reciprocal trefoil repeat. The second had slight wear and repair but better color. (See color insert) ....
(1) Est. $9,000/12,000; sold for $12,100 (2) Est. $6,000/9,000; sold for $15,400.

Caucasian Brocaded Rug (c. 1885, 8'11" ×5'6"). Four rows of seven polychrome bordered and diamond-figured squares upon a red ground with an allover diamond pattern, all in shades of dark and rose red, white, green, tan, rust, brown, and light and royal blue. Good condition. ....
.... Est. $4,000/6,000; sold for $4,125

Caucasian Horse Cover (c. 1875, 8'8" ×4'9"). Brocaded figural flat weaves with soumak details are known in the trade as *vernehs*. This outstanding example has horizontal rows of polychrome horses and riders alternating with processions of caparisoned camels on a dark brown ground sprinkled with small animals and geometric figures, all within a narrow, dark brown border ornamented with connected figure-eight motifs. Vivid shades of red, ivory, dark and medium blue, jade, and camel. Woven in two panels joined horizontally, fringed at one end. Good condition. (See color insert) .... Est. $8,000/10,000; sold for $27,500

Caucasian Brocade and Soumak Rug (c. 1875, 6'1" ×4'4"). This one-piece *verneh* has a central vertical row of stylized birds and double-headed animals on red within a dark blue border and an outer red border displaying the same figures with the addition of fantailed birds, all enclosed by narrow ivory guards with simple flower and vine repeats. Added fringe; good condition. ....
.... Est. $5,000/7,000; sold for $4,400

SW Persia, Quashqai, Flat-Woven Horse Cover (c. 1885, 5'8" ×5'4"). Woven in two pieces, the top half is densely covered with polychrome quadrupeds and fantailed birds within numerous narrow borders, below which are three rows of small horned animals. The remaining third of the cover is unornamented save for three horned animals marching in lockstep. A gold border with a pretty geometric repeat encloses the entire piece. Vivid shades of red, rose-pink, light and medium blue, jade, gold, and ivory. Original tassels in red, dark blue, gold, green, and ivory. Very good condition. ...Est. $8,000/10,000; sold for $9,350

SW Persia, Luri Mixed Technique Rug (c. 1900, 3′9″×3′9″). The dark blue flat-woven ground is divided into symmetrical ivory-bordered compartments centered with polychrome rosettes in pile, all enclosed within a reciprocal trefoil border and barber-pole guards. Polychrome tasseled ends. Very good condition. .... Est. $600/900; sold for $1,980

West Turkestan, Uzbek Main Carpet (c. 1910, 10′×6′4″). Three rows of Memling guls separated by stars, cross-centered diamonds, and a variety of other geometric repeats set in banded rows on an abrashed red ground within a narrow star border along the sides; boxed stars along the top and bottom fringed ends. Colors include dark blue, red, ivory, and gold. Good condition. .... Est. $1,500/2,000; sold for $3,025

COMMERCIAL CARPETS,
1875–1930

Upon hearing the phrase "oriental carpet," the average person pictures a room-size rug made in Persia and richly ornamented with swirling floral patterns. The rug that fits this mental image has a balanced design developed by an artist and woven with dyed-to-order wool supplied to skilled weavers working in an urban workshop under contract. Even the finishing stages of clipping and washing are carried out by specialists. The fact of its being a commercial product reproduced in quantity, perhaps in a variety of popular sizes, matters little to someone wishing a handsome floor covering, and indeed, why should it?

The court carpets of the 15th–17th centuries were workshop extravaganzas made for a wealthy and aristocratic clientele; today rug workshops thrive in a dozen or more countries, producing rugs to suit every taste and pocketbook. Here we will be looking at rugs made between roughly 1875—when, if you will remember, entrepreneurs began organizing weavers to supply the needs of a growing and prosperous market in the West—and 1930, when Eastern traditions began being supplanted by transient Western color and design fashions. (An extreme example are the Chinese Art Deco rugs, long consigned to attics, which are now making a comeback.)

Most of the rugs categorized as commercial *were* in fact made in Persia—known as Iran only since 1935—but workshops in Turkey and India and later in China were also active during this period. Many of these rugs, distinguished by the attention given to design details and the technical skill of their weaving, are justly highly valued. The majority were intended as floor coverings; the much smaller production of modestly sized, extremely finely knotted silks are best reserved for display as wall hangings or table covers.

As you read through the list of carpets below, bear in mind that, according to the trade magazine *Decorative Rug*, "the word quality is used in the oriental rug industry to grade a rug's weave as to degrees of fineness. It is a descriptive rather than a judgmental term." In other words, given a selection of rugs all made with equally good materials, the more coarsely woven examples, no matter how attractive or serviceable they may be, are automatically considered of lower quality than more finely knotted pieces which may, in fact, not wear as well.

Note: Decorative commercial carpets offered at auction are more likely to have been "fiddled" than smaller collectible rustic and tribal rugs. Consult the auction house experts concerning any tinting, painting, or reduction in size that may have been done to carpets that interest you. Obviously, you shouldn't pay as much for an altered or painted carpet as you would for a similar unaltered example, but temper your decision with common sense: a rug destined for placement under a dining room table can afford to have areas of central wear, as these will hardly be seen; missing borders, which would be obvious in a dining room, might be unnoticeable in a living room in which edges are largely hidden by couches, chairs, and side tables.

TURKISH CARPETS

Throughout the 19th century, a cottage industry producing great numbers of traditionally patterned rugs prevailed in Turkey and, for the most part, still does. Finely knotted commercial carpets, woven in response to the revival of interest in oriental rugs, were made in only a few urban workshops, the output both in design and palette bearing little resemblance to the colorful, sturdy rustic rugs now commanding very respectable prices from collectors.

GHIORDES

A weaving center for centuries, its early reputation for elegantly designed prayer rugs was so respected that copies were made in many other Turkish weaving areas, considerably hampering contemporary attempts at attribution. Toward the end of the 19th century and into the early 20th, the weaving had become commercial, with room-size rugs being made, along with coarse-textured, synthetically dyed prayer rugs in familiar patterns, which, when artificially aged, were often passed off as antiques. Now out of fashion, a good, if worn, old example can be had for surprisingly little.

Ghiordes Prayer Rug (early 19th century, 6′×4′4″). Dark blue blossom-filled *mihrab* beneath a pale blue-green floral arch, the whole banded top and bottom with carnations. Secondary floral borders on ivory flank the wide ivory border patterned with stylized tulip clusters. Oxidized browns; damage to selvage; end guards missing. .... Est. $4,000/6,000; sold for $5,225

HEREKE

The workshop rugs made in Hereke, 40 miles from Istanbul, were originally produced in a court manufactory established there in the mid-19th century. Designs borrowed from Ottoman and Persian Sefavid court rugs have been woven as finely as 800 knots per square inch. Ghiordes prayer rug designs have also been copied. Unlike other Turkish rugs, the knots are often asymmetrical; the materials range from all wool to all silk; the dyes and workmanship are impeccable. The best Herekes are very expensive, but the examples sold at auction during the past two years were not of this quality.

Hereke Carpet (c. 1930, 9′4″×6′9″). A Mughal-inspired design of a flower-centered acanthus-leaf lattice on a rose-red field with a well-resolved, floral, rose red primary border within floral guards. Signed. Good condition. ....
....Est. $4,000/5,000; sold for $4,400

Silk Hereke Rug (c. 1900, 7′9″×6′6″). Scalloped medallion with delicate tracery of green, red, rose, and blue flowering vines on a peach ground within scalloped, green-edged spandrels. Cypress trees and vines on a peach primary border enclosed by meandering vine-and-rosette jade green secondary borders. Red, peach, and green silk warps. ......Est. $15,000/20,000; sold for $26,400

KONYA

The 13th-century Seljuk carpets—the oldest known Turkish rugs—were made in Konya. A cottage industry continues to thrive in the area, and the name has been attached to some attractive commercial carpets produced during the rug revival period.

Carpet (c. 1875, 12′4″×8′6″). On a lustrous, madder red ground, a gul-like green pendanted medallion within a delicate barber-pole hexagon from which stylized flower clusters in ivory, gold, and plum are suspended. Stylized leaves and blossoms ornament the sawtoothed light blue spandrels; polychrome cartouches are unevenly spaced along the gold primary border enclosed by meandering vine guards. Symmetrically knotted, 42 per sq. in., on wool foundation; short striped kilims at ends. Good condition. ....
.... Est. $25,000/30,000; sold for $29,700

OUSHAK (USHAK)

The venerable Oushak name is unfortunately also attached to a large output of "rug revival" carpets, typically very coarsely woven in large sizes, originally in harshly bright synthetic colors and later in pastels that paled further in use. The symmetrical knots, ranging from 16 to 40 per sq. in., are tied on a wool foundation. Only occasionally does one recommend itself from an otherwise forgettable crowd and then more for its decorative than collectible potential.

Carpet (c. 1910, 12′×9′). Light blue leaf-ornamented scalloped medallion and spandrels, with palmettes and flowering vines in shades of rose, salmon, celadon, and dark jade symmetrically placed on a tan field. Meandering vine borders guard the warm brown palmette and rosette primary border, all enclosed by a trefoil outer border. Generally good condition. ....
....Est. $4,000/6,000; sold for $3,000

SIVAS

A center of rug weaving in Central Anatolia since the 19th century, the commercial weaving here—done in jails as well as city workshops—had finer knotting and a less exuberant coloration than Turkish village weaving.

Rug (c. 1900, 6'3"×3'7"). A Sivas rug of the refined Zara type with vertical vine-meander stripes of varying widths within a dark brown primary border of stiffly vine-connected rosettes and palmettes. Very finely and symmetrically knotted on a wool foundation in subdued reds, golds, green, blue, brown. Good condition; slight color run. .... Est. $2,500/3,500; sold for $6,600

CAUCASIAN CARPETS—KARABAGH (QARABAGH)

Unlike the traditionally patterned Caucasian rugs village-woven for commercial buyers, the designs of many late-19th-century workshop Karabagh rugs made in the southeastern section of the region were clearly influenced by foreign fashions. Of finer weave than village Karabaghs, the workshop variety can often be identified by their large size and a penchant for the pinky purple shades of red characteristic of cochineal-derived dyes. Old rugs have a wool foundation with each row of symmetrical knots separated from the succeeding row by two shoots of weft.

Karabagh Hunting Carpet (c. 1910, 16'4"×6'10"). On a dark blue ground, a large-scale floral pattern in the French style is arranged in two long, loose rows; between each are leaping stags and figures in European-style hunting costumes. Cabbage roses bloom densely on a dark blue primary border enclosed by two pairs of narrow guards. A characteristic Karabagh shade of bright pink-red predominates, along with golds, tans, light blue, and green. Good condition. .. ..Est. $8,000/10,000; sold for $8,800

Karabagh Runner (c. 1890, 18'5"×3'5"). Elaborate floral garlands in the French style on a blue-black ground along with scattered cabbage roses and a variety of filler motifs. Reds, gold, tan, and sharp yellow. Very good condition. .... Est. $3,500/4,500; sold for $7,150

PERSIAN CARPETS

The carpets included here are considered the most collectible of the commercial class of carpets made, roughly, between 1875 and 1930. Although some of the rugs may have been woven on village rather than workshop looms, their nontraditional designs were obviously either supplied or strongly influenced by commercial contractors.

Carpets were woven in so many locations in Persia that an across-the-board survey is not feasible. The famous finely knotted rugs from Qum and Nain were omitted because weaving did not begin in those cities until the late 1930s, and in any event, their sterile, mechanical look argues against their being considered collectible. Readers wishing a more encyclopedic treatment should consult the annotated book list in the Resource Guide.

BIDJAR (BIJAR)

The sturdy, coarsely woven scatter-size rugs with a salt-and-pepper back seen in millions of Western homes were woven in Hamadan, a well-known weaving area northwest of Kashan. Although often appealing and "affordable," few of these rugs are as collectible as those made in the Kurdish weaving towns to the north and west of Hamadan, one of which is Bidjar.

The classic Bidjar rug has vegetable-dyed wool symmetrically knotted on a wool foundation. The thick warps—cotton in more recent examples—are alternately depressed to the degree that one of each knot's nodes is entirely hidden. Given the springy quality of wool, the high average knot count of these old Bidjars—144 per sq. in.—required the two wefts between each row of knots to be beaten in with unusual force, thus producing a tightly packed structure of unequaled density.

Bidjar triclinium carpet,
Northwest Persia, c. 1875,
19'8" × 11'6", $19,800.
PHOTO © 1991
SOTHEBY'S, INC.

Examples of these very hard-wearing old rugs are also included among the rustic Persian Kurdish weavings listed elsewhere; here we will look only at those Bidjars whose designs were clearly commercially inspired even if woven in a domestic setting.

Triclinium Carpet (c. 1875, 19′8″ × 11′6″). Abrashed madder field in middle panel with polychrome floral sprays and ivory swirls, flanked by two narrower Herati-filled indigo panels, all topped by a wider panel with medallion format on a Herati-patterned indigo ground. Even wear. ....
....Est. $15,000/20,000; sold for $19,800

Medallion Carpet, Persia (c. 1885, 11′×6′7″). Probably made for the St. Petersburg market, French-influenced full-blown roses (*gol-farang*) decorate the blue-ground medallion, the red field, and the blue spandrels and surround. The red main border contains swirling vines; a plain red outer border acts as a frame. Good condition. ....Est. $8,000/10,000; sold for $13,750

Palace-Size Garus-Design Carpet (c. 1885, 25′6″ × 15′). Outstanding example of a design derived from 17th-century Kurdish carpets. On a lustrous, dark blue ground are stylized palmettes within vinelike lattices enlivened by realistic flowering plants in red, gold, green, ivory, camel, and three blues. The ivory main border is swirled with red and blue palmettes and leaf motifs and gold cloud bands; the flower-and-vine meander minor borders have narrow red guards. Good condition. .... Est. $50,000/75,000; sold for $44,000

Bidjar Garus carpet, Northwest Persia, c. 1885, 25′6″ × 15′, $44,000. PHOTO © 1991 SOTHEBY'S, INC.

Garus-Design Carpet (c. 1885, 17′9″ × 11′4″). With similar coloration and design as above but not as grandly spaced. Some floral elements and minor borders in ivory. Uneven wear. ....Est. $6,000/8,000; sold for $17,600

French-Style Long Rug (c. 1875, 12′8″ × 6′9″). Swirling red vinery punctuated with ivory carnations and blue and green birds, interspersed with bouquets and circlets of red roses, the whole framed by narrow guard borders and an ivory main border of connected leaves, gold florets, and full-blown roses. Vegetable dyes. Shows some wear. ....Est. $6,000/9,000; sold for $7,700

Medallion Rug (c. 1885, 7′ × 5′). Ivory-centered, blue-pendanted medallion on a gracefully Herati-decorated red field. Leafy vines fill curvilinear blue spandrels within a leaf-and-rosette ivory primary border with narrow floral guards. Vegetable dyes. Evenly worn. ....Est. $2,500/3,000; sold for $3,500

FERAHAN (FEREHAN, FEREGHAN)

The trade has applied this name to a class of distinguished old rugs woven in the Arak district, mostly in traditional repeating designs, principally the Herati. Ferahans are asymmetrically knotted, over 100 per

Ferahan carpet, Western Persia, c. 1875, 9′8″ × 7′, $17,600. PHOTO COURTESY OF CHRISTIE'S EAST.

sq. in., on a cotton foundation with wefts dyed pink or blue. Their excellent vegetable dyes commend antique examples to collectors. (See also Ferahan Sarouk under Sarouk.)

Herati-Patterned Carpet (c. 1900, 12′2″×8′8″). The gold, red, ivory, and light blue Herati-covered medium blue ground is centered with a small red, blue, and gold geometric stepped medallion, whose design is repeated, quartered, in the modest spandrels. Blue and gold guard borders enclose the flowering vine, leaf, and palmette main gold border. Vegetable dyes. Slight wear. ....
....Est. $7,000/9,000; sold for $7,700

Flower and Vine Small Carpet (c. 1875, 9′8″×7′). Warm honey-cream ground bears diagonal rows of graceful green vines bearing blue, rose, and red flowers, enclosed by a honey-cream border with a flower meander, guarded by light blue floral guards. The overall impression one of great refinement. Vegetable dyes. Small breaks, repairs, and slight loss to one end border. ....
....Est. $15,000/20,000; sold for $17,600

Ferahan Prayer Rug (c. 1880, 6′9″×4′5″). A stylized and flamboyant polychrome tree-of-life fills the ivory prayer niche flanked by elaborate columns leading to spandrels swirled with blue and red flowering vines. The madder red primary border decorated with vines and palmettes is guarded by flowering vines on navy. Evenly worn. ....Est. $5,000/7,000; sold for $5,500

HERIZ

The province of Azerbaijan in northwest Iran is home to the robustly patterned rectilinear medallion rugs known generically as Heriz. Also woven here are the similar but more finely woven type labeled in the trade as Serapi, and the distinctive, often spectacular, rustic-looking Bakshaish carpets. Although these rugs are for the most part a cottage industry, some of the designs, like those of the Bidjars mentioned above, have more to do with Western fashion than tradition. Symmetrically knotted and woven with varying degrees of fineness on a cotton foundation, very coarse examples are more appropriately labeled Gorevan.

A very beautiful, finely knotted class of silk rugs is also said to have been woven by Heriz weavers, an attribution denounced by at least one scholar who claims these rugs are Tabriz products which, in recent years, have been labeled as Heriz because of the drawing power of the name with contemporary buyers. But as long as they continue to be tagged by dealers and auction houses as Heriz silks, collectors seeking these lovely rugs are advised to inquire after them by that name, whatever their true origin may be.

Art Nouveau Carpet (c. 1900, 10′3″×7′6″). Although the leaves and vegetable-dyed blue, red, rose, and gold Shah Abbas palmettes of this rug are traditional, their arrangement on the cream ground is much more akin to European art nouveau taste than to Oriental. The vine-and-palmette red primary border is wholly traditional, as are the flowering vine guards. The awkwardly resolved border corners indicates a village loom origin. Even wear. ....
.... Est. $50,000/70,000; sold for $55,000

Heriz carpet, Northwest Persia, c. 1900, 10′3″ × 7′6″, $55,000.
PHOTO © 1991 SOTHEBY'S, INC.

Cypress Tree Carpet (c. 1900, 14′10″×10′7″). A dressy rug bearing a deli-cately flowered grid of vines enclosing rows of polychrome cypress trees—elements of which are borrowed from the Bid Majnum pattern—on a cream ground. The golden-tan main border is decorated with leafy flowering vines in reds, blues, and cream; the floral guard borders are red and dark blue. Nicely resolved border corners. Partial end borders; cut and reduced in size. ....
....Est. $15,000/20,000; sold for $26,400

ISFAHAN (ISPAHAN, ISPHAHAN)

Isfahan is a beautiful city in central Iran where carpets were made for the Sefavid dynasty. Two centuries later, finely woven carpets—200–400 asymmetrical knots per sq. in. on a cotton foundation—again began to be woven here, but the materials used in Isfahan rugs made after World War II—a period not discussed here—are considered better than those used at the beginning of the weaving revival.

Medallion Carpet (c. 1920, 12′×8′5″). A scalloped plum and dark cream circular medallion bearing dark blue pendants centered with roses on a dark cream ground, swirled with medium-blue leaves and plum flowering tendrils. The navy-grounded spandrels are decorated with elaborate floral motifs, including rose-centered palmettes, and bordered by stylized vines and palmettes on plum. Two floral guards are cream; two are navy. Good condition. ....
.... Est. $12,000/15,000; sold for $17,600

JOSHAGAN (JOSHOGAN)

North of Isfahan is the venerable weaving town of Joshagan, whose rugs dating from the mid-19th century typically display a floral-cluster-enclosing lattice design.

Joshagan, Central Persia, c. 1875, 6′5″ × 5′3″, $23,100. PHOTO
COURTESY OF CHRISTIE'S EAST.

Rug (c. 1875, 6′5″ ×5′3″). On a gold ground, finely drawn clusters of flowers enclosed by a medium blue lattice within a dark blue main border bearing a classic palmette, rosette, and vine repeat. Slight wear. ....
....Est. $20,000/25,000; sold for $23,100

KASHAN

About 100 miles south of Isfahan lies Kashan, which is also famed for the fine carpets and other textiles woven there during Sefavid times. Turn-of-the-century Kashans, tightly woven of wool or silk, sometimes in combination, are highly regarded in today's rug trade—particularly the wool-pile carpets distinguished as *Mohtashem*, a label variously interpreted to refer to a master weaver and a superior grade of wool. Although woven on cottage looms, the elaborate curvilinear designs were supplied by commercial contractors. The best Kashans boast velvety wool with tight asymmetrical knots, 300–400 per sq. in., on a cotton foundation. Alternate warps are deeply depressed; double wefts are typically blue. Kashan rugs are appropriate for formal, dressy interiors, with the silk-warped, silk-pile examples reserved for wall or table decoration.

Kashan carpet, Central Persia, c. 1850, 10′ 10″ × 8′ 4″, $13,750.
PHOTO © 1991 SOTHEBY'S, INC.

"Mohtashem" Kashan Rug (c. 1885, 7′5″×4′6″). Rust and medium blue medallion on a navy field, enclosed by medallion-shaped broad ribbons of pale orange and jade and rust spandrels. A cartouche within the scrolled-leaf-and-palmette navy border bears an inscription. Even wear. ....
....Est. $5,000/7,000; sold for $13,750

"Mohtashem" Kashan Rug (c. 1885, 7′4″×4′4″). Brick red and royal blue pendanted medallion enclosed by bold arabesques on a floral decorated cream ground within a royal blue vine-and-rosette main border. Flat-woven ends embellished with silk. Good condition. ....Est. $6,000/8,000; sold for $9,500

Silk Carpet (c. 1900, 10′4″×6′11″). A stepped red, gold, and blue pendanted medallion on a flower-and-vine-swirled cream field. The curvilinear spandrels are banded in red, blue, and gold; the flower-and-palmette gold main border is guarded by narrow floral borders of red and blue. Good condition. ....
.... Est. $12,000/15,000; sold for $17,600

"Mohtashem" Kashan Rug (c. 1900, 6′11″×4′5″). Well-proportioned pendanted dark blue palmette-and-flower-decorated medallion on a cream ground bearing pretty flowering vines. Sheaves of flowers fill the dark blue spandrels; geometric borders guard the primary dark blue border bearing a formal array of floral motifs with perfectly resolved corners. Small repiled area in one corner.
.... Est. $10,000/15,000; sold for $15,950

Kashan Carpet (c. 1850, 10′10″×8′4″). An exceptionally handsome, generously scaled carpet, with a pendanted flower-and-palmette navy medallion on a rosy madder red ground enclosed by honey-colored palmette-decorated and leaf-edged spandrels. Two flower-and-vine red borders guard the stylized navy palmette-and-flowering-vine main border. Time-softened vegetable dyes. Well worn throughout. .... Est. $10,000/14,000; sold for $13,750

"Mohtashem" Kashan Carpet (c. 1885, 17′3″×11′10″). Humans on foot and mounted on horse and camel make their way with difficulty through the host of wild and domestic animals marching in polychrome rows across this large carpet within a dark blue field in a jungle of stylized flowering trees. A classical vine-and-palmette border, reds and blues on golden tan, properly takes a back seat to the activity it encloses. Stains, wear, restoration, ragged areas of selvage. ......
.... Est. $40,000/60,000; sold for $82,500

"Mohtashem" Kashan Carpet (c. 1920, 11′2″×8′2″). A well-proportioned formal carpet with a pendanted red medallion on a flower-ornamented cream field and dark blue spandrels. Delicate floral motifs fill the red guards; palmettes and flowering vines are meticulously resolved at the corners of the dark blue primary border. Good condition. ....Est. $20,000/25,000; sold for $31,000

Small Silk Runner (c. 1920, 4′10″×1′9″). Graceful, symmetrically balanced flowering leafy vines and palmettes cover the gold ground enclosed by a dark blue floral primary border and two ash rose flower-and-vine guards. Shows some wear. .... Est. $3,500/4,500; sold for $4,180

KERMAN

This formerly isolated provincial city was also a Sefavid weaving center, but it later gained fame for its shawl production, at one time rivaling that of Kashmir. The traditional Kerman rug of the revival period is short-piled and asymmetrically knotted on a cotton foundation with a density sometimes exceeding 400 knots per sq. in., rarely fewer than 140. Alternate warps are deeply depressed, and the Kerman uniquely has three wefts.

The designs used in the city workshops and surrounding villages were professionally conceived and are distinguished by their delicacy of both ornament and coloration. A lovely magenta shade of red obtained from cochineal is characteristic of many turn-of-the-century Kermans. Rugs particularly finely woven are known in the trade as Ravar—sometimes, wrongly, as Laver—Kermans, after a town supposed to be their source. These refined old rugs have nothing in common with the thick-piled, detached-floral and open-field pastel varieties designed in later years for the American market.

Tree-of-Life Carpet (c. 1900, 10′9″ ×8′8″). Medallion-shaped flowering tree-of-life on a claret field flanked by celadon green cypress trees and swirling cream floral vines within cream, claret-edged spandrels. Five elaborate floral borders, the primary one displaying densely flowering vines on a claret ground. Shows slight wear. ....Est. $8,000/10,000; sold for $8,800

Prayer Rug (c. 1875, 6′ ×3′10″). A stylized tree-of-life flanked by two dark blue cypress trees and a myriad of colorful, realistic flowering plants fills a stepped cream prayer niche under two flower-decorated dark blue spandrels. Stalks of henna flowers intertwined with vines ornament the dark blue primary border. Vegetable dyes in rose, rust red, apricot, olive, yellow. Shows wear. ..
.... Est. $1,500/2,000; sold for $3,575

Kerman prayer rug, South Persia, c. 1875, 6′ × 3′10″, $3,575. PHOTO COURTESY OF GROGAN & COMPANY.

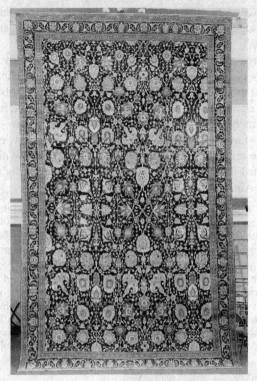

Ravar Kerman carpet, South Persia, c. 1850, 21' 10" × 13' 6",
$13,200. PHOTO © 1991 SOTHEBY'S, INC.

Ravar Kerman Vase Carpet (c. 1850, 21' 10" × 13' 6"). Arguably a Tabriz carpet, this three-plane lattice design has a background of flowering plants on a
blue field within a leaf-and-palmette blue main border flanked by decorative
guard stripes. A borrowed and somewhat simplified version (no vases) of a classical 17th-century Kerman format. Vegetable dyes. Shows wear; cut and reduced
in size. ....Est. $6,000/8,000; sold for $13,200

MAHAL, SULTANABAD

Woven in the Arak district, best known for Sarouk rugs, Mahals and
Sultanabads were largely a workshop production controlled by European
firms like Ziegler. Both symmetrical and asymmetrical knots were used
in these rugs, which, like the Sarouk, have a cotton foundation but are
more coarsely woven and display a much less pronounced depression of
the alternate warps. The designs tend to be sprawling versions of traditional floral motifs, but the best of them, thanks to good vegetable dyes,
are admirably suited as decorative carpets for informal settings.

Sultanabad carpet, Western Persia, c. 1885, 9'9" × 8'3", $12,000.
PHOTO COURTESY OF SKINNER, INC.

Ziegler Mahal Carpet (c. 1880, 11'4" ×8'10"). A lustrous rust ground covered by a very relaxed version of the Kerman vase design enclosed in a wide gold border prettily sprawled with flowers and leafy vines and two narrow rosette-decorated medium-blue borders. Vegetable dyes. Some wear. ....
....Est. $9,000/12,000; sold for $8,250

Sultanabad Carpet (probably Ziegler) (c. 1885, 9'9" ×8'3"). Abrashed, unornamented royal blue field with rectilinear red spandrels decorated with large-scale flowering vines within a wide abrashed red primary border with rosette, leaf, and palmette repeats, guarded by two narrow bands of trefoil motifs. Vegetable dyes. Generally good condition. . Est. $14,000/16,000; sold for $12,000

MALAYER

Lying south of Hamadan and west of Arak within a broad rug-producing area, Malayer produced rugs that, unlike their Hamadan cousins, were apt to be double-wefted. Seen mostly in scatter to area sizes with medallion-centered formats, they are as finely knotted and elegantly designed as Ferehan Sarouks, for which they are frequently mistaken. The foundation is typically cotton, and the pile is close-clipped.

Malayer rug, Western Persia, c. 1885, 5'6" × 6', $22,000. PHOTO
COURTESY OF CHRISTIE'S EAST.

Rug (c. 1885, 5'6"×6'). A floral-ornamented and pendanted ivory medallion
is centered on an abrashed dark blue ground ornamented with flowering vines
and palmettes and flanked by honey-color, vine-decked spandrels. The tan primary border has a delicate flower-and-vine meander within ivory floral guards
and a bold reciprocal trefoil outer border. Good condition. ....
.... Est. $20,000/25,000; sold for $22,000

QASHQAI

The weavers living in the Fars province bordering the Persian Gulf in
the south of Iran are generally considered as belonging to tribal groups.
Many weavers of the Qashqai group, however, can more accurately be
described as workshop workers who, for 100 years or more, have lived
largely settled lives. Fine old examples of these well-made, beautifully
colored, and eminently collectible rugs are hotly competed for. Generally asymmetrically knotted on a wool foundation—occasionally silk-
warped—the knot density averages 150 per sq. in.

Qashqai millesfleurs rug, Southwest Persia, c. 1875, 6′1″ × 4′2″, $28,500. PHOTO COURTESY OF CHRISTIE'S EAST.

Silk-Warped Millesfleurs Rug (c. 1875, 6′1″ ×4′2″). Derived from a classical Mughal prayer rug design, a flower-filled vase on a cream ground is surrounded by an ascending network of diverse flowering stalks. The vase, stylized here, floats above a scalloped red plinth, also filled with flowering plants, as are the red spandrels. Narrow gold carnation borders guard the deep aubergine main border of rosettes interlocked by flowering vines. Vegetable dyes. Dog-eared corner; small break. .... Est. $25,000/35,000; sold for $28,500

SAROUK

The carpets bearing this name were woven in west central Iran, in and around the city of Arak, formerly Sultanabad, where workshop weaving was instituted in the second half of the 19th century. The best of these decorative rugs—known in the trade as Ferahan (Ferehan, Fereghan) Sarouk—were made mostly in floral-ornamented area sizes bearing elegantly drawn medallions. They are characterized by a short, tightly woven, velvety wool pile asymmetrically knotted, 100–200 per sq. in., on a cotton foundation with depressed alternate warps.

The modern Sarouk, a different kettle of fish altogether, has a longish, thick pile woven in detached floral spray designs developed for the American market after World War I. This generation of Sarouks has blue-dyed cotton wefts. Typically, the ground color varies from deep rose to maroon, achieved in early examples by bleaching a red considered too bright, repainting the pile with darker colors, and "restoring" the dulled pile to an artificial brilliance. Later rugs of this type were spared this torture, but if considering one, be wary.

Carpet (c. 1875, 10′8″×7′3″). On a deep blue ground a central axis of seven flower-derived motifs in gold, red, blue, green, and cream is flanked by palmette-bearing vines radiating from a narrow trefoil border. Enclosed by two gold floral guards, the dark blue primary border of palmettes and graceful flowering vines boasts perfect corner resolutions. Vegetable dyes. Shows slight wear. ....
.... Est. $20,000/25,000; sold for $22,000

Garden Carpet (c. 1875, 9′11″×6′9″). Four rows of cypress, fruit-bearing and flowering trees in blues, reds, gold, green, and peach on a honey ground, are drawn with a delicacy reminiscent of the best Kermans. Two pairs of guards enclose a midnight blue primary border closely strewn with a variety of classically derived floral motifs. Vegetable dyes. Shows wear; loss to ends. (See color insert) .... Est. $10,000/15,000; sold for $12,100

Sarouk carpet, Western Persia, c. 1875, 10′8″ × 7′3″, $22,000.
PHOTO COURTESY OF CHRISTIE'S EAST.

Rug, Ferahan Type (c. 1885, 6′8″ ×4′3″). A lobed and pendanted dark blue floral medallion and spandrels placed to striking effect on an abrashed honey ground. A navy primary border of meandering palmettes, rosettes, and flowering vines has a pair of narrow red floral guards. Vegetable dyes in reds, blues, greens, and golds. Shows slight wear. ......Est. $6,000/8,000; sold for $4,800

Millesfleurs Prayer Rug, Ferahan Type (c. 1885, 6′10″ ×4′6″). A cloud of gracefully drawn polychrome flowers rises from a vase set upon a narrow stepped plinth in a cream prayer niche flanked by abrashed blue-green floral spandrels. Trefoil guards enclose a flowering-vine-swirled navy border. Vegetable dyes. Good condition. .... Est. $8,000/12,000; sold for $20,900

Rug, Ferahan Type (c. 1900, 6′7″ ×4′4″). A lobed and pendanted midnight-blue floral medallion floats on a cream ground ornamented with graceful, prettily colored floral vinery within blue floral spandrels, the whole enclosed by a madder red floral border with imperfectly resolved top corners. Vegetable dyes. Shows slight wear. .... Est. $6,000/8,000; sold for $9,075

Rug, Ferahan Type (c. 1885, 6′10″ ×4′6″). A midnight blue floral medallion with double pendants in blue and green on a red field enclosed by elongated midnight blue spandrels and palmette-and-vine-ornamented main border, with red and ivory guard stripes. This attractive, sensitively drawn format is also seen in larger sizes. Three small repairs; otherwise good condition. ....
.... Est. $3,500/4,500; sold for $3,250

Ferahan Sarouk, Western Persia, c. 1900, 6′7″ × 4′4″, $9,075.
PHOTO © 1991 SOTHEBY'S, INC.

Five Sarouk Carpets (c. 1920, each approx. 9′×12′). A representative selection of good commercial Sarouks of the type described above was sold at auction in 1989–90. Four had red grounds, from light to medium, the fifth a rich dark blue. All featured nontraditional detached floral sprays of varying degrees of delicacy; all were in good condition and none had been painted. ....Est. $7,000/12,000; sold for $8,800–9,900

TABRIZ

This well-known center of workshop weaving is situated in the far northwest corner of Iran. The rugs presented here have a symmetrically knotted wool pile, 200–250 per sq. in., on a cotton foundation, which is typically short and bristly. Silk Tabriz rugs are rather finer and occasionally knotted asymmetrically. Curvilinear and rectilinear medallion designs predominate on the wool carpets; the silks are often woven in a prayer format.

Medallion Carpet (c. 1885, 17′×11′4″). Tabriz rugs display medallion designs in both curvilinear and rectilinear formats; this is a striking example of the latter: a series of Herati-ornamented, delicately pendanted hexagons and spandrels of graduated sizes and differing ground colors—red, dark blue, and cream—are imposed one upon another and accented by a single broad, brick red, unornamented hexagonal band. Six narrow guards flank the red main border with palmette, rosette, and vine-decoration. Shows minor wear. ....Est. $15,000/20,000; sold for $13,200

Sarouk carpet, Western Persia, c. 1920, 9′ × 12′, $8,800. PHOTO COURTESY OF CHRISTIE'S EAST.

Tabriz silk prayer rug, Northwest Persia, c. 1885, 5′5″ × 4′3″, $6,050. PHOTO COURTESY OF CHRISTIE'S EAST.

Animal Carpet (c. 1885, 16′6″ × 12′9″). The brick red pendanted medallion, dark blue field, and flanking red spandrels are all crowded with animals and birds among flowering plants and trees. The primary red border packed with floral motifs is flanked by four guards, two with a repeat calligraphic motif on dark blue. Typically subdued coloration. Shows some wear, stains. .... Est. $30,000/35,000; sold for $26,400

Silk Prayer Rug (c. 1885, 5′5″ × 4′3″). Lustrous dark blue ground with columns and well-drawn stylized lamp suspended from cream, vine-tendriled prayer niche. The cream rosette-and-vine decorated primary border has three pairs of narrow floral guards, the whole distinguished by its quiet coloration and formal appearance. Shows wear. .... Est. $3,000/4,000; sold for $6,050

Silk Rug (c. 1885, 5′2″ × 4′1″). Borrowed from Arak, this popular design incorporates a pendanted, rosette-shaped, rayed medallion, one half of which is repeated at each end, with flowering stalks protruding into the abrashed cornflower blue field from multiple floral guards. The dark blue primary border bears an array of floral motifs. Good condition; reselvaged. .... Est. $7,000/10,000; sold for $13,200

TEHERAN

The present-day capital city of Iran was never an important weaving center, and its well-made workshop rugs are apt to be labeled as Isfahan. Asymmetrically knotted, about 200 per sq. in., on a cotton foundation, the double wefts may be pink or blue.

Rug (c. 1920, 6'7"×4'5"). The ivory ground is covered in a pleasing version of the Herati pattern in red, green, gold, and blue. Narrow vine-and-palmette guard borders flank a sea green primary border with rosettes and palmettes linked by meandering vines. Good condition. ..... Est. $4,000/6,000; sold for $3,520

Rug (c. 1900, 7'×4'5"). A well-made but rather mechanical version of the Garus design noted under Bidjar above, and with a similar primary border. Red, ivory, gold, green, and medium blue on a midnight blue ground. Good condition. .... Est. $10,000/14,000; sold for $17,600

INDIAN CARPETS

Except for the exceptionally accomplished and distinctive early weaving characteristic of the palace workshops, collectors have had little interest

Agra carpet, India, c. 1885, 22'2" × 13'8", $75,900. PHOTO
© 1991 SOTHEBY'S, INC.

in Indian rugs. Although well woven of generally superior materials, the designs of later carpets are so derivative of foreign traditions they are routinely labeled Indo-Ispahan or -Kerman or -Tabriz—even Indo-Chinese.

The "jail carpets" from the venerable carpet-weaving center of Agra, where, in the mid-19th century, the British placed looms in the prisons, are often more interesting than other Indian carpets of this period. Like the cotton prison-made dhurries, native fauna were frequently incorporated into the designs, perhaps reflecting a yearning for the outside world. Of moderate density, they are asymmetrically knotted in wool on a cotton foundation.

Agra Carpet (c. 1885, 14′6″ × 11′7″). Large-scale, geometricized Herati-like motifs in rows alternating with shield and gul shapes in deep carmine red and dark olive on a greenish tan field further ornamented with red and green vinelike traceries. Greenish tan cartouches on a carmine primary border; angular flowering vine motifs in the guards. Partial ends, stains, restorations. ....
.... Est. $30,000/40,000; sold for $33,000

Agra Floral Carpet (c. 1885, 23′6″ × 17′6″). The honey-gold field of this very large carpet is covered with rows of colorful and realistic one-directional flowering plants reminiscent of classical Mughal rugs, except the plants are much more closely packed. The primary carmine red border has cypress trees alternating with flowering stalks; there are several guards of varying widths and types. Nicks in ends, repiled areas, staining. ....
.... Est. $20,000/30,000; sold for $44,000

Agra Tiger Carpet (c. 1885, 22′2″ × 13′8″). A carmine red circular medallion is centered on a honey field with carmine-bordered dark olive spandrels. The medallion, spandrels, and field are ornamented with the Herati motif, but in the field version, realistically drawn and colored snarling tigers replace the traditional curved leaves. Two red flowering vine guards flank an elegant primary honey border of dark blue cartouches ornamented with red calligraphy interspersed with rosettes. Good condition. Est. $50,000/70,000; sold for $75,900

CHINESE CARPETS

The designs of commercial Chinese rugs made between 1875 and 1930 range all over the lot, from slightly stylized versions of traditional patterns to peacock-decorated Art Deco creations. Chinese rugs of this era were relatively coarsely and asymmetrically knotted—averaging 30–65 per sq. in.—on a cotton foundation. The wool used for the pile is lustrous, thick, and moderately long. Before the introduction of chrome dyes around World War I—earlier than in most rug-weaving areas—Chinese rugs were famed for the shimmering variations of their indigo blues. Aside from blue, the palette used in traditional rugs was limited to tans, yellows, ivories, peach, and occasionally a rather washed-out red.

Chinese carpet, c. 1885, 11′6″ × 9′, $7,150. PHOTO © 1991
SOTHEBY'S, INC.

Peony Blossom Carpet (c. 1885, 11′6″ ×9′). A traditional peony and scrolled-vine motif in saffron and cream covers a lustrous medium-blue ground within a saffron border ornamented with peonies and vines in shades of blue enclosed by a wide blue edge. Good condition. .... Est. $7,000/9,000; sold for $7,150

Art Deco Carpet (c. 1930, 11′7″ ×9′3″). A lobed, trefoil-edged unornamented indigo field displays Art Deco–style peacocks in each corner of the tan surround. A collectible period rug for 1930s decor, without a trace of Chinese influence save for the blue field and wide blue outer and only border. Good condition. .... Est. $3,500/4,500; sold for $3,850

CONTEMPORARY COLLECTIBLE RUGS

Like everything else collectible, oriental rugs have had their ups and downs in popularity. Many of the rugs being collected today were produced during the booming 19th-century revival fostered by a new appreciation of oriental rugs in the West, which was sparked by the paintings of a group of well-traveled artists known as the Orientalists.

By the turn of the century, dealers had begun a diligent search for old rugs to satisfy a more sophisticated market that developed during the 1880s, and the 1920s saw a tidal-wave surge in prices paid for classical carpets by highly competitive, well-heeled collectors.

The 1929 crash ushered in a long period of economic drought accompanied by wrenching changes in aesthetic as well as social attitudes, including a taste for clean, uncluttered lines and neutral colors promoted by a "less is more" mentality. Oriental rugs, seen as too busy and too bright, were banished to the attic in favor of calm expanses of carpeting. Rug collectors who maintained their interest through the 1940s and 1950s acquired rugs now considered world-class for sums that today would be insufficient to buy dinner for four at a top-rated restaurant and bought antique bags for less than the cost of a bottle of decent—not great—wine.

The era of the 1960s and 1970s witnessed, in addition to a bemusing variety of ways to prepare granola, a rebirth of interest in crafts and folk arts. Idealistic Americans returning from Peace Corps service in exotic places brought back with them a lively appreciation for the weaving arts they had seen practiced on a village and tribal level, and the new demand thus introduced was soon commercially supplied.

Many of the rugs produced for this folk art market are a mishmash of borrowed popular designs and cheap synthetic dyes debased further by bleaching and glossing. There are, however, some notable and shining exceptions, which, having already caught the rug world's attention, are worthy of yours. Collectors of antique traditional rugs often choose these honest new rugs for furnishing their floors; others find them worthy of collection regardless of any practical considerations.

Some of these enterprises are native cooperative ventures; some are promoter-driven; but whatever the engine that sparks them, in the case of the five I have chosen to present there is a sensitive appreciation of

local history and craft as well as the possibilities and limitations of rug
weaving as a viable cottage industry in the 1990s.

Retail outlets for these contemporary collectible rugs are not only
limited but subject to change; for that reason, only primary sources will
be supplied. New rugs are generally priced on a flat rate per-square-foot
basis; except for the occasional uniquely wonderful piece, this pricing
applies to all the new collectible examples discussed in this chapter.
Collectors wishing to learn more about any of the rug projects described
should direct inquiries to the dealers profiled below.

DOBAG

The introduction of cheap, easily applied but stridently colored and unstable synthetic dyes during the 19th-century boom years led to a sad
decline in quality—particularly in Turkey—and in the prices paid the
weavers by wholesale buyers. The craft, however, continued to be practiced and taught, and this, together with the persistence of design traditions, encouraged a return to the use of natural dye methods and, when
feasible in terms of supply, hand-spun, lanolin-rich local wool.

DOBAG, a Turkish acronym that stands for Natural Dye Research and
Development Project, was the pioneer venture. All others were inspired
by it and have benefited from the technical expertise DOBAG provided

*DOBAG rug, Yuntdag region,
Turkey, 1987, 7'8" × 4'8",
$1,700.* AUTHOR'S COLLECTION.

the two weaving cooperatives established with its guidance in 1981 in northwestern Turkey.

The vibrant vegetable dyes used for the rugs produced by the DOBAG villager-owned and -administered cooperatives are an outgrowth of the research and experimentation of a German chemist and rug scholar, Dr. Harold Böhmer, whose work was sponsored by Marmara University in Istanbul. The designs used for DOBAG rugs are traditional designs surviving in rugs given over many years to local mosques, but the choice and combination of motifs and colors in a particular rug are those of the woman or women who wove it.

DOBAG rugs have had no chemical or aging treatment of any kind. The low sheen of the hard-wearing long-staple wool is natural, and the rich, subtly shaded vegetable colors will mellow gradually over time. Each rug is registered with the cooperative: the number is recorded on an attached leather tag guaranteeing its quality and accompanied by a card bearing the rug's dimensions, knot count, and the names of the weaver and her village.

Gayle Garrett has been importing DOBAG rugs since 1986 for her Washington, DC, firm The Rug Project. She has supported and publicized the Turkish cottage weaving industry through lectures and tours and, most notably, through the symposium she organized in 1987, *The Fabric of Daily Life*. It included a widely acclaimed exhibition of over 100 DOBAG rugs at the Washington headquarters of The World Bank.

Ms. Garrett chooses her rugs one by one at the cooperatives. As they approach their tenth year of operation, it has become clear that DOBAG rugs are collectible, not only on the basis of intrinsic merit but because weavers whose work is consistently distinctive deserve the same special regard by collectors as that of superior potters or silversmiths. Accordingly, the quality of each piece determines its price within The Rug Project's rather narrow retail range. Stock on hand at any given time includes mat, scatter (including prayer formats), and area rug sizes up to 8 × 10 feet. Knot density averages 56 to 63 per square inch. Special orders can be placed, including sizes 8 × 10 and larger, with colors and designs chosen in consultation with Ms. Garrett.

The Rug Project shows rugs in Washington by appointment; rugs can also be purchased on approval on the basis of a description and color photograph. Payment, which is requested before shipment, is refunded, less shipping costs, if the rug is returned within a previously agreed-upon time period.

Return to Tradition, an attractive retail store that opened in San Francisco in 1989, is the only other DOBAG rug specialist dealer in the United States. Return to Tradition prices its DOBAG rugs on a uniform per-square-foot basis. This works out, on average, somewhat higher than the prices of The Rug Project, with the exception of those rugs Ms. Garrett considers outstandingly superior. As of 1991, Return to Tradition's flat rate for pile rugs was $58 a square foot; flat-woven rugs, $39. These prices are, of course, subject to change according to prevailing economic conditions.

WOVEN LEGENDS: THE AZERI PRODUCTION

Spurred by the appearance in 1982 of a few naturally dyed rugs in the Istanbul market, a young American dealer in old rugs, George Jevremovic, embarked on a career as a Turkish rug entrepreneur. His Philadelphia-based firm, Woven Legends, which is now the largest U.S. importer of Turkish rugs, is the umbrella under which his new rug enterprises cluster. Azeri, the name chosen for the production he organized in Eastern Turkey, produces room-size pile rugs in sizes 6 × 9 to 12 × 20 and runners. The knot count and handle is comparable to that of the DOBAG rugs. But although Jevremovic unhesitatingly credits DOBAG for the benefits its reintroduction of natural dyes brought to Turkish village weaving, he had ideas of his own concerning design.

Rugs made in the early days of the DOBAG cooperatives have been

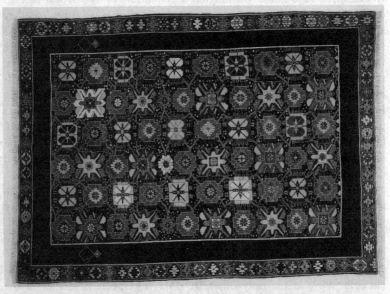

Azeri carpet, Turkey, 1990, 7' 10" × 10' 11", $4,800–$5,200, a production of Woven Legends. PHOTO COURTESY OF WOVEN LEGENDS.

criticized for what some saw as a slavish adherence to the traditional design vocabulary; some other new village productions have been taken to task for their rote copies of designs foreign to the weavers. The Azeri rugs straddle the line, borrowing for one rug from popular Persian designs, for another from Central Asian themes, with southwest Persian tribal and Caucasian and tried-and-true Turkish motifs thrown in for good measure. For the most part it works, perhaps because Azeri weavers are encouraged to adapt foreign motifs to their traditional taste; perhaps, too, because the exuberance of the palette and quality of the hand-spun wool remain wholly Turkish. This is not accomplished entirely without risk: at their best, Azeris are very, very good; occasionally, if the adaptions and spacing are clumsy and the colors ill-chosen, they can be downright horrid.

The success the Azeri production is enjoying is unusual in a market whose acceptance of off-beat products is normally slow and reluctant. In this case, however, the quality of the materials—no chemical glossing here either—and the cheerful spontaneity of the designs have won plaudits from collectors and dealers alike, and the Woven Legends booths at the national wholesale markets are invariably sold out. Interestingly, Azeri rugs are generally stocked by dealers whose primary business is in antique rugs. The knot count is comparable to the DOBAG rugs; the cost, ranging from $5,400 to $8,000 for a 9 × 12 (as of late 1990), is appreciably less than a similarly sized antique rug, and its suitability for a heavily trafficked area is appreciably greater. The names of dealers offering Azeri rugs may be obtained from the Woven Legends headquarters.

GANGCHEN

Tibetan rugs have been another success story, but until recently it was not, for the most part, due to adherence to tradition.

When Tibetans escaped to Nepal during the Chinese takeover of their homeland in 1959, a carpet production center was soon organized as a means of providing employment to the refugees while providing Nepal with needed hard currency. By the early 1980s the industry was well established, but although the wonderful long-staple Tibetan wool and sturdy, if coarse, structure of the rugs won favor with dealers everywhere, the demands of Western taste forced significant changes. Traditional designs and bright synthetic colors soon gave way to open-field designs and sophisticated Westernized floral motifs knotted in earthtoned, vegetable-dyed wool paled further with chemical washes. Decorators loved these tasteful, plush, durable, and reasonably priced small rugs; collectors sighed regretfully and chose the Turkish village rugs for their floor furnishings.

By the late 1980s a desire to return to the old weaving traditions had become manifest. To that end, an enterprise known as InnerAsia Trading was established for the purpose of "revitalizing Tibet's rug weaving heritage, developing a viable business and generating extra income for the Tibetan weavers and wool-producing nomads."

The moving spirit behind this revitalization of the Tibetan rug industry, once again able to flourish in its homeland, is Kesang Tashi, an American-educated member of a distinguished Tibetan entrepreneurial family. He switched to rug manufacturing in Lhasa from a career in banking in New York. "The time was ripe," he says, "and I took the plunge."

Tibet is economically backward even by third world standards, with endless frustrations and complications encountered in achieving the sim-

Gangchen rug, Tibet, 1990, 3' × 6', $900–$1,100. "FLOCK OF CRANES" IS A REPRODUCTION FROM INNERASIA TRADING COMPANY, EXCLUSIVE NORTH AMERICAN IMPORTER OF CARPETS FROM TIBET.

plest aim. Fortunately, Tashi and his partner, George Doubleday, persevered, their hopes sustained by the excellence of the wool produced by the aboriginal sheep of the Tibetan plateau; the availability of skilled weavers, both male and female; and a reservoir of traditional rug motifs that other new productions had largely neglected.

Color choices and the selection and presentation of motifs are always critical factors in regard to market acceptance, but since oriental rugs now appeal to more than one kind of market, InnerAsia shrewdly decided to place its eggs in more than one basket.

Gangchen, the name chosen for the production, means "snowland." Gangchen rugs are made in Tibet with hand-spun, long-staple, lanolin-rich Tibetan wool richly colored with both natural and high-quality Swiss synthetic dyes. The knots are asymmetrical, and the density ranges from 40 to 80 per square inch, in keeping with the difference between loosely woven village rugs and those made in Gyantse and Lhasa workshops.

The rugs are woven in carefully reproduced traditional Tibetan designs: dragons, tigers, cloud bands, geometrics, and florals. I was particularly taken with one depicting a flock of cranes in a stylized landscape. They retailed in early 1991 for $50 to $60 a square foot in sizes ranging from 3 × 6 to 9 × 12. Runners and oversize carpets can be made to order.

A Gangchen folk art line inspired by the Turkish DOBAG experiment is in the process of organization. Assuming that all goes as planned, it will offer one-of-a-kind, vegetable-dyed pieces growing out of the weavers' experiences and reflecting their aesthetic sensibilities.

AFGHAN TURKOMAN RUG PROJECT

The need for an Afghan rug project similar to DOBAG became apparent to rug dealer-scholar Chris Walter in the course of his work with Turkoman weavers among the Afghan refugees encamped in Pakistan. Rug weaving has always been an important part of Turkoman tribal life, and for the displaced refugees it became not only a crucial source of income but a means of maintaining cultural identity.

The aim of the project is to produce an authentic and beautiful rug through the reintroduction of vegetable dyes, hand-spun Afghan wool, and traditional designs not included in the sadly limited repertoire used by Turkoman weavers for the commercial market. Start-up funds were granted in part by an organization called Cultural Survival, which, like Chris Walter himself, is based in Cambridge, Massachusetts. Essential assistance is provided in Pakistan by Jora Agha, a Turkoman from northern Afghanistan widely respected among his own people and knowledgeable about all local aspects of the rug business.

*Afghan Turkoman Project,
Pakistan, 1990, Dudin prayer rug
reproduction, 3' 11" × 5' 10".
Price NA.* FROM THE COLLECTION
OF WILLIAM MOR.

The Afghan Turkoman project, still in its infancy, turns out only 100 to 150 rugs a year in 3 × 5, 5 × 7, 6 × 9, and 8 × 11 sizes. Runners and room-size rugs are also available. Weaving, shearing, and washing—soap and water only—is done in the Haripur Refugee Camp in Pakistan; artificial aging and chemical glossing are not allowed. The retail price per square foot as of early 1991 was about $37.

Inquiries about the purchase of one of these handsome, well-made, and authentic new Turkoman rugs should be addressed directly to Chris Walter at the address given below.

TURKISH KILIMS

In recent years, the American rug market has been flooded with small kilims, the majority of which are made in Turkey. Whether their acceptance stems from the enthusiastic reception accorded contemporary Indian dhurries, also flat-woven, whose peak of popularity seems to have passed, or a trickling down of the fervor for antique kilims shown by collectors, I hesitate to say. Whatever the reason may be, these widely available, loosely woven, inexpensive scatters, while satisfactory as furnishing accents, are in a different class altogether from the new kilims considered collectible.

Marian Miller, a highly regarded New York specialist in antique kilims, is enthusiastic about a small Turkish production from Oushak and Manisa supervised by an old-time Turkish dealer she greatly respects both for his eye for color and his knowledge of design gained through long experience with antique rugs.

Turkish prayer kilim, Western Anatolia, 1990. 3′6″ × 5′1″, $600. PHOTO COURTESY OF MARIAN MILLER RUGS.

The weave of these all-wool kilims is tight and fine, and the motifs are much livelier and more inventive than the run-of-the-mill patterns that, Ms. Miller told me, the weavers refer to by the Turkish word for "dumb." The wool, although machine-spun, is of high quality; both vegetable and synthetic dyes are used for the vibrant colors. The average size is 3′6″ × 5′6″, and the prices range from $450 to $900 as of this writing. The *mihrab* of the 3′6″ × 5′1″ prayer kilim pictured here ($600) displays yet another version of the tree-of-life design discussed in the chapter on motifs.

Turkish kilim, Yüncü design, 4′7″ × 6′9″, $900. PHOTO COURTESY OF TURQUOISE GALLERY.

The Turquoise Gallery in New York City is another good source for better-than-average Turkish kilims. The production featured here is woven of vegetable-dyed wool on linen warps; traditional patterns are available in area-rug sizes. There are occasional bright white accents in cotton. The pictured kilim is a design associated with weavers of the settled Yüncü tribal groups of Western Anatolia. As of early 1991, the retail price for this piece, which measures $4'7'' \times 6'9''$, was $900. A $3'5'' \times 5'4''$ kilim with wide, bold elibelinde-patterned end borders was $700.

Exceptional contemporary Turkish versions of the enchanting floral kilims of the traditional Romanian or Bessarabian type are occasionally available from Marian Miller and, in a slightly different weave, from Woven Legends. (See color insert.) These finely woven pieces demand superior weaving skills, employing as they do both eccentric wefting and supplementary wefts for various of the design elements, and in both cases availability is quite limited. These lovely vegetable-dyed kilims average 4×6, and the prices range from about $900 to $1,200.

SOURCES FOR THE RUGS
PROFILED ABOVE

DOBAG RUGS

The Rug Project
4814 MacArthur Boulevard, NW
Washington, DC 20007
(202) 965-2834
Note: Call for appointment.

Return to Tradition
3319 Sacramento Street
San Francisco, CA 94118
(415) 921-4180

AZERI RUGS

Woven Legends
4700 Wissahickon #106
Philadelphia, PA 19144
(215) 849-8344

GANGCHEN RUGS

InnerAsia Trading Company
112 East 37th Street
New York, NY 10016
(212) 689-6886
Note: By appointment only;
write for brochure.

YAYLA TRIBAL RUGS:
AFGHAN TURKOMAN
PROJECT

Chris Walter
308 Broadway
Cambridge, MA 02139
(617) 576-3249

TURKISH KILIMS

Marian Miller Kilims
148 East 28th Street, 3rd Floor
New York, NY 10016
(212) 685-7746
Note: Call for appointment.

Turquoise Gallery
Seyfullah Turkkan
132 East 61st Street
New York, NY 10021
(212) 759-6424 (phone and fax)

OTHER DEALERS IN CONTEMPORARY COLLECTIBLE RUGS

The following dealers are direct importers of contemporary collectible rugs. Consult the Resource Guide lists for additional sources.

Turkish Village Rugs
Bergi Andonian
102 Madison Avenue
(at 29th Street)
New York, NY 10016
(212) 532-4688

Turkish Village Rugs and Kilims
Saul Barodofsky
Sun Bow Trading Company
108 Fourth Street
Charlottesville, VA 22901
(804) 293-8821

ORIENTAL RUG CARE

CLEANING YOUR ORIENTAL RUG

When I suggested to a woman visiting my rug booth at a Connecticut antiques show that her oriental scatter rugs could safely be washed in a solution of neutral detergent and water, she blinked in disbelief.

"Tea is what they use to clean rugs with," she corrected firmly.

"They," I assumed, referred to authentic rug merchants, the ranks of whom obviously could not include a female of Gaelic descent like myself. Nevertheless, I was amused by this latest addition to the list of rug-cleaning secrets of the Orient generously shared with me during the two-day show: new-fallen snow had been mentioned several times and vinegar twice, but I had been spared sauerkraut juice, an aromatic German recipe, and the romantic but risky instruction from Victorian England advising immersion of one's rugs in the clear, cold waters of a rushing mountain stream.

There seems to be something quirky in human nature that rejects simple solutions in favor of the complicated, the unlikely, and the arcane—a remnant of a primitive, mythic past, perhaps. The contemporary corollary is the insistence on applying to household furnishings museum standards that, although technically correct, are inappropriate to the situation. Some readers may object to this and succeeding chapters dealing with oriental rug care and repair on the grounds of their not being exacting enough in regard to materials and techniques. In my opinion, however, the average busy householder, who is perfectly able to differentiate between lukewarm and cool water when washing a rug, might very well abandon the whole business if exhorted to use water of, say, no more than 86° F, adjusted to a pH of 5.

The tested and conservative methods presented in this chapter are in fact *more* exacting than those employed by oriental rug cleaning firms, whose principal advantage is wide experience with all types of rugs and rug-cleaning problems and the ability to handle rugs of a size impossible to manage in the home environment. In the instructions and advice that follow, I have attempted to distill the best of current wisdom, tempered with my own strongly pragmatic turn of mind, but only you can decide what makes the most sense to you and for your particular circumstances.

THE IMPORTANCE OF PERIODIC CLEANING

The frequent inspection and cleaning of oriental rugs, whether used as floor furnishings or wall hangings, should be included in any household maintenance program. Grit trapped in carpet pile can quickly cause visible wear through abrasion, particularly on rugs piled with soft wool, like the Pakistani "Bokharas" or those with corrosive black or brown dyes, which are characteristic of many old Baluch tribal rugs.

Dirt allowed to settle and compact around the knots at the base of the pile restrict the ability of the foundation to adjust to the subtle tensions caused by changes in temperature and humidity and may eventually cause it to weaken and break. Rugs used as wall hangings will not, obviously, suffer abrasive wear, but dust and greasy cooking smoke, if allowed to accumulate over long periods, will dull the colors and luster.

VACUUM CLEANING

New or sturdy old rugs can be vacuumed once a week; antique and loosely knotted older orientals should be vacuumed only once or twice a month and in the direction of the pile only. A carpet sweeper may be used for the weekly once-over. There are several small, lightweight, and efficient models currently available that are handy for quick cleanups of all kinds. If a rug is very fine or fragile, purchase a square of plastic screening, tape the edges, and place it on top of the rug before vacuuming; this will protect delicate or loose pile fibers from the direct pull of powerful suction.

Small rugs can be shaken instead of vacuumed, but gently does it. If you snap them like a bullwhip, you could crack the ends and edges or cause the foundation to separate and tear. Periodically—at least once a year for large rugs—it is a good idea to vacuum the undersides of your rugs and inspect the foundation for mildew, insect eggs, and moth damage. This type of thorough cleaning is particularly necessary for rugs whose ends or edges are concealed under furniture, where drifts of lint, dust, and food crumbs are apt to accumulate. Failure to clean these areas is equivalent to hanging out a free-room-and-board sign for insect pests: not infrequently at auctions one sees an otherwise lovely rug with a sofa-length strip nibbled down to the foundation.

Moth damage is an even greater hazard on wall-hung rugs because of the easily accessible and protected egg-laying environment created by the space between the wall and the back of the rug, so remember to occasionally take down any hanging rugs for inspection and brushing or vacuuming.

SURFACE CLEANING

In the course of a year, your rugs may acquire a dulling film composed of dust and greasy smoke that resists removal by vacuuming. Assuming your maintenance program has been conscientiously observed, you should be able to revive the color and luster of your rugs with a simple surface cleansing of the pile with snow or detergent suds.

The only advantage snow has over suds, and only for the country dweller, is that it's more fun. The next time a winter storm hits your area, take your rugs out and place them pile-side down on a clean stretch of snow. Press them into the snow with the flat side of a broom, but try to avoid covering the back of the rug. When you pick up the rug and shake it out, you'll be amazed at the amount of dirt left behind on the snow. Before replacing the rug on your floor, towel-dry any residual moisture left by melting crystals trapped in the pile fibers.

To clean the pile surface of your rug with suds, add a neutral detergent to a bowl of lukewarm water and work up thick suds by repeated squeezings with a clean sponge. Apply *only* the suds to the pile with a strong wiping motion. Rinse the sponge in clean water after each application of suds to remove the dirt you have wiped up. After suds have been applied to the entire surface, go over the pile with a clean damp sponge to remove all traces of suds and loosened grime. Towel dry if necessary.

WASHING VERSUS DRY CLEANING

The wet or dry cleaning of a rug, especially a large one, is a stressful process and should not be part of your yearly maintenance program unless a combination of kids, pets, and heavy foot traffic produces an unusual amount of dirt and grit that cannot be removed satisfactorily by vacuuming and surface cleaning. There are, however, some situations that demand it as a matter of course:

1. Dirty and possibly moth-harboring rugs acquired at auction, from an antique shop, or through inheritance.

2. Rugs requiring repair—wool colors should not be matched to a dirty rug.

3. Rugs with small areas markedly cleaner than the rest of the rug, due to the removal of spots or stains.

When an oriental rug requires a thorough cleaning, wet washing is preferred to dry cleaning because the chemicals used in the dry cleaning process tend to remove the natural oils and patina from wool and give white wool a yellowish cast. But before you decide to slosh your scatter rugs and tribal trappings in the bathtub, there are a few facts about rug fibers in general and oriental rugs in particular, that should be kept in mind:

1. Vegetable fibers, like cotton and linen, become stronger when wet; animal fibers—wool and silk—weaken. This means that a heavy, wet wool rug can withstand less stress, less pulling and hauling, than the same rug can when dry.

2. Silk rugs, including wool rugs with significant amounts of silk in design details, should be dry-cleaned by an experienced professional. *There are no safe exceptions to this rule.*

3. Bleeding dyes, generally reds and blues, are not necessarily a sign of poor-quality synthetics. Insufficiently rinsed naturally dyed wool may also bleed if water was in short supply for rinsing the wool after it was dyed. Always test dyes for fastness as later described. This test is not 100 percent reliable—the dyes may be fast in the test area but unreliable elsewhere—but it will pinpoint bad risks in the great majority of cases. If your rug fails the test, or if there are signs of past dye runs on the pile or staining on the fringes, you should have it cleaned by a commercial firm experienced in handling oriental rugs.

4. Any rug larger than about 3 × 6, regardless of the dye quality, will be difficult to wash properly in a bathtub. Unless it is quite thin, a rug folded in half or thirds will not only become unwieldy when wet but difficult to rinse entirely free of suds. If you have access to a clean, paved driveway and convenient hose outlet, a large rug can be washed with the aid of a squeegee mop to work the suds through pile and across the back and to squeeze out the suds while rinsing. However, unless you also have a satisfactory place to dry your rug and the assurance of two or three days of brisk, sunny, dry weather, you run the risk of mildew, or, in the case of a rug with a cotton foundation, dry rot.

5. Do not be tempted to use a carpet-washing machine of the type available for rent at hardware stores or to hire a firm that specializes in cleaning wall-to-wall carpeting. The treatment is too harsh for orientals, and it is very difficult to dry a large wool carpet *in situ*.

6. Finally, whether you wash your rugs at home or send them out to a professional firm, take the time to overcast and secure with stout button thread any damaged areas—holes, frayed ends and edges, and the like—so as to protect the pile knots from erosion during the cleaning process.

THE WASHING PROCESS

First, remove as much dirt as possible by turning the rug facedown and gently beating the back with the flat side of a broom to dislodge dirt that may have compacted around the pile knots. Follow by a thorough vacuuming of both sides, then test the dyes as follows:

1. Apply a few drops of the water and detergent solution you plan to use to each area of color. Allow it to sink in.

2. Blot firmly with a clean white cloth or paper towel.

3. If there is no evidence of color transfer, you may proceed with washing as described below.

Some authorities recommend routinely adding acetic acid in the form of white vinegar to the wash water to set the dyes, but this advice is sound only if one is sure the dyes are acid dyes. If one or more color is a basic dye, the acid may dissolve rather than set it; on the other hand, since the early basic dyes were for the most part fugitive, not enough color may remain from them to be worth worrying about.

Another factor affecting the stability of dyes during the washing process is the temperature of the water. Textile conservator James Rice, in his Textile Museum monograph on historic textile colorants, writes: "Some dyes are soluble at relatively low temperatures, while others will not dissolve until the water boils . . . this accounts for some cases of color change in cleaning when one of the components escapes before others in relatively cool water." This may also explain why rugs that have survived numerous washes may bleed during a succeeding one in which the water was warmer than before. Still another complication is the as yet undetermined role aging plays in the susceptibility of rug dyes to dissolution under varying and unpredictable conditions. In short, be prepared to remove your rug from the wash water immediately upon any sign of a color run, then thoroughly blot and dry on a flat surface to minimize the possibility of loosened dyestuffs staining adjacent color areas.

After testing, the next step is to fill your tub one-third to one-half with cool water and add 2–4 tablespoons of a mild hand-dishwashing detergent:

Although soap, a combination of fats and alkali, is probably more effective than detergents for removing dirt from heavily soiled textiles, it is not recommended for use on oriental rugs because dyed animal fibers can be harmed by alkaline solutions. Synthetic detergents are generally of two types: built and unbuilt. Built detergents contain varying amounts of alkaline chemicals to enhance cleaning action and sudsing, soften water, and brighten colors. Almost all powders and liquids formulated for laundry and dishwasher machine use are built detergents, as are those marketed for the hand-washing of woolen garments, and should not be used for your rugs.

Unbuilt detergents, among which are the hand-dishwashing liquids, may contain some brighteners but are near neutral in solution. The Textile Museum in Washington, DC recommends the neutral anionic detergent W. A. Orvus, a Proctor and Gamble product available through a conservators' supply house listed in the Resource Guide. An anionic detergent allows oil-attracting molecules to surround particles of dirt and pull them into the water. Even if you have only a couple of rugs to wash, it might be worth the trouble to send for some Orvus because it will also do a dandy job with what television advertising has dubbed "fine washables."

Orvus paste is quite viscous, so be sure it is well dispersed before immersing your rug. There is, by the way, no "correct" amount of detergent one should use. The quantity depends on the particular detergent, the softness of your water, and the amount of water needed to immerse the article you plan to wash. As a general rule, it is always better to use less and add more than to be overwhelmed with suds that will leave a dust-attracting film if not *thoroughly* rinsed out.

If your water is very hard, do not add to the wash or rinse water any softener containing the alkalies commonly known as sal soda, washing soda, or TSP (trisodium phosphate). Sodium hexametaphosphate, available under the brand name Calgon—do not mistake for it Calgon*ite*, a detergent formulated for dishwashing machines—is nearly alkali-neutral and may be used to discourage the scummy deposit characteristic of hardwater washing, but use it sparingly: excessive softening of the water may allow the detergent to remove the wool's natural lubricants along with the dirt. If your water is heavily chlorinated or commercially softened it may be alkaline enough to make it inadvisable for use with rugs colored with late-19th- and early-20th-century acid dyes. In these cases, your best bet is an experienced professional rug cleaning firm. You could, of course, collect rain water, but that is hardly practical for city dwellers and a bit much even for country folk, unless you happen to be a back-to-nature type with a rain barrel.

The washing process continues as follows:

1. Immerse the rug in the wash water and gently rub both the pile face and the back with a soft brush or sponge to loosen the dirt. If the water becomes dirty, drain and refill. Repeat the entire process until the water shows little discoloration.

Note: As your rug absorbs water it will become stiff and bumpy. Do not panic: it will resume its normal pliancy when dry.

2. Rinse the rug with cool water until the water running out of it is entirely free of suds. A hand-held shower spray will facilitate this process.

3. Sponge and drain as much water out of the rug as you can before removing it from the tub. Then, on a flat surface, blot or squeegee any remaining excess.

To dry, elevate the rug slightly. Do not hang or drape a rug unsupported between chairs or sawhorses. A wet rug, even a small wet rug, can be surprisingly heavy. The extra weight of the water can distort the foundation, creating wrinkles and sags; if the rug is old and brittle, the weight might cause it to tear. A clean window screen placed beneath it outdoors in a shady area with ample air circulation would be ideal; indoors, a fan, supplemented by a forced air heater in winter months, may be used. Drying may take one to three days depending on the size of the rug, its thickness, and the drying conditions.

Occasionally smooth the pile in its natural direction with a soft brush while drying.

Note: If the pile of your rug when dried seems a bit dull and lifeless, you may be tempted to treat it with lanolin, which is recommended by some authorities as a way of restoring a natural gloss to wool fibers. This can cause more problems than it might solve. Dead fibers are unable to absorb lanolin, and since it is fatty and sticky, even a thin and carefully dispersed solution will trap dust and dirt. It may also attract insects: a friend of mine who bought a lanolin-rich rug in Morocco found a large colony of plump maggots thriving on the oily wool when she unrolled it at home.

FURTHER CONSIDERATIONS CONCERNING HOME VERSUS PROFESSIONAL WASHING

At this point, some readers may be fretting about my admonition to leave the cleaning of silk rugs and rugs with unstable dyes to professionals, when this is precisely the kind of instruction they were hoping to find. Actually, the question in these cases is not whether you *could* do the cleaning but rather whether you *should*. Aged, dyed silk, in particular, is very tricky to work with, and all textile conservation bulletins approach the subject with the wariness of a high-strung horse on a wooden bridge.

The cleaning techniques professionals employ are not in themselves arcane, but the assessment of the problem presented by a given rug requires considerable hands-on experience. And if dry cleaning an entire rug is required, ask yourself whether you really want to undertake at home a process involving the use of flammable fluids on absorbent fibers, which will release while drying unpleasant and possibly dangerously noxious fumes over a period of several days.

What it comes down to, really, is the exercise of common sense. I have washed upward of 50 Baluch tribal weavings, and I now know just by looking at rugs of this type which ones may present cleaning problems. However, some years ago, when I acquired a rare, prison-made Indian pictorial dhurrie, I tested all of the dyes because they were unfamiliar to me. One of them, a dark brown, proved to be extremely unstable in water, so I entrusted the dhurrie to a textile conservation center, where it could be cleaned on a suction table—a device that pulls the cleaning solution and dissolved dirt out of the fabric, thereby depriving unstable dyes of a medium in which to spread.

Do not conclude from the foregoing that washing problems occur only with old rugs. According to the Rug Renovating Company in New York—founded in 1896 and the largest facility of its kind in the United States—new foreign, chemically washed oriental rugs, especially the lesser-quality Chinese, Indian, and Pakistani rugs, may suffer pile distortion and color changes when washed. Many cleaning companies refuse responsibility for such changes and warn customers accordingly. The most common complaint is the yellowing of ivory and white wools; but other colors sometimes become mottled, and when generally accepted methods of spot and stain removal are applied to these rugs, permanent alterations in color may result.

For More Information

Included in the Resource Guide in the back of this book are sources of washing compounds and the names and addresses of textile conservators and professional oriental rug cleaners (firms with equipment suitable for the washing and drying of large carpets) as well as individuals who will undertake the hand-washing of fine, small pieces. Consult oriental rug dealers in your area for additional recommendations.

SPOT AND STAIN REMOVAL

Should you ever contemplate buying a bargain-priced stained rug, think again: you must know what caused a stain before you can make an intelligent decision about how to remove it. Accepting stains of unknown composition, age, and previous treatment is asking for trouble and, in the end, no bargain.

If a guest spills wine on your cherished Kazak, spring into action. When it comes to removing soil from an oriental rug, immediate treatment is always your best and safest bet, for the longer soil or a stain remains on a rug the harder it will be to remove. If you can manage the cleanup with a lighthearted air, without making the offending guest feel like a boor, you may save yourself considerable postfestivity despair.

The removal of soil and its stains from a rug may require three separate procedures:

1. Immediate removal of the bulk of the soiling material by lifting or blotting it up before it has a chance to seep into the rug fibers.

2. Dissolving and washing out the residue with the aid of solvents.

3. Minimizing the effect of any residual stain by first rendering it colorless and then, if necessary, restoring the original color with dye or paint.

REMOVAL OF THE SOILING SUBSTANCE

The first step is the removal of as much of the soiling substance as possible by mechanical means. To accomplish this you will need:

1. A spatula or flexible dull-edged table knife.
2. A coarse-toothed comb.
3. Heavyweight paper towels or clean *cotton* rags, preferably white.
4. An absorbent powder like fuller's earth, available at drugstores.

Procedure

Thick, gooey stuff should be *lifted off* the rug with a spatula or similar flat-bladed tool. Jelly, paste, grease, ice cream, and animal feces and vomit fall into this category. Try not to press the offending matter into the pile. If the pile is long, what remains may be largely combed out with a coarse, blunt-toothed comb, but be careful not to loosen the pile knots.

Liquids should first be *blotted up*. This should be done gently with a patting and lifting motion to avoid either spreading the liquid outward or forcing it down into the pile. The object is the removal of as much liquid as possible before the fibers have a chance to absorb it; therefore, *do not rub*. Let the absorbency of the toweling do the work, and be generous with your use of it. Unless you are sure the cloth discards saved for household use are 100 percent cotton, use paper towels for blotting: cotton in combination with synthetics has very limited absorbency.

Another way to remove liquids is through the use of an absorbent material like fuller's earth. When applied to a wet spot, it draws up the soiling substance, which then can be brushed or vacuumed away when it has dried. Do not, however, use any of the commonly recommended substitutes on oriental rugs: talcum powder's fine particles tend to sift into rug fibers, making removal difficult, and cornstarch residues are an open invitation to hungry insects.

SPOT AND STAIN TREATMENTS

Once you have removed as much foreign matter as possible by mechanical means, a complete cleanup may require the use of solvents and bleaches. These can, if incorrectly chosen and applied, affect the dyes, the fibers, or both. Unfortunately, it is difficult to determine with complete accuracy the chemical composition of the dyes used in any given rug short of laboratory analysis. For centuries natural dyestuffs were the only source of color; but since the mid-19th century, synthetic dyes have been used extensively, often in combination with natural dyes. In addition, many late-19th- and 20th-century rugs have been chemically treated after manufacture to suit Western tastes, that is, bright colors bleached to fashionable pastels, with darker shades obligingly painted back in again if the result is *too* pale. Wool pile made limp and dull by all of this mucking about is then subjected to lusterizing processes that impart an attractive, if temporary, sheen to the pile. What this all adds up to in the context of spot and stain removal is that in the absence of certain knowledge of the dyes your rug contains and the chemical treatments it may have received, you should proceed very cautiously indeed.

To begin with, you should identify the fibers used in your rug because solvents and bleaches that are safe and effective on a vegetable fiber like cotton may prove harmful when applied to wool and silk. Rugs may be all wool, all silk, wool pile on a cotton foundation, wool and silk in various combinations, all wool with areas of white cotton in the pile, and so on. Sometimes, in cheap rugs, rayon or mercerized cotton is knotted into wool pile to impart a silklike luster. When in doubt as to what fiber or fibers you are dealing with, the following tests may be useful:

Wool burns slowly, with a sputter, and gives off the odor of burning hair. When the flame is removed, wool shortly ceases to burn. The residue is a brittle, blackish-brownish shiny coil that crushes easily into a powder. Wool yarns have a characteristic fuzziness, especially when new, which is clearly apparent under moderate magnification. The wool in antique rugs will be much less fuzzy as the result of decades of wear.

Silk also burns slowly, sizzling rather than sputtering, with the unpleasant odor of burning feathers. Its ash consists of small shiny beads, rather like wool but lighter and even more easily powdered. Pure silk pile and flat weaves have a distinctive cool, fluid feel or *handle*, an alive quality, peculiar to silk, that some people find vaguely repellent and others find decidedly sexy.

Cotton burns rapidly with a clear and even yellow flame. It produces smoke with the odor of burning leaves or paper and continues glowing long after the flame is extinguished. It leaves a fine, pale gray ash. Cotton fibers are smooth and obedient and have a softer, more pliant feel than most wools used in rugs, with the exception of camel and, rarely, mohair and cashmere. Cotton is found in the foundation structure of the finest antique Persian carpets and the majority of modern rugs.

Rayon melts when given the flame test and smells rather like burning rubber. Rayon made from cellulose acetate is the type most likely to have been used, so the cleaning instructions for cotton apply.

DISSOLVING SOIL RESIDUE AND REMOVING STAINS

The solvents and bleaching procedures recommended here are time-honored methods found in one form or another on every authoritative list. There are no space-age miracles. Some familiar methods may not be included if there is a possibility that harm to rug dyes or fibers may result; some common soils and stains may not be included if they require treatment best left to professionals.

Warning: Do not attempt to clean silk rugs with any home treatments. Old dyed silk fibers, long exposed to the light and dry heat conditions of the average home, are apt to become brittle and fragile. Prudence dictates avoiding placing a silk rug where it can be spilled upon. But if a spill occurs, immediate first aid of the sort previously discussed under mechanical soil removal should be applied so as to remove as much of the spillage as possible. Any residual staining should be referred to experienced professionals.

Soil Solvents

The terms "soil" and "stain" are not synonymous. Soil is a foreign substance that, although it may dirty a rug, may be lifted, brushed, blotted, or readily dissolved in water and washed out. Stains are caused by soil that has combined chemically with the fibers or dyes and therefore must be altered chemically to be removed or minimized. Obviously, it is very much to your advantage to avoid converting a simple spot of soil into a stubborn stain, either by delaying its removal or by hasty, ill-considered applications of familiar household solvents.

In the course of doing research for this chapter, I discovered that the removal of soil from textiles with water in combination with detergents is a surprisingly complex process, the understanding of which helped me realize why certain cleaning techniques are effective while others, seemingly as practical and sensible, are not.

Soil may be held by fibers in various ways: (1) mechanically, as when particles of foreign matter become lodged between the fibers, (2) by absorption, and (3) by chemical reaction, as in urine stains. By adding a detergent to water, the surface tension of the latter is lowered, making it "wetter." This wetting action of detergents allows water to permeate greasy surfaces more easily, and for this reason as much soil and spillage as possible should be removed *before* applying a detergent solution, which could have the undesirable effect of hastening the penetration of staining substances into the fibers. Dirt that has become embedded or absorbed into fibers can be washed out by a detergent solution, but stains created by a chemical reaction can only be neutralized or bleached.

Because of the practical impossibility of determining the composition of all the dyes in any given rug as well as any previous treatments it may have had, only a very limited number of solvents can be recommended safely. For all treatments you should have on hand the following:

Clean white cotton rags or paper towels.
Soft brush for smoothing pile.

Glycerine for pretreatment of some spots, available at drugstores.

Water, cool to lukewarm. Never use hot water as this may convert simple soil into a permanent stain or cause otherwise stable dyes to run. If your water supply is heavily chlorinated or commercially softened, keep a gallon of distilled water on hand to eliminate the possibility of an adverse alkaline reaction.

Neutral detergent. Soap and the majority of laundry detergents contain alkaline substances that may be harmful to some dyes, so it is important to use as near neutral a detergent as possible. Choose a type formulated for hand-dishwashing, as these contain few additives, or use the Orvus paste discussed in the preceding chapter if the size of your collection warrants the expense.

Trichloroethane and perchloroethane. This relatively safe, clear liquid oil solvent is widely available under the trade name Carbona. Carbona is also marketed in a spray can, which is more expensive and contains other, unknown, ingredients. Stick to the bottled liquid and use only in a space that can be well ventilated.

Note: There are some other commonly available solvents which should never be used on the absorbent pile of rugs because they are extremely flammable (naptha and benzine), have dangerously poisonous fumes (carbon tetrachloride), or may float away otherwise stable dyes (alcohol).

Procedure

Since rug dyes can be affected by solvents, always test them first in an inconspicuous place by rubbing the dyed wool with a white cloth moistened with the solvents, including water and detergent mixtures, that you plan to use. If an appreciable color transfer occurs, obtain the services of an experienced professional oriental rug cleaner; if only a trace of color is transferred, the advantage of prompt treatment may outweigh the possibility of a minor dye run. Only you can decide if the spotting or staining is serious enough to warrant some risk.

Pretreatment

If several hours have elapsed between the mechanical removal of the soil and treatment with a solvent, the residue may have hardened enough to make pretreatment with glycerine advisable, especially on rugs with dyes of dubious fastness. A little glycerine applied to the spot and left for about 30 minutes will soften and lubricate the soiling material so that it may be more easily dissolved by the appropriate solvent.

Treatment A—for nongreasy soil:

1. Test dyes as recommended above with a mixture of cool water and neutral detergent, ½ teaspoon to 1 pint.

2. If there is no transfer of color, wet the spot with the water and detergent mixture.

3. Blot dry.

4. Continue wetting and blotting with dry sections of the rag or paper towel until no trace of soil is picked up.

5. Sponge with plain, cool water and blot as much moisture from the pile as possible.

6. Finish by gently brushing the cleaned area of pile fibers in the same direction as the pile in the rest of the rug. If possible, elevate the damp area so that air circulation under it will speed the drying process.

Note: Do not be alarmed by the stiffness of the damp area. This will regain its normal flexibility when dry.

Treatment B—for greasy soil:

1. Test dyes first with Carbona as well as with detergent and cool water, mixed 1/2 teaspoon to 1 pint. Carbona will damage rubber products, so if the test allows you to proceed, either remove the rug from any rubber or rubberized pad or protect it with several layers of paper or cloth.

2. Apply Carbona generously and lift up both the solvent and the dissolved grease by blotting or wiping it *up*, not *in*, with a clean cotton rag or paper toweling. *Avoid inhaling the fumes and ventilate the room as much as possible.*

3. Once you have removed as much grease as possible with the oil solvent, sponge the cleaned area with detergent and lukewarm water, mixed 1/2 teaspoon to 1 pint.

4. Sponge with plain cool water and blot as dry as possible.

5. Finish by brushing the pile and elevating the cleaned area, if possible, to speed the drying time.

Treatment C—for combination soil

1. Test dyes as above with both Carbona and the detergent and water mixture.

2. Sponge area with detergent and lukewarm water, 1/2 teaspoon to 1 pint, to remove sugar and food coloring. Blot up the moisture before proceeding to next step.

3. Apply Carbona to dissolve grease or fats. Blot up—do not rub in—with a clean cloth or paper towel. Repeat if necessary.

4. Sponge area with detergent mixed with cool water, 1/2 teaspoon to 1 pint. Blot dry.

5. Sponge with plain cool water and blot as dry as possible.

6. Finish by brushing the pile and elevating the cleaned area to speed drying time.

TREATMENT OF SPECIFIC SOILING SUBSTANCES

Acids See stain treatments, next section.

Alkalies See stain treatments, next section.

Animal soil Feces and urine should be removed as quickly as possible by mechanical means followed by Treatment A (for nongreasy soil). If several hours elapse between the accident and your discovery of it, staining may occur. See stain treatments in next section.

Blood Treatment A. If stain persists, see next section.

Butter, oils Treatment B (for greasy soil).

Candle wax Use Carbona-saturated cotton swabs to loosen; lift off with knife blade.

Chocolate Treatment C (for combination soil).

Coffee, tea With cream or milk, Treatment C; without, Treatment A. If stain persists, see next section.

Fruit juices Treatment A. See next section if stain persists.

Furniture polish Treatment B. If the polish contains color, use fuller's earth to absorb and contain the polish before applying the solvent. If staining occurs, see next section.

Glues Remove as much as you can mechanically, then call your local dry cleaner for advice, as formulas and treatments vary widely.

Gravies Treatment C.

Hand lotions Treatment C.

Ice cream Treatment C.

Ink If spilled, blot up as much as you can as carefully as possible to avoid spreading the damage; then consult your local dry cleaner about how best to deal with the specific ink involved. Treatments suitable for one kind of ink may set another.

Iron rust The tips of metal furniture legs may leave rust rings, especially in the course of a humid summer. See stain treatments in next section.

Liquor Treatment A. For red wine and punches, see also stain treatments.

Mayonnaise Treatment C.

Medicines Blot up as much as you can as quickly as possible. Medicines are tricky because of the difficulty of determining the composition of the base and coloring matter. In general, try Treatment C on oily medicines, Treatment B on syrupy compounds. If staining occurs, see next section.

Mildew See Special Problems below.

Milk Treatment C.

Paint See Special Problems below.

Sauces Treatment C.

Skunk odor See Special Problems below.

Soft drinks Treatment A.

Road oil, tar Scrape up as much as possible. If the material has begun to harden, soften with glycerine as directed in Pretreatment, above, and follow with Treatment B.

Table syrups Treatment A.

Urine See "Animal soil" above.

Vomit Remove as much as possible by mechanical means. Follow with Treatment A; then, because vomit contains powerful acids, see stain treatments in next section.

SPECIAL PROBLEMS

Mildew

Mildew is a whitish-grayish parasitic mold that flourishes in damp, warm, poorly ventilated, and dimly lighted areas. Its growth is characterized by an unpleasant musty odor and spotty discoloration. If mildew has invaded your rugs or you suspect its presence in a rug bought at auction, it is essential that the spore growth be stopped before it weakens rug fibers.

First, thoroughly vacuum the rug both front and back. Do this outdoors if possible to avoid scattering the mold spores in the house. Promptly seal and dispose of the cleaner dust bag.

Next, thoroughly air the rug on a dry, breezy day to eliminate dampness and mustiness and inhibit the growth of any remaining spores. If the mildew invasion was significant, the rug should be sponged or washed or, if the dyes are not fast, dry cleaned. Of course, the best way to deal with mildew is to discourage its onset. See the section on rug storage for a fuller discussion of treatment and deterrents.

Paint

Paint spills present a truly frustrating problem: the safest course is to leave its removal to a professional cleaner; but by the time one can get the rug to the cleaner, the paint will have hardened sufficiently to make a difficult problem worse. With this in mind, the most practical approach is the prompt removal of as much of the spill as possible by mechanical means. Then test the dyes as earlier described: if the paint is of a type that can be cleaned from brushes with water, use Treatment A. If it is an oil-based paint, sponge with turpentine and follow with Treatment B. If the paint has begun to set, pretreatment with glycerine may facilitate its further removal with a solvent; but don't use paint thinners or removers containing alcohol, as this may lift the dyes. If an unsightly residue remains, call your dry cleaner for advice. He will need to know what kind of paint was spilled and how you have treated it.

Skunk odor

This is not a common problem, but when it occurs it can create more alarms and excursions than a Laurel and Hardy comedy. The tried-and-true remedy for removing skunk odor from its unhappy canine recipient is a dousing of tomato juice. I've tried it and it truly works, but its use on rugs a frantic dog has rolled on may cause a stain that lingers longer than the odor of skunk. The safest course is to sponge sparingly with Carbona only where necessary, then blot dry. Follow with a sponging with plain cool water and blot as dry as possible. If the next day is dry and sunny—skunk spraying invariably happens at night—the rug would benefit from a good airing, but be prepared for the memory to haunt you on humid days for several weeks thereafter.

STAIN REMOVAL

Sometimes it just isn't possible to attend to soiling and spills immediately. Sometimes the problem may be undetected for hours or days, especially if the culprit was an unreliable pet or a child reluctant to confess. In short, stains can occur in even the most competently managed households, but with proper treatment they can often be reversed or at least minimized.

Stains may result from a deposit of color from a spill (blood, red wine, fruit juices, medicines, furniture polish, etc.) or from a chemical reaction left either untreated or improperly treated (iron rust, urine, vomit). A color-deposit stain will require bleaching; chemical stains must first be neutralized, then bleached if staining persists. But before you whip out your trusty bottle of Clorox, please bear in mind that many commonly available household cleaning agents can seriously damage and discolor rug fibers and dyes. Accordingly, never use any of the following on oriental rugs:

Chlorine bleaches (sodium hypochlorites).
Washing sodas, including sodium carbonate.
Trisodium phosphate, or TSP, a principal ingredient in many heavy-duty household cleansers.
Laundry liquids or powders containing alkaline builders.

Unfortunately, despite advertisements to the contrary, there is no such thing as a universal stain remover. Stains that persist after all of the soiling substance has been removed are the result of a chemical reaction. The nature of that reaction, acid or alkaline, would in ordinary circumstances determine what should be applied to neutralize it, but there may be other factors to consider.

Textiles stained with an acidic substance like vomit or fresh urine ordinarily require the application of a neutralizing alkaline solution; but if the textile dyes are acid, an alkaline solution may cause them to bleed. The same holds true for basic-dyed textiles stained with alkali: an acid solution applied to neutralize the stain may dissolve the dyes. For our purposes, then, one should choose the mildest agent in the most dilute form capable of doing the job.

Substances with acid or alkaline properties exhibit a wide range of activity: the typical mineral acid, such as sulfuric or hydrochloric, is violently reactive with many substances, including cotton, and strong alkalies like lye, (i.e., sodium hydroxide) can severely damage wool and silk fibers. But no matter how concentrated a solution of a mild alkali like sodium bicarbonate (baking soda) may be, it will never attain the degree of caustic activity of a dilute solution of lye; similarly, acetic acid is weakly active in comparison to hydrochloric acid.

Because the chemical makeup of the dyes in your stained rug may be unknown, you should initially apply the mildest available neutralizer in the hope that the color damaged by the stain can be restored without provoking the side effect of an undesirable color change in adjacent areas. If a mild solution of the neutralizer you have chosen is ineffective, you will have to decide whether the need to remove the stain outweighs any negative effect a stronger solution might have on unstained portions of the rug. If you decide that it does, test the stronger solution in an inconspicuous area colored with the same dyes as the stained section.

With the foregoing in mind, the following can be used with caution and should be included among your cleaning supplies:

Hydrogen peroxide in a 3 percent solution available at drugstores. It should be stored in a dark, cool place to maintain effective strength.
Sodium hydrosulfite, a color remover packaged as a powder and available under the Rit and Tintex labels.
Ammonia, household strength, for neutralizing acids.
White vinegar (acetic acid) for neutralizing alkalies.

Some useful accessories are:

White cotton rags or paper toweling.
2 or 3 watercolor brushes of varying fineness.
Medicine dropper.
Uncolored wooden toothpicks or similar narrow, blunt-ended tool.
Discarded toothbrushes.
Small-headed stiff brush of the type used to apply shoe polish.
Metal cuticle pusher, the type with blunt edge on one end and arrow-shaped point on the other.

Procedure

The usual admonition about testing dyes before applying any treatments applies; although in the case of stains complicated by dye runs, the dyes are obviously not entirely fast or they wouldn't have run in the first place. If the bleeding is extensive and pervasive, there is little or nothing you can do to correct it with home remedies. Never buy a rug in this condition, and if it happens to one you already own, consult an experienced oriental rug cleaner. If, however, the dye run is noticeable only in isolated areas of white pile, it may yield to Treatment 2 described below.

Treatment 1—hydrogen peroxide bleach. Apply peroxide directly to the stain with a medicine dropper. Work the liquid into the pile with a watercolor brush, being careful to stay within the stained area. Allow the peroxide to remain for several hours, but check frequently to be sure the rug dyes are not being adversely affected. After treatment, sponge the area well with plain cool water and blot dry.

Treatment 2—sodium hydrosulfite color remover. This should be used with caution—only if the peroxide treatment is ineffective and only on white or ivory areas of pile. Moisten the stain with warm—not hot—water, using a dropper to confine the moisture to the stained area. Apply the sodium hydrosulfite powder directly and carefully to the moistened area—the blunt, shovel-like end of the cuticle pusher is ideal for this purpose—and work it into the pile with a plain wooden toothpick or similar tool. This treatment works quite fast if it is going to work at all, so after about 10 minutes sponge the area carefully and thoroughly with cool water. Blot dry.

Treatment 3—for acid stains. Use household ammonia diluted ½ strength with plain cool water. Moisten the stain with cool water, then, after first testing its action on the dyes in an inconspicuous spot, apply the dilute ammonia with a dropper and tamp with a brush to work it into the affected fibers. The tamping action can be compared to driving a thumbtack with a light hammer. Ammonia is alkaline, so do not allow it to remain on wool for more than about 15 minutes. Sponge the area with plain cool water, then carefully apply a solution of half white vinegar and half cool water to neutralize the ammonia and restore any color that may have been affected by it. Finish with a thorough sponging with plain cool water. Blot dry.

Treatment 4—for alkaline stains. Use white vinegar diluted ½ strength with plain cool water. Moisten the stain with water, then, after testing its action on the dyes in an inconspicuous spot, apply the dilute vinegar with a dropper. Tamp gently with a brush to neutralize the alkaline stain and restore color affected by it. If the vinegar appears to affect the dye colors, sponge the area with cool water to which a few drops of ammonia

have been added. Finish with a thorough sponging with plain cool water.
Blot dry.

TREATMENT OF SPECIFIC STAINS

Animal Soil

Feces Once you have removed as much as possible as directed under
"Removal of the Soiling Substance," apply Treatment 4. If a stain
persists, follow with Treatment 1.

Urine Fresh urine stains are acid, but as they age, they become alkaline.
On a fresh deposit, use Treatment 3 and apply Treatment 1 if some
staining persists. If yellowing of white pile is still noticeable, try Treatment 2.

If Treatment 3 is ineffective because of the age of the deposit, try
Treatment 4 followed by Treatment 1, and if necessary Treatment 2,
to minimize yellowing.

Urine stains on indigo blues are very difficult to treat successfully
for complicated reasons involving the chemical processes of dyeing
with indigo. One textile conservation authority advises that if left alone
and given enough time, the color may return to the original hue. This
does not mean you can omit sponging the area with cool water after
blotting up as much urine as possible; it means that further treatment
may be ineffective. This is a case where painting to disguise an unsightly stain is a reasonable option.

If you catch a puppy in the act, blotting followed by an application
of soda water, which combines a mildly alkaline substance with water
in a single treatment, may be sufficient to counteract the fresh, relatively weak acid content. Unfortunately, the residual odor, even when
too faint to be detected by humans, may continue to attract the offending pet, and anything strong enough to kill it presents risks. Try
masking the odor with a carpet freshening powder, as animals tend to
shun chemical fragrances.

Blood Treatment 3, followed if necessary by Treatment 1.

Coffee, tea Treatment 1. If stain persists on white or ivory pile, try
Treatment 2.

Fruit juice Pretreat with glycerine to loosen the staining material and
follow with Treatment 4. If necessary, apply Treatment 1 or, on white
or ivory pile only, Treatment 2.

Polishes If a color stain remains on white or ivory areas after the spot
removal treatment detailed in the preceding section, try Treatment 2.
If the polish color has stained a dyed area, anything that will remove
the polish dye will also affect the rug dyes. If the spot is not large, it
could be bleached and painted; if extensive, the stained wool could be
replaced, a job for a professional.

Iron rust First try applying a paste of table salt and white vinegar. Work the paste into the stain. After 30 minutes, thoroughly sponge it out with plain cool water. Repeat if necessary. If rust stains persist on white or ivory pile, try Treatment 2.

Vomit Vomit contains strong acids that should be neutralized as quickly as possible with Treatment 3. If the acids have begun to affect the dyes, this treatment may restore them, but if the process is well advanced, the area will probably have to be painted.

Wine, red Pretreat with glycerine as described in the preceding section on spot removal, then apply Treatment 4. If staining persists, try Treatment 1.

It should be noted that the treatment of any spot or stain, whether successful or not, may present you with a new problem: the creation of a small area of pile noticeably cleaner than the rest. You can, of course, wash the entire rug, but if the rug is relatively clean, you can drab the area by judiciously applying ashes or charcoal from a burned match rather than subject the rug to the stress of a largely unnecessary washing.

For More Information

If you are unable to remove a stain using the methods suggested here, consult an experienced oriental rug cleaning establishment recommended by a local rug dealer or included in the Resource Guide in the back of this book. For valuable rugs, an alternative is a textile conservation service, names of which will also be found in the Resource Guide. In either case, describe the situation and the methods you have employed and inquire what the approximate cost might be for whatever treatment is suggested. Do not expect a firm estimate until the rug can be seen and evaluated.

UNDERLAYMENTS

In the years before World War II, the sort of people who accumulated oriental rugs were likely to be wealthy enough to maintain servant-staffed houses with many amply dimensioned rooms where rugs could be seen and enjoyed but rarely walked upon. In those well-ordered households, the children lived in the nursery, the dogs in a kennel, and both were suffered to join the family only for brief, well-mannered visits. Given such hot-house conditions, it was easy to maintain a fine, lustrous-piled rug in mint condition for fifty or more years.

Today wear caused by constant foot traffic and stains deposited by imperfectly trained pets is taking a drastic toll of old rugs, particularly the little tribal pieces too often used as door mats or to line old Bowser's basket. If you buy or inherit a small antique rug in good condition but have no sheltered floor space, consider displaying it on a wall, as described in the next chapter. If it is a fine old silk piece, you really have no reasonable alternative; unless treated as wall hangings they will wear rapidly and ruinously. But even a sturdy new or used rug bought to furnish your floors will probably require a protective pad beneath it, the type depending on the size and weight of the rug and the use to which it will be put.

A large rug bought for a living room, bedroom, or dining room should be equipped with a dense, firm pad to cushion the weight of furniture standing on it. This is particularly necessary for a dining room carpet subject to the repeated sliding of chairs and feet, and for that reason it will also benefit from a half-yearly reversal of its position to distribute the wear.

A light scatter rug or a large but thin carpet on a polished floor adds up to a potential accident in any room of the house. To protect your family and guests from needless injury you must provide a nonskid underlayment. Do not attempt to anchor lightweight rugs by tacking them directly to the floor, by applying latex, or by gluing nonskid strips to their backs.

Although oriental runners are not the best choice for stair coverings, they are undeniably attractive when used to accent a graceful stairway. It is essential, however, that the rug chosen for this purpose be free from holes, splits, and badly worn or weakened areas that could be caught and torn by high heels. Stair rugs may be fitted over flat carpeting or provided with a thin underlayment, but in either case they should be secured with wooden or metal stair rods (see Resource Guide), which will allow the rug to give a bit with the push and pull of stairway traffic. This movement is necessary: if the rug is tacked directly to the treads or sewn to an underlayment, it will tend to tear under stress rather than adjust to it. To further extend its years of safe use, a stair rug should be shifted slightly up or down once or twice a year to distribute wear.

A pad protects the foundation of a rug from both the abrasive action of grit trapped between it and the floor and the wear caused by repeated rubbing against uneven flooring. This latter problem can be a serious one in antique houses with wide handcrafted floor boards and in rooms and hallways surfaced with stone or tile. A pad will also cushion a rug against hard-soled and high-heeled shoes, and although it cannot eliminate the dents caused by the feet of heavy furniture, it can at least buffer the mortar and pestle effect of a vulnerable textile trapped between furniture and an unyielding floor.

TYPES OF RUG UNDERLAYMENTS

There are two schools of thought about the proper kind of rug cushion. Traditionalists, particularly old line rug dealers, are loyal to the hair and jute pad, the one that looks like a coarse and hairy brown felt. Newer versions have a rubberized bottom to guard against slippage. If cost is a significant consideration, jute is your best bet. However, jute pads are heavy and awkward to move; they have a tendency to shed clingy bits of hairy stuff; and if you intend to store your rugs, they make very bulky, mildew-prone rolls that will absorb moisture like a thirsty camel.

The preferred pad is a densely compacted rubber or synthetic cushion, ⅛ inch to ¼ inch thick, available either in rug-size widths or narrow strips that can be joined by duct tape to make up the required width. Although expensive compared to jute, these paddings provide a firm, secure cushion that is also clean, lightweight, and durable. The synthetic variety is also mildew-resistant, an important consideration if you intend taking your rugs up in summer. Pads of this type may be obtained from dealers who specialize in oriental and other fine area rugs. Some dealers provide free ¹⁄₁₆-inch flexible sheeting with the purchase of a rug—the type I have seen most often is a rather nasty shade of mint green. But although these sheetings are reasonably good for anchoring a rug, they provide almost no cushioning.

There are other kinds of padding materials stocked by retailers of bulk carpeting that should be avoided unless there is no alternative easily available to you. These include bubble padding and expanded plastic foam padding.

Bubble padding is a thin layer of rubber or comparable synthetic material pressed into large puffy bubbles and backed with a mesh netting. The rubber layer is so thin it dries out in a comparatively short time, and the brittle edges then break down into a fine powder. Another drawback is that lightweight rugs tend to "copy" the bubble pattern, resulting in a curious effect rather like seersucker on a grand scale.

Expanded plastic foam padding is very lightweight and is manufactured in a variety of thicknesses for use under wall-to-wall carpet installations. Although mildew- and rot-resistant, it is too compressible to provide firm cushioning for oriental rugs, and because of its extreme lightness, it tends to shift under foot. A cosmetic objection is that since it is made only in very pale colors, the effect created by rugs sliding on this padding is that of a white petticoat dipping unevenly below the hemline of an otherwise smartly turned-out woman.

Carpeted rooms present the owners of oriental rugs with a unique difficulty. Until recently, scatter and area-size could be used satisfactorily only on very low-loop or flat-faced carpeting, because the tufts in cut-pile types will inch a small rug across its surface just like the legs of an upside-down caterpillar. I once purchased for my bedroom a luxuriously thick, cut-pile carpet in a soft camel-hair color as a background for a couple of antique Baluch prayer rugs. They looked wonderful when I first put them down, but within an hour the little rugs had scooted noticeably out of place, and by the end of the day they were creeping under the bed like a couple of naughty puppies anticipating a scolding. Now, thanks to products developed specifically to counteract this problem, orientals may be used in combination with wall-to-wall carpeting.

The following underlayment materials were on the market as of early 1991. Call the manufacturer or wholesaler for a retail supplier in your area. If the underlayment of choice is no longer available, or if your choices are very limited, I want to emphasize that any type is better than none. Its dimensions should be the same as the rug, minus 1 inch all the way around. Rug dimensions, by the way, ordinarily exclude the end finishes, with the exception of those with significant flat-woven skirts, like most old Turkoman and Baluch pieces, which should be protected to within 1 inch of the edge.

Underlayments for use between rugs and hard-surfaced floors:

Rug Anchor II: Carpet Cushion Corporation, 261 E. Lancaster Avenue, Wynnewood, PA 19096; (215) 649-1600

Rubber sheeting available in four thicknesses ($\frac{1}{16}''$, $\frac{3}{32}''$, $\frac{1}{8}''$, and $\frac{1}{4}''$) to suit every rug need. Excellent quality; neutral color.

Dura Hold: No-Muv Corporation, Inc., 5801 Phillips Highway, Jacksonville, FL 32216; (904) 739-3636

Synthetic fiber compound-bonded to waffle-patterned rubber backing, at $\frac{1}{4}$ inch thick enough to provide good padding. Moisture- and mildew-resistant; lightweight yet sturdy; dark neutral color.

Underlayments designed to prevent the movement of rugs placed on carpeting:

Kwik-Stik: American Non-Slip Products, Inc. 2924-A Amwiler Road, Doraville, GA 30360; (404) 449-3015

This is a thin, lightweight, and odorless synthetic material treated with a specially formulated water-soluble adhesive on both sides.

Rug-To-Rug: Rug-Hold, 350 Fifth Avenue, Suite 6608, New York, NY 10001; (212) 239-0135

A Swiss product similar to that described above.

Go-Between: Jade Industries, Inc., 261 Lancaster Avenue, Wynnewood, PA 19096; (215) 649-1600

A dense, rigid product whose toe-stubbing thickness ($\frac{1}{2}''$) makes its use under small rugs unwise. For larger rugs, however, it would be quite effective in controlling movement on carpets.

No-Muv: No-Muv Corporation, Inc., 5801 Phillips Highway, Jacksonville, FL 32216; (904) 739-3636

This is another dense, thick, and rigid product, to which the same reservations as noted above apply.

DISPLAYING YOUR COLLECTION

When all of your floors have been splendidly furnished and each chair and couch has accumulated its quota of artfully draped tribal trappings, the next step is the creation of a display area where your finest pieces can be hung properly lighted and viewed to their best advantage. Few of us have space enough to display more than one or two wall-hung rugs at a time, but that is all to the good: frequent changes of rug displays will discourage dust from settling and insects from setting up housekeeping.

Another benefit conferred by a vertical display area is that it allows one to buy with a clear conscience—and, one hopes, for less money— fine antique rugs too fragile to use as floor coverings. This can include fragments with exceptional color and design like the mid-19th-century 3 × 15-foot Turkish kilim panel I found in a rural New England antique shop. One end of this handsome piece had been damaged beyond repair, but it was long enough to allow me to cut off the top 6 feet for a dramatic wall-mounted display, turn the next 2 feet into a striking pillow, and bestow the remaining undamaged portion upon a grateful textile collector to whom I owed a favor. Most fruitful $50 I ever spent.

Most houses are unsuited to the hanging of very large rugs. Not only are the mechanical problems daunting, but once one has gone to the considerable effort of hanging a large carpet, it is all too easy to postpone taking it down again, to the eventual detriment of the rug. Wool fibers are subject to stretching if the moisture content of the wool or the atmospheric humidity is high, and under these conditions a large rug whose weight is unsupported except at the top can stretch considerably over time. If the fiber extension is moderate, it may eventually retract to its original dimension once taken down, but too great a percentage of stretch may distort a rug beyond recovery.

Since rug warps are stronger than the wefts, pieces chosen to hang for display, except for small mats and big faces, should always be suspended vertically. If the rug must be hung sideways because of the design or the limitations of the wall space available for this purpose, it would be prudent to limit the display period, especially if the rug is an old one with fibers less able to respond well to stress than a new and supple rug.

Few handmade rugs are dimensionally true—nomadic tribal pieces are often noticeably skewed—and it is harder to make them hang flat than to lie flat. A rug suspended with rings or clamps attached to wall hooks often presents a visually untidy effect unless one is willing to tinker at tedious length with the placement of the hooks. Even if a successful arrangement of hooks is finally achieved for one rug, it is unlikely to suit another's peculiarities, and suspension for long periods from rings or clamps subjects the warps to unequal stress that in time can cause waves or scallops to form between the suspension points.

THE VELCRO DISPLAY SYSTEM

The most satisfactory method for displaying rugs employs Velcro, a patented fastening material that consists of two strips of woven nylon: one is faced with tiny hooks and the other with fluffy fibers with which the hooks interlock in much the same fashion as a burdock fastens itself to the tails of hapless horses. Velcro is available at almost any notions counter in black, white, and beige—additional colors may be found at specialized stores—and in four widths: ⅝ inch, ¾ inch, 1 inch, and, less commonly, 2 inches. The expense is not insignificant considering that once you have mounted a length of the hooked Velcro strip on the wall, half the cost of subsequent purchases is wasted, except in a special circumstance I will discuss later. Nevertheless, the ease of hanging and adjusting rugs using this method far outweighs the cost of materials.

1. Determine how high the wall-mounted Velcro strip must be to accommodate your longest rug, then see if your shortest rug can be hung from the same point without having to crane your neck to view it properly. If you have any leeway, try to achieve a happy medium; if not, you may choose to attach mounting strips at two or more heights.

2. Cut a wooden batten to fit the width of the wall space selected. If you live in a house with conventional wood framing, secure it if possible into the framing studs, which are normally placed 16 inches apart; if your house or apartment is of brick or concrete construction, consult your local hardware store or the building superintendent about the most practical way to attach battens to the wall in question.

3. Paint or stain the battens the same color as the wall to reduce visual clutter.

4. Closely staple or tack to the mounted batten a hooked Velcro strip long enough to receive the widest rug you plan to display.

5. Attach the fluffy-faced Velcro strip along its top and bottom edges directly onto the back side of the top edge of the rug with moderately long stitches of stout button thread of a blending shade; or sew it first onto a cotton twill tape, which is then sewn to the rug. The latter extra step might be prudent if your rug is old and fragile or if you plan to hang a rug for long periods of time. If the weave is tight, you will need

a strong, sharp needle, a thimble and possibly a small pliers with which to pull the needle through.

Note: To determine the top of a rug with an allover pattern, run your hand over the pile. The smooth feel runs towards the bottom of the rug, where the weaver began; the rough feel runs toward top, where the Velcro should be attached.

6. Attach the rug to the wall mount by firmly pressing the tapes together. If the rug hangs unevenly, and it probably will initially, the strips can be pulled apart here and there to make the necessary adjustments. For maximum positioning flexibility, use the 2-inch wide Velcro tape on the wall mount.

DISPLAYING FRAGMENTS, MATS, AND TRIBAL TRAPPINGS

Fragments of rugs suspended without a backing look rather forlorn; the same piece mounted on a neatly covered panel achieves instant respectability. Permanently mounted fragments of museum quality require, and deserve, fabric-covered stretchers and frames made to order for a particular piece. For display in the home, a fabric-covered, unframed panel of Homasote or plywood is an easy and inexpensive alternative more appropriate for the purpose than a frame, which is a bit fussy for a coarsely woven textile like a rug.

Homasote is a type of building panel suitable for both interior and exterior applications. It is made of 100 percent recycled processed paper and is available at very reasonable cost in $4' \times 8' \times \frac{1}{2}''$ panels, known as 440 board, at building supply outlets. Its advantage over plywood is that $\frac{1}{2}$-inch plywood is appreciably heavier and 20 percent higher in cost than Homasote, and thinner panels tend to torque and look flimsy when wall-mounted. Homasote's disadvantage is that since it is a relatively soft material, ordinary staples used to attach the fabric covering may pull out. Be sure you have a staple gun capable of driving staples with legs at least $\frac{5}{16}$ inch long. If you can find the type of staple designed to mount ceiling panels—with slightly offset legs and superior holding power—so much the better.

Although Homasote is easily sawed, a full-sized panel is a bit awkward to transport. Determine what size you need beforehand and ask to have it cut to order at what is usually a modest additional cost.

Your next step is to choose a fabric covering for the cut panel. Most museums and galleries use linen or monk's cloth, but I chose a matte nylon upholstery fabric with a surface texture just fuzzy enough to connect with the otherwise discarded lengths of hooked Velcro tape, which I sewed to the tops of pieces selected for panel display. To my pleased surprise, the kilim fragment mentioned earlier clung to the textured nylon

not only along its top edge where the hooked tape had been sewn—which
I had expected—but throughout its length, almost as if glued. The attachment of heavier-pile pieces, however, usually has to be augmented
with T-shaped upholstery pins unobtrusively added along the top and at
the bottom corners. To be sure of achieving a similar result, take a test
strip of the hooked Velcro with you when shopping for your panel covering.

If you choose a neutral color for your panel cover, bear in mind that
the white and ivory portions of old rugs are usually quite a bit darker
than one realizes: placed against too pale a hue they will look drab and
dirty instead of pleasingly antique. If you doubt the accuracy of your
visual memory, don't haul your rugs around with you: instead, match
the wool colors to the sample paint strips available in a tremendous range
of colors at all paint stores. Fabric remnants are usually much less expensive than lengths cut to order from a bolt, but be sure the piece you
select is wide enough and long enough to overlap the panel on all sides
by about 3 inches.

You will need a second pair of hands to help you cover the panel with
the fabric you have chosen. One person cannot pull the fabric sufficiently
taut and simultaneously staple it into place. If the material has substantial
body or texture, it may be difficult to achieve neat corners without a bit
of snipping and sewing, but don't do any cutting until you have studied
the situation carefully. One mistake may force you to discard the entire
piece.

After the panel has been covered, it should be mounted to the wall by
nailing or screwing through the fabric and panel and into the studding
with large-headed fasteners spaced about 1 foot apart in an area that will
be concealed by the smallest of the pieces you plan to display. If the
mounting is to be temporary, investigate fixtures used to hang mirrors
of comparable size and weight. The object is to create a smoothly covered matte surface held tight to the wall yet projecting sufficiently to
convey the impression of a vertical stage set apart from it. The effect is
a subtle one, but it will lend the pieces you display an air of specialness.

LININGS

If you plan to hang a rug for appreciable lengths of time, it is advisable
to shield the back from dust and insect damage. Materials chosen for
lining should be lighter in weight than the rug and preshrunk to eliminate
any possibility of shrinkage should it become damp due to high humidity,
as this would create uneven tensions.

Lining a rug can be a maddening process if the lining material is in
the least slithery. A well-washed old bed sheet is an ideal choice for

texture, weight, stability, and, for most wall-hung pieces, size. If you don't have one, any thrift shop should be able to oblige you.

Hem on all sides a lining piece just large enough to cover the entire rug minus the edges and ends. Tack the lining with linen or button thread at the top, just below the Velcro fastening strip, and all along the sides with moderately large, loose stitches, leaving the bottom end unfastened. Then hang the rug for a few days to see if any signs of uneven tension develop, such as puckering or pull. Once you have made any necessary adjustments, which may include tacking the lining here and there to forestall sagging, the bottom may be stitched into place.

DISPLAYING FRAGILE OR DAMAGED RUGS

A very worn or damaged antique rug may require a little something extra in the way of support to prevent the rug's own weight from pulling weakened warp threads to the point of separation. The easiest and least expensive way to accomplish this is to tack strips of the fuzzy-sided Velcro across the back of the rug at 1- to 2-foot intervals and then attach to the wall battens stapled with the hooked mating strips at the corresponding wall heights.

WALL RACKS FOR VISIBLE RUG STORAGE

Dedicated collectors may choose to combine the functions of storage and display by devoting an entire wall to this purpose. At the Textile Museum in Washington, DC, the storage rug racks consist of wooden uprights placed along the walls at 4-foot intervals, although tighter spacing may be indicated if your collection consists largely of small pieces. From the uprights, arms 3 feet long extend horizontally at 1-foot intervals, but in a home situation you may have neither the space nor the need for arms that long. The upright members are mounted so that the top rests against the wall and the bottom is 1 inch away from it, which tilts the arms just enough to keep the rolled rugs placed across them from sliding off. With this system, a large rug may extend across several arms; a small rug, only two. And unlike rugs piled on shelves, it is seldom necessary to move more than one or two to get at the piece you have chosen to display.

Museums use metal or acid-free tubes to roll rugs on, but a satisfactory substitute for home use are the cardboard tubes used for shipping and displaying upholstery and drapery fabrics. Ask a local fabric retailer to save discards for you. Whether or not you use tubes, rugs should be rolled in the direction of the pile and with the pile side in.

LIGHTING

Lighting wall-hung rugs with two to four instruments will enhance the natural luster of the pile and emphasize the charm and artistry of the design. In fact, this enhancement effect is so pronounced, one should never bid on rugs on impulse during an auction that has not been previewed: flaws, even quite pronounced ones, are remarkably minimized by theatrical lighting.

You can either have elegantly designed track lighting professionally installed or achieve satisfactory results at much less cost with mass-produced do-it-yourself track lights requiring only a screwdriver and a standard wall outlet. The only drawback to the latter is that unless your home is suited to the high-tech look of exposed electrical cords, it may take a bit of ingenuity to conceal or minimize their clutter.

Because of justifiable concern about the long-term effect of light upon textiles of unusual historic and aesthetic interest, conservators severely restrict both the wattage and type of lighting used for museum displays. Collectors with qualms about the illumination of home displays might consider installing dimmers and reserving the highest levels of light for special occasions.

RUG STORAGE

The proper storage of oriental rugs is not easy to manage in the average domestic environment. Hot dry attics and cool dry cellars can cause problems, and closets are apt to be too small or already overcrowded. That leaves only the storage facilities offered by your local dry cleaner or a second look at your home to see if satisfactory storage space can be found or created. But first, let's back up a bit and determine whether or not you will want to store your rugs at all.

Even if your interest in rugs begins and ends with the sensible desire to furnish your home with a few attractive pieces, there are two practical reasons for deciding to store your rugs on a seasonal basis. The first is that the rugs that look so warm and glowing in winter may make your home seem stuffy and overfurnished in summer. The second reason is threefold and has as much to do with your rugs' well-being as your own: Rugs will last longer if exposed to family traffic only part of each year; the necessity for a periodic inspection for damage and a thorough cleaning becomes virtually automatic when rugs are taken up for summer storage; then, when they are put down again in the fall, you will fall in love with them all over again.

FINDING SPACE

Most houses have closets with an inconveniently high top shelf relegated to the domestic detritus known as it-may-come-in-handy-someday. This includes games bought for children who are now away at college, hats too dowdy even for funerals, and boxes of papers relating to community projects long since accomplished. Clean out those shelves, buy a sturdy, well-balanced step-stool, and alert the family that henceforth this area is for rug storage only. Since collectors are apt to accumulate smallish pieces—easier to handle and display—one or two such areas, approximately 1 × 2 × 6 feet will hold a respectable number of rolled scatters and tribal trappings. Under-bed storage is suitable for larger rugs, provided that the rugs are well wrapped and mothproofed. Another possibility is to make rug storage part of the decor by building museum-style racks against the wall of a study or bedroom. If combined with a lighted display panel, the effect can be quite handsome.

ROLLING AND WRAPPING FOR STORAGE

Rugs to be stored over a season should first be vacuumed front and back for any insect-attracting spills: food spills principally, but animal urine residues are also very appealing to moths. These should be dealt with according to the instructions in the section on spot and stain removal before the rugs are rolled for storage.

1. Make note of how your rugs are placed on the floor so that you may reverse their position when you put them down again. This will distribute the wear more evenly over the years.

2. Roll the rugs with the pile inward and in the direction of the pile to prevent crushing and crimping of the fibers. This is particularly important in the case of large, thick rugs. To determine the pile direction, run your hand over the surface: the smooth feel is with the pile; the rough feel is against it.

3. Do not fold a rug in half or thirds before rolling, as this will create unsightly creases that will be difficult to remove and, if the rug is old and dry, may crack the foundation.

Dealers often fold and roll large rugs into squat cylinders, but this is done to make them easily accessible for frequent display to customers. Museums customarily store rugs by rolling them on tubes, which are then placed on racks or across long pegs projecting, slightly angled, from the wall. This system is useful for large and valuable collections as it prevents the rugs from compressing each other, as would be the case if they were stacked for long periods without support.

Museum standards for textile conversation include the use of acid-free papers, boxes, and tubes, but unless your collection includes fragments of classic rugs, this would be gilding the lily in the context of temporary home storage.

You should, however, assiduously avoid using plastic to wrap your rugs because most plastics seal in moisture, which in turn promotes the growth of mildew, especially in hot, dark, airless storage areas. Use instead large sheets of heavy brown wrapping paper. Most hardware and variety stores stock paper of this sort, and if handled with reasonable care, it may be used over and over again. After sprinkling or spraying with one of the insect repellents discussed later, the rug should be rolled, wrapped, and securely sealed with one of the many excellent tapes now available for home use.

STORAGE PROBLEMS

Rugs stored for as long as a season, especially summer, should be protected against the following: (1) insect damage, (2) rodents, (3) dry rot, (4) mildew, (5) excessively dry heat.

Insects

Clothes moths. The two most common clothes moths, the webbing moth *(Tineola bisselliella)* and the casemaking moth *(Tinea pellionella)* look very much alike. The adult moths are yellowish or buff in color and have a wingspan of about ½ inch. They are not strong flyers and are not attracted to bright light; instead, they may be seen flitting erratically in dim corners. Female moths usually lay from 200 to 300 tiny pearly eggs upon a material the larvae can feed on, which includes all animal products and, as mentioned earlier, urine residues. The egg-hatching period is about four to eight days in summer, but may take longer in cooler weather.

The webbing moth spins a silky coverlet, usually concealed in a fold or crevice, under which the white-bodied, dark-headed larvae feed and then pupate at the conclusion of the feeding period. Its life cycle is variable, extending from three months to a year.

The casemaking moth larvae construct a small portable case of the woolen material it feeds upon. The case enlarges and is dragged about as the larva feeds. But after the feeding stage has concluded, the larva attaches the case, in which it will pupate, in a secluded place. The length of the life cycle is extremely variable: depending on the food supply, temperature, and humidity, it may require from two months to four years.

Carpet beetles. Four species of small, oval dermestid beetles, which may be either solid black or mottled with white, brown, yellow, or black. The larvae have gold, brown or black bristles terminating in a tuft of long hairs, and grow to be ¼ to ½ inch long, depending on the species.

Although the adult beetles—commonly known as Buffalo moths or bugs—feed on pollen and vegetable matter, museum curators are constantly on the watch for their larvae, which can consume insect collections and the wool, hides, and fur of stuffed animals in a very short period of time.

According to the U.S. Department of Agriculture and the conservators at the Merrimack Textile Museum, carpet beetles are more abundant in many areas than clothes moths and are often the cause of damage attributed to moths. The adult beetles fly readily and can enter houses through cracks as well as open doors and windows. Their destructive larvae may be deposited either as eggs by the adult females or carried into homes on secondhand furnishings. Although it may be possible to prevent beetle larvae from damaging rugs through the use of products mentioned later in this chapter, a significant infestation may require fumigation by a professional exterminator.

Control of rug-damaging insects. To control clothes moths and carpet beetles, rugs being prepared for storage should be sprinkled with paradichlorobenzine flakes or crystals at the USDA-recommended rate of at least 1 pound per 100 cubic feet of space; then the rugs should be rolled and securely wrapped to retain the vapor. An alternative treatment may be provided by Crispell's liquid mothproofing solution, details of which may be found at the end of this chapter. Do not substitute the cheaper and somewhat more easily available napthalene "moth balls" for paradichlorobenzine. Napthalene is not as effective, and conservators suspect that long-term use may cause color changes in rug dyes.

Concern about insect damage should not be limited to stored rugs. Rugs kept in rooms with little traffic and portions of large carpets that extend under furniture are also subject to moth and beetle infestation and can suffer extensive damage in a surprisingly short time. A friend of mine, a resident faculty member of a New England preparatory school, returned from a three-week Christmas vacation to find a wool Tunisian wall hanging infested with casemaking moth larvae and riddled with holes. Additional larvae were discovered on and behind all of his other rugs, and the cracks in the wooden wall behind the badly damaged hanging were stuffed with pupating larvae. All of this occurred in a small two-room apartment which, though attractive and tidy, was thoroughly dusted and vacuumed about as often as could be expected of an overworked young bachelor.

In short, even actively used quarters can harbor hordes of destructive insects if their food source remains undisturbed, and their ranks can include cockroaches and crickets attracted to rugs sauced with neglected food spills and crumbs. If you discover larvae on your rugs, brush them off—outside if possible—and follow with vacuuming front and back. If the rug is relatively small, place it inside a plastic bag and pop it in the freezer for at least 48 hours, then brush out the frozen dead moths and larvae.

Because of the constantly evolving standards of acceptability regarding insect sprays, I am reluctant to recommend any commonly available brands sold for mothproofing. Either order a supply of Crispell's solution, which was formulated specifically for oriental rugs, or consult a local exterminator for the names of approved brands.

Cedar-lined closets and chests, although certainly useful as storage areas, should not be relied upon for complete protection from the ravages of destructive insects. A New York City dealer suggested wrapping rugs in newsprint because, he said, the inks would act as a repellent. But I have found no proof of their effectiveness, and the extremely high acid content of printing inks argues against their involvement with the long-term storage of textiles.

Worst of all is the recommendation to place saucers of feathers among stored rugs because moths supposedly vastly prefer a feather diet to all others. This balmy notion first appeared in 1922 in a respected handbook by Kendrick and Tattersall and was cheerfully repeated as gospel in an otherwise useful guide published in 1980. Not only is the premise unsubstantiated, but it ignores the question of what the larvae eat once they have consumed the favored feathers.

Rodents

Damage caused by mice, rats, and squirrels seeking nesting materials can sometimes be a concern, especially in old rural houses with dry wall foundations and less than airtight attics. If you have had rodent invasions in the past, your best bet is to store rugs in a commercial facility unless you can ensure a rodent-free storage area through the use of poison baits or traps or by preparing an enclosure of coarse metal screening.

Dry Rot

According to one of the auctioneers I consulted, dry rot is a significant cause of value-robbing damage to cotton-wefted or -warped rugs consigned to auction by private owners. The culprit is an airborne, microscopic plantlike fungus that feeds on cellulose fibers, principally wood but including cotton. Although its insidious growth can be arrested, its effect is irreversible. The alternate wetting and drying of fibers leads to the rapid growth and spread of dry rot. Although an infected rug may *look* perfectly normal, the affected fibers become brittle and will eventually crack and disintegrate when subjected to stress. That is why you will sometimes see dealers at auction previews lean close as they carefully bend particular rugs back and forth at various points, listening for the telltale "chut-chut" or cracking of a weakened cotton foundation.

Storing a rug in winter in a damp, cold place that becomes warm and moist in summer invites the growth of dry rot; therefore, cellars, garages, and leaky attics should be avoided as storage areas. If you have rugs where they occasionally become damp, such as an entry hall or bath area, they should be taken up and allowed to dry thoroughly, front and back, before being replaced. The practice of standing large potted plants on rugs is a common cause of severe damage. Even if you are scrupulous about emptying the overflow out of the saucers in which the pots stand, the airless moisture trap created beneath them can rot out a rug in an alarmingly short time. Either place the pots elsewhere or upon a rack that will allow air circulation beneath them.

Although the animal fibers, wool and silk, are not subject to dry rot—indeed, wool requires a certain degree of moisture to remain supple—the silk content of rugs made in the 19th and early 20th centuries may deteriorate if allowed to become damp because the dyeing processes employed during that period increased the natural tendency of silk fibers to become brittle and eventually shatter when exposed to high levels of either moisture and dryness.

Mildew

Mildew is a thin, often whitish fungal growth that also requires moisture in which to thrive. The spores are likely to develop in hot humid weather in poorly ventilated spaces on rugs that are soiled or stored in plastic bags or plastic-coated wrappings.

Unlike dry rot, mildews attack just about anything, with the exception of some synthetics; and as they grow, they become unsightly and can cause considerable damage. Mildew molds leave greenish-gray or grayish-black splotches that will eventually weaken rug fibers, and their strong musty odor is difficult to dispel.

Atmospheric humidity is beyond our control, but the problems attendant upon its pervasive dampness can be mitigated by the following:

1. Drying the air through the use of air conditioners or dehumidifiers. In closets, a continuously burning electric light bulb may provide sufficient heat to discourage the growth of mildew.

2. Moisture-absorbing chemicals such as silica gel or activated aluminum may be obtained at hardware and building supply stores under various trade names. To use, hang in a cloth bag or place in an open container in the storage area. Both of these chemicals can be recycled by drying out at 300 degrees in a vented oven for several hours, then cooling before reusing.

Mildew can be deterred by the vapors of paradichlorobenzine, which is also the only insect repellent recommended by the textile conservators I consulted. Use no less than 1 pound per 100 cubic feet, replenishing the supply periodically to ensure a sufficient supply of effective vapor.

In the eastern half of the United States, where high humidity is virtually synonymous with summer, rugs can develop mildew even on the floor, especially in small, airless rooms and hallways and under furniture. Brush or vacuum off any surface growth—if possible outdoors to prevent scattering of the spores inside the house—then seal and dispose of the vacuum cleaner bag.

Sun and air will stop mold growth, but if you discover it during a prolonged spell of hot, humid, overcast weather, dry the rug front and back with a forced-air heater or, if the rug is quite small, with a hand hair dryer. If you are using a jute rug pad, this too may require vacuuming and drying. Then, during the next spell of dry weather, expose rug and pad to the sun after sponging the affected areas with the suds of a neutral detergent—as described in the section on rug washing—followed by their removal with a water-dampened sponge. Unless city dwellers have the luxury of a large sunny window, they will have to settle for an electric heater and fan. In either case, the rug and pad should be completely dry before replacement.

Unfortunately, the mustiness characteristic of mildew is very persistent. Sponging and airing may help, but on dank days be prepared for a cryptlike smell well into the fall heating season. Avoid artificially perfumed, sweet, floral room deodorants: they can be nauseating in combination with the lingering odor of mildew. Instead, try pungent incense sticks like balsam fir or piñon pine.

Dryness

Excessively high heat can also be damaging, especially to rugs containing significant amounts of silk. Wall-hung rugs are apt to become dry in the upper third, where heat rises and concentrates; dulled pile and a brittle foundation may be the price your rug pays for being placed too near a source of heat, in front of a large unshaded window with a southern exposure, or stored in an unventilated attic where summer daytime temperatures can soar well above 100 degrees.

Additional Information About Crispell's Liquid Mothproofing Solution

This colorless, odorless, nonflammable solution is virtually the only product on the market today specifically formulated for mothproofing oriental rugs. It has been used successfully by the rug trade for about 20 years on all types of rugs. The only problem encountered has been with post-1926 "lustre-washed" Kermans, which have experienced staining and graying of colors. This solution is *not* an insecticide: it renders wool inedible but will not kill moths, larvae, or eggs already present that could migrate elsewhere. Before treatment, therefore, rugs and trappings should be thoroughly vacuumed and washed (see section on rug washing).

The solution is available from the Chatalbash Rug Co. (see Resource Guide) at a cost in early 1991 of about $12 a gallon plus shipping. A quart will mothproof a rug of about 50 square feet: one-third for the back, two-thirds for the pile. More may be needed for a very thickly piled rug, less for a worn one. The liquid should be applied with a hand or power sprayer with a glass or plastic reservoir. A vacuum cleaner spray attachment is ideal for this purpose.

Rugs should be both clean and dry before being treated. Place rugs facedown on a flat surface, which, if indoors, should be protected with heavyweight paper or plastic sheeting. After applying the solution according to the directions on the container, drag an old-fashioned broom across the rug to break up any beading and allow the solution to penetrate the fibers. When the surface has dried—if weather conditions are unfavorable, a fan will facilitate the process—turn the rug pile-side up and repeat the process. Do not fold or roll a treated rug until completely dry. Rugs should be retreated after washing.

For additional information and names of other suppliers write or phone Crispell's Oriental Rugs, 20 Adriance Avenue, Poughkeepsie, NY 12601-4922; (914) 454-5500.

REPAIR, RESTORATION, AND CONSERVATION

Compared to other works of art and fine craftsmanship, the treatment oriental rugs are expected to endure is really quite unreasonable. Would we cut down a painting by Canaletto to fit the space between the dining room windows? Do we feed the family pet from an antique Meissen bowl? Yet splendid old runners are blithely butchered to suit the dimensions of apartment hallways, and we literally wipe our feet on finely woven 19th-century Sarouk mats.

I'm not suggesting that all rugs be taken out of domestic service and hung reverently on artfully lit walls; but unless aesthetic and monetary value and ongoing usefulness are of no interest, every rug owner has very practical reasons for learning how to distinguish use from abuse. Once a rug's edges and ends break down to the point where the pile knots are no longer secure, or when a weak spot in the foundation abrades into a hole, the situation has already deteriorated beyond the point where the average rug owner has the time, materials, skill, and knowledge to make acceptable repairs. Rebecca Venable, who writes on restoration for the trade journal *Rug News*, summed it all up back in 1981 in one sternly succinct phrase: rugs are not ruined in a day or restored overnight.

One of the purposes of this section will be to acquaint owners of rugs in good condition with techniques that will help keep them in their present fine state of repair. These maintenance measures can be done at home with basic needle-and-thread skills and easily obtainable materials; yet because they are time-consuming, they can be expensive to have done professionally.

But what about the rug that was worn or damaged before you acquired it? The rug you inherited or picked up for peanuts at a house sale or an exceptional example affordable because of its problems? In cases like these, the most important part of the repair is the assessment of the rug as an entity. Once that has been dealt with, the type and quality of repair best suited to it will be much easier to decide.

First of all, is more of the rug in reasonably good condition than in need of repair? If not, but the rug has outstanding color and design, then mount or hang it as you would a fragment. If only small and scattered areas of the original glory remain, you could incorporate them into pillows, vests, or pocketbooks.

Next, the *quality* of the rug should be determined in regard to its age, rarity, design execution, historical significance, and quality of the fibers and dyes. You may wish to seek advice from a knowledgeable collector—another good reason for joining a rug society—or museum curator. A dealer or a rug specialist at one of the major auction houses can also provide information, but you may have to pay an appraisal fee to get it.

The *structure* of a rug can affect both the solution of a repair problem and its cost, which is often the explanation for the seemingly inexplicable variation in prices dealers are willing to pay for damaged rugs at auction. For example, the edges of old Baluch rugs are wrapped with goat hair of a type rarely available in this country; if the original edges are missing, a dealer knows that the cost and extra work involved in adhering to authenticity will outweigh the price he can get for all but the finest Baluch work.

Caucasian and village Turkish rugs, on the other hand, are not only highly popular with collectors but are among the easiest to repair. They are relatively coarsely Turkish-knotted, and the colors and wool are fairly easy to match, which allows reknotted areas to blend readily into the original.

Finely woven Persian rugs can be very difficult to reweave, especially if the warps lie on two levels as they do in densely structured types like old Bijars and Kermans, which is why it may cost appreciably more to repair a hole in a worn, mediocre old Bijar than in an antique Kazak worth thousands more.

Chinese rugs present the greatest repair challenge because of the problems encountered in matching Chinese wools. I am told that a reknotted repair that blends perfectly at one angle of light will most likely be very apparent in another light, no matter how skillfully the repair itself has been done.

The rug's *primary purpose* should be defined: do you consider it as a floor furnishing only or as part of your collection? If the latter, did the expectation of eventual profitable resale affect your decision to buy it? If no longer serviceable as a floor covering, is it small and handsome enough to be used without repair as a wall hanging?

Finally, there is that intangible element best defined as *point of view*. An example of this is the friend who referred apologetically to an antique Heriz in his Federal Connecticut home as a "beat-up old thing we really must replace." This lovely old carpet has obviously seen better days, but it suited its 19th-century setting much better than would a newer rug in mint condition. And since the market value of this worn rug had been further reduced by the removal of a substantial portion of one corner, it was a prime example of a severely damaged rug not worth expensive repairs that could have been markedly improved with a little paint and the overcasting of frayed edges.

Once the condition, quality, and proposed use of a damaged rug have been defined, the appropriate level of repair can be considered. If professional repairs are not required or must be delayed, some basic preventive measures not only can but should be undertaken at home to prevent further damage and additional expense. These include overcasting ends to arrest the unraveling of wefts; stabilizing edges that have loose or missing sections of the original overwrapping material, and securing and backing holes and tears. Techniques and materials will be discussed in the following section. Rug painting, the method of last resort, will be treated separately.

Treatments beyond the competence of most collectors fall into three broad categories: functional, restoration, and conservation:

FUNCTIONAL REPAIRS

The aim of functional repairs is to return a damaged rug to useful service in the home. At its best, this type of repair approaches true restoration: fiber type, weight, ply, and color are closely matched to the original warp, weft, and pile fibers; and the workmanship is such that the repaired area can be detected only upon close examination. Work of this quality is expensive, so it is important to resolve the following questions before embarking upon a costly program of professional repair:

1. Will the market value of the repaired rug compensate for the cost of repairs?

2. Does the decorative or sentimental value of the rug outweigh monetary considerations?

Unless you are familiar with the rug market, the only way the first question can be answered is by having the rug appraised and its repaired value estimated by an experienced dealer. Consider the fee as part of the cost of repairs.

An auction bargain can become very expensive once repair costs are added, so if you have your eye on a fine but damaged rug being offered at auction, it would be worth paying a fee to a free-lance rug repairer to attend the auction preview and provide you with an estimate.

Established dealers usually have competent craftspersons on the premises who do custom repair work in addition to readying old rugs for sale. Since repair work is a necessary adjunct to a successful dealership in old rugs, the cost, although always high, will be competitive. Some dealers include the price of repairs in the old rugs they sell, so if you are considering buying a rug with problems, be sure you know what its price includes and that both you and the dealer agree on the type and extent of repairs included.

Be sure that whoever does your repair work is not only skilled but conscientious. If the skill of the repair person is not readily ascertainable or if the estimate is higher than anticipated, contract to have the work done in stages so that the quality of the work can be reviewed before you commit yourself to further expense. Don't be shy about discussing your expectations: as you will learn later, there are some cost-cutting measures that are acceptable and others that aren't.

At the low end of the functional repair ladder is a type best described as stitch-and-patch, which is acceptable only for rugs that have suffered irreversible harm but are still useful as furnishing pieces. This includes rugs that have been awkwardly reduced in size and rugs with extremely worn pile or with holes in foundations weakened by dry rot. In the last case, a patch cut from a similar rug or a neat darn may be the only practical solution. A collectible rug's original size should never be reduced; however, the appearance of a worn furnishing rug can sometimes be markedly improved by removing severely frazzled edges and ends or by cutting and rejoining—known in the trade as cut-and-shut—in order to eliminate a large hole or disfiguring stain that cannot be painted out.

RESTORATION

The goal of a restorer is to recreate the original condition of a rug through the virtual duplication of the materials, the weaving of the foundation, and the knotting of the pile. An expert restorer will often spend as much time studying the construction of a rug and matching colors and fibers as it takes to do the actual restoration work.

Richard Newman, a Manhattan-based craftsman, says that a close study of rug structure is like deciphering a code. Once he becomes familiar with the subtle interrelationships between the warps, wefts, and knotting that characterize not only the type of rug given him to repair but the style of the weaver of that particular rug, the actual process of restoration is like playing a well-rehearsed song. Every element falls into place in rhythmic progression without strain or hesitation.

Although the performance of this song of restoration is extremely expensive, if you own a carpet of exceptional quality or rugs that represent tribal design and weaving skill at its characteristic best, you could consider it a capital investment. Short of a worldwide collapse, the choicest examples of any of the arts often increase in value at the same time that the merely good ones are declining.

CONSERVATION

Conservation of a rug possessing significant historical or design interest requires that the methods of display and of chemical and mechanical preservation affect its integrity as little as possible. Strictly interpreted, this rules out the removal or addition of materials, which the process of repair or restoration necessitates and in the doing blurs the historic information contained in the rug's original materials and structure. Even a worn and damaged rug with little market value may, if it is old enough and rare enough, be worthy of conservation; so if you have inherited any antique rugs, it would be wise to have them assessed by an expert eye before turning them over for stitch-and-patch repairs.

You may wonder why a rug considered to have little value or interest in the past should now be thought a possible candidate for conservation. Well, it could, for instance, be a type of tribal rug of which only a few are represented in Western collections. Even a battered rug becomes important to conserve for technical analysis and study if it provides an essential link in the design progression of a particular weaving group or contains a unique combination of motifs and colors.

Then, too, tastes and opinions change in rugs as they do in everything else. It is not always easy to predict what future generations will consider important or beautiful. Even as I write, textile curators are acquiring rugs containing early synthetic dyes because they represent a significant chapter in the history of weaving, and a few collectors have already begun speaking of "classic early synthetics" because at the same time the scarcity of fine old rugs drives prices up, it changes the standards of acceptability.

Scientific conservation of an object presupposes treatment, storage, and display under strictly controlled conditions, as prescribed by a specialist. Informal conservation can be undertaken by collectors through the exercise of a prudent policy of limited use in an environment with moderate temperature, humidity, and light-level ranges and of having repairs made with reversible techniques.

The question of whether a rug should be repaired, restored, or conserved is complicated and often controversial. When all is said and done, the final decision rests with the owner, who, unfortunately, is not always as informed as one might hope. Not long ago, on a visit to a carpet and tile shop near my home, I noticed a fine old Baluch rug rolled up in a corner. The proprietor told me it had been brought in for repairs, which he had undertaken reluctantly—he admittedly knew nothing about oriental rugs—because the insistent owner was a valued customer. These "repairs" entailed cutting off the rug's exceptionally beautiful brocaded skirts and replacing the characteristic goat-hair-wrapped edges—with glued-on cotton twill binding, no less—because both were somewhat frayed and the owner wanted to "tidy the rug up a bit." The sorriest part of it all was that an acceptable, workmanlike repair job would probably have cost very little more than this needless butchery.

If you decide *your* rugs could use a little tidying, I hope the following sections will enable you to make informed decisions based on an intelligent assessment of the problems and of the repair options available to you. For the venturesome, a marvelous book offering step-by-step instruction in rug repairs on an advanced level is included in the Resource Guide in the back of this book. But before you snip a single warp or weft thread or remove a knot of pile, please consider the following:

1. The average rug owner is unlikely to have a sufficient variety of discardable worn rugs or fragments suitable for practicing and perfecting repair skills.

2. The variety and colors of fibers necessary for a first-rate major repair may be difficult to acquire in small quantities.

3. Rug repair is a slow and painstaking craft requiring a high degree of patience, a keen sense of observation, and the kind of temperament that relishes work involving the exact duplication of small details.

4. A carelessly or incorrectly performed *irreversible* repair can do more harm than good.

SIMPLE HOME REPAIRS

Since the primary audience for this guide is beginning collectors, I will not discuss except in passing those problems whose repair requires a familiarity with rug structure beginners are unlikely to possess. A list of tools and materials required for the basic repairs presented here will be found at the end of this section. To readers interested in pursuing the craft beyond this elementary stopgap level, I unhesitatingly recommend Peter Stone's *Oriental Rug Repair*, which may be obtained from booksellers listed in the Resource Guide at the back of this book.

RUG REPILING

Although replacing lost, worn, motheaten, or discolored pile is a task more demanding of patience than of skill, there are too many variables among rugs to allow a general approach to the subject. If all rugs were knotted coarsely and all knots were lined up on a single plane and easily accounted for, a beginner's knowledge of rug structure and a few glib paragraphs of mine might suffice; unfortunately, this is not the case.

In addition to familiarity with structure, an acceptable repair requires wools matched to the original in texture as well as color: light reflected from a long, thick glossy pile will not have the same value as light glancing off a short, fine, less lustrous pile dyed exactly the same color. The difference can, in fact, be startling. Unless one is willing to spend the money necessary to amass a wide variety of wools, not to mention the time needed to blend and re-ply them to effect an exact match, a repiled area will betray itself no matter how skillfully copied the knotting technique may have been.

An alternative to knot replacement in very worn rugs is a type of rug darning known as *kashmiring*, which covers the exposed warps and, assuming the color match is good, can approximate the look of the adjoining low pile closely. It is, however, a cosmetic or conservation repair and should not be substituted for pile replacement in an otherwise sound and serviceable rug. This technique is described in greater detail in a later section on conservation methods.

Speaking of conservation, at the risk of offending fellow cat owners I feel obligated to point out that cats that develop a fondness for exercising clawed paws on rugs can literally destroy a low-piled fragile carpet in short order. If you find the thought of declawing too horrible to contemplate, either hang your antique rugs or resign yourself to a battle of wills your cat is almost certain to win.

REPAIRING FLAT WEAVES

Since flat-woven rugs have no knots to assist in containing damage, a small hole in a flat-woven rug will usually enlarge more rapidly than it would in a pile rug. Damage to flat weaves used as floor furnishings should therefore be promptly attended to even if the resulting "repair" is less than expert. In the long run, it will be cheaper to have your small repair redone than a large hole rewoven from scratch.

If you are unable to trace out the pattern of the weave—some are quite complex—a neat darn accomplished with a blunt tapestry needle and needlepoint yarns reasonably well color-matched will temporarily suffice. Do try, however, to approximate as closely as possible the tension of the original weave so as to minimize the strain on adjacent areas. The

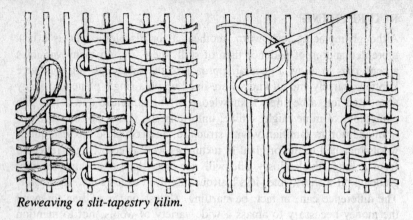

Reweaving a slit-tapestry kilim.

Reweaving a soumak flat weave.

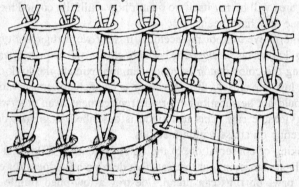

names of craftspeople qualified to do flat-weave restoration will be found in the Resource Guide.

EDGE AND END FINISHES

The first areas of a rug to show wear are usually the edges and ends. Even some brand-new rugs have unraveling ends due to careless or hasty finishing. Anchoring these weak points requires more time than skill. If consigned to a professional, the cost will be high; the collector who elects to do them at home will not only stand to gain in self-satisfaction, but in the doing will learn more about the way rugs are constructed than any book can teach. It is an ideal task to accomplish while television-viewing: tedious but requiring little judgment in the process.

Many people think rug edges and ends serve a function that is primarily cosmetic, like a frame around a picture. But a picture removed from its frame remains intact; a rug so deprived will inexorably disintegrate. A pile knot here and a weft thread there can add up to a very expensive repair job by the end of a year. Because it is so important to attend to the first signs of damage, one should, ideally, possess a work box kept stocked with well-chosen materials and the solemn sense of duty that impels one to do a proper repair in timely fashion.

Perfection being in short supply in this imperfect world, I suggest instead you seize the moment when both your mood and available time are in happy conjunction and use anything you have on hand. Overcasting the edges of an antique Ladik prayer rug with lavender acrylic knitting wool may offend your sensibilities, but arresting further disintegration takes priority. Amends can be made when you acquire satisfactory materials.

Fortunately, it isn't necessary to know much about rugs to do simple edge and end repairs *as long as you allow the rug to guide you*:

1. Don't remove any more of the original material than is necessary: the color, weight, ply and style of application of the original finish helps establish age and origin.

2. Don't apply a finish of your own devising because it's easier or, in your opinion, more attractive than the original. Rug repair, and especially rug conservation, is an inappropriate field for creative needlework.

Edges

There are four fairly distinct stages of edge disintegration:

1. *Breakage, loosening, and minor loss of the fibers used in overcasting.*

The overcasting material protects the edge warp structure, and although it is often distinctive or decorative, it is not an integral part of the structure. Its replacement, therefore, is the easiest of the edge repairs and can be accomplished successfully by anyone willing to first match the original material in color and density and then copy the tension and angle of the existing, adjacent material.

If the damaged overcasting is itself not original, you may choose to reovercast the entire edge with a more suitable material. If, however, the replacement nearly duplicates the original, you need redo only the damaged portion.

The fuzziness and plumpness of new overcasting can be corrected by applying a flame to the former—a quick pass with a kitchen match or lighter should do the trick—and a wooden mallet to the latter, preferably in that order.

2. *Small sections of the edge warp cords have become separated from the wefts extending from the rug foundation and woven into or around them.*

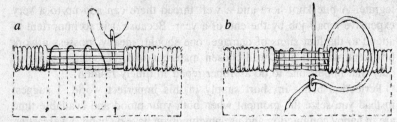

(a) Securing a single bundle of edge warp cords into the foundation of a rug; (b) overcasting exposed edge warp cords.

This repair can also be done at home. First, pull or clip away any broken bits of overcasting and wefts clinging to the side cords. Then, before proceeding further, take the time to closely inspect the weft-weaving technique used originally to secure the edge cords to the foundation warps. The more closely you can duplicate the damaged wefts in both weave and color, the less visible your repair will be.

Thread a large-headed, sharp-pointed needle with a stout linen or button thread color-matched as closely as possible to the broken wefts. Knot the end.

Insert the needle on the back of the rug. Draw it through up to eight sound foundation warps (if the weave is tight, you may need a small pliers to pull the needle through) and, depending on the number of cord-bundles in the original edge finish, loop the thread around a single bundle

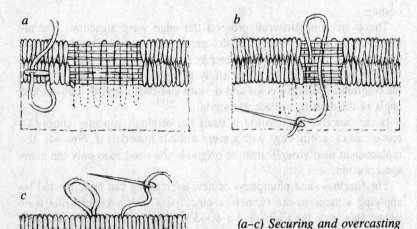

(a–c) Securing and overcasting a damaged double-cord edge.

or over and under two or three or more. Then return the needle and new weft thread through sound warps into the body of the rug.

Repeat the process along the length of the damaged section, taking pains to maintain the original tension. A thread drawn too tightly can cause puckering; if left too loose, gaps may occur.

Finish the repair by overcasting as described above in No. 1.

3. *Sections of the warp cords comprising the edge have not only separated from the wefts securing them to the foundation warps but are severely frayed or broken.*

This problem presents several technical challenges: first, the edge cords must be duplicated—which in most cases involves the respinning and plying of wool threads—then joined inconspicuously both vertically and horizontally to the remaining warps, a task that should be done on a frame and under carefully adjusted tension so that the new edge will lie smooth and flat, without bulges or puckers. This repair is best undertaken by a professional.

4. *Broken edge warp cords are missing in part or entirely, and the exposed, loosened pile knots have begun to erode.*

When edge damage is this extreme, a proper repair exceeds the ability of all but the most determined amateur, especially if the damage includes a dog-eared corner.

Rug owners are often shocked to learn that reconstruction of edges, eroded guard borders, and dog-eared corners is more difficult, and therefore more expensive, than the reweaving of a hole in the middle of a rug. If professional repairs must be delayed, either take the rug out of service or retard further erosion of the pile knots as follows: (a) Closely overcast the damaged area with wool or stout thread, or (b) fold cotton twill tape around the damaged portions, attaching it as neatly as possible front and back with large, loose zigzag stitches. The tape can be dyed if the color difference is extreme. You may be tempted to apply an adhesive tape: *don't*!

False Edgings

Are there any acceptable alternatives to the above procedures? In regard to the first two and the relatively simple problems described above, both of which can be easily remedied at home, the answer is no.

Complex edge repairs on a rug in generally good condition should be undertaken by a professional, but if the rug has additional serious problems—unevenly worn pile, for example, or unsightly dye runs—you might consider a handmade false edge, a ready-made edging, or machine overcasting. Personally, I would have no qualms about having a false edging applied to a decorative but otherwise undistinguished worn rug if the alternative was unsightly edges and a continued erosion of pile, but it must be pointed out that the choice of any of these less expensive alternatives can create a new problem in the place of the one it was intended to solve.

This new problem originates with the cutting away of what remains of an original edge to make way for a new one. If the pile knots have already begun to loosen along the edge, this may include a portion of the border guard stripe as well. In either case, the largely invisible but structurally important weft reversals that the edge structure was designed to protect will be irreversibly compromised. A false edging, which is attached *to*, rather than incorporated *into*, the newly trimmed edge, may in time require occasional reinforcement with a few turns of button thread to prevent it and the warps to which it is precariously attached from pulling loose under the normal stress of household use.

Because false edgings of one kind or another are so much less costly than reconstruction, the average journeyman repair person may assume this is what you want done unless instructed otherwise. It is desirable, of course, to match any type of edging as closely as possible to the original, but an expert won't be fooled by a false edge no matter how cunningly devised.

Ends

In general, the ends of all oriental rugs, new as well as old, should be securely overcast, as shown, to prevent the unraveling of wefts and eventual loss of pile knots, unless the warps are firmly braided or knotted across the entire width. However, although the loss of original rug end finishes is always regrettable—especially if distinctive or decorative—as long as there is enough of a stub end left to firmly secure so as to prevent

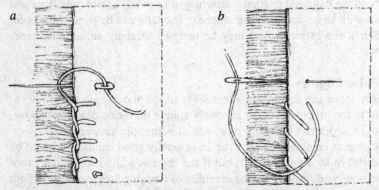

(a) Right: This is the recommended way to overcast the ends of rugs to prevent the loss of wefts and knots. (b) Wrong: This method will not sufficiently secure wefts and knots against working loose from the foundation.

the pile knots from working loose from the warps, the structural integrity of the rug will be preserved. Whether that justifies lopping off worn or partially missing end finishes and overcasting the remainder depends on the rug in question: if it is a fine antique Baluch with long, elaborately brocaded skirts, reconstruction may be warranted; ordinary fringes may be treated more cavalierly, depending on the extent of the loss.

1. *The fringe is unevenly worn and has no distinctive features.*

If the wear does not extend into the wefts or the edge finishes, the warp ends that make up the fringe can be artfully evened by snipping off a few at a time so that the result has the slight imprecision characteristic of a handmade rug. Remove no more than is necessary to minimize the damage, and try to resist the temptation to remove a perfectly good length of fringe at one end to match what is left of the other.

To soften the bluntness of the newly cut ends, comb out the fibers with a fine-tooth comb or suede brush. Finish by overcasting.

2. *The uneven fringe wear extends into a section of plain weave.*

Some village and tribal rugs have sections of warp and weft plain weaving between the body of the rug and an end fringe, which in this instance is a secondary finish and usually quite short. The plain-weave strip may be purely functional and only ½ inch to 2 inches long; in others, Baluch and Turkoman rugs in particular, it may be an elaborately decorated 6 inches or more.

If the plain weave is functional, or the decoration consists of no more than plain-woven stripes repeating the colors of the pile, the wefts can be removed one by one, gently prying them out with a blunt needle, until an undamaged row of wefting is reached. Secure this row by overcasting before turning your attention to the fringe. This should be judiciously evened as described above, with special attention to teasing out the crimped look of warps from which damaged wefts have been removed.

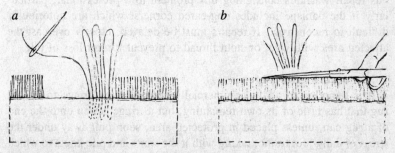

Replacing a section of missing fringe. (a) Anchor new yarns an inch into the foundation; (b) trim new yarns to the length of the existing fringe.

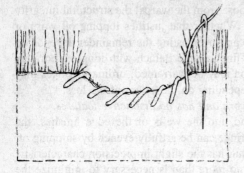

Until a professional repair can be done, a gouged edge should be closely overcast to prevent further erosion of rug fibers.

3. *A section or sections of fringe have been cut, torn, or chewed off along the edge of the pile, but the remaining fringe is undamaged.*

In this case, new warp threads must be manufactured and anchored into the foundation, then trimmed and the ends teased out as described above.

If the warp fiber is wool, hand-spun knitting or needlepoint wools can be used, depending on the texture of the original warps. If white and brown wools were combined in a single warp, you can achieve a similar barber-pole effect by plying together strands of similarly colored wool. If the fringe to be replaced is cotton, it can probably be matched to cording used in macramé craft work.

The new fringes, whether of wool or cotton, may have to be tinted to blend with the original fringe. The most effective method involves a solution of permanganate crystals. Its preparation and use will be described later in this chapter.

4. *The damage to the fringe extends into the body of the rug, causing a loss of pile.*

The technical challenges involved in making a stable and inconspicuous repair warrants consigning this problem to a professional, particularly if the damage includes dog-eared corners, which are notoriously difficult to reconstruct. If repairs must be delayed, closely overcast the affected area with wool or stout thread to prevent further loss of pile.

Manufactured Fringes

It is tempting to add a commercially manufactured fringe to an old rug that has little of its own remaining, but a fringe sewed onto the end of a rug can, unless placed in protected area, soon pull away under the stress of daily foot traffic, taking with it the wefts and pile knots to which it was attached.

However, if you are unable to accustom yourself to the appearance of a rug without fringes, a variety of styles of uniformly good quality are

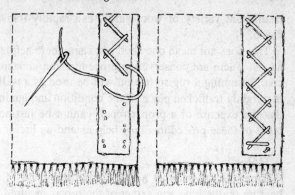

*Attaching a
stiffening strip to
a curling edge.*

available by mail order from a reliable source listed at the end of this chapter. Remember that these fringes are cotton and therefore are unsuitable for rugs with wool warps.

CURLED CORNERS AND EDGES

Rugs with turned-over edges and corners curling like a breaking wave are not only unsightly but potentially dangerous, especially if the afflicted rug lies in a busy passageway. Tacking a curling edge or corner to the floor will succeed only in eventually separating it from the rest of the rug, and steam-pressing curls into submission is at best a temporary remedy. The most effective approach is to counteract the curling tendency with a strong backing material.

A cotton twill tape may suffice for a lightweight or limply curled rug, but a rug of any substance will in time bend even a stoutly woven fabric to its will. What is needed, I have finally concluded—and have since had confirmed by other sources—is a dimensionally stable material that can be attached to the curling portion of the rug without damaging the foundation. Satisfactory choices include dense cardboard, linoleum, thin vinyl tile or masonite, or a sturdy leather like cowhide, all of which can be sewed—never glued!—to the underside of the rug with linen or button thread once holes have been drilled or punched in the backing strip as illustrated.

HOLES, SPLITS, AND TEARS

Holes, splits, and tears often seem more alarming than they are in fact because, unlike damaged edges and ends, they disrupt the overall harmony of the rug design. Actually, hole repairs usually present a skilled, well-equipped craftsperson with fewer technical problems than the reconstruction of a severely dog-eared corner. On the other hand, an eager, inexperienced collector, with only book knowledge of structure and an insufficient variety of wool yarns, can rapidly transform a flaw into a fiasco.

This does not mean one need just stand there helplessly wringing one's hands. There are conservation procedures an amateur can safely undertake, assuming a rug so treated will be used as a wall hanging or placed in a lightly trafficked place. If the condition and quality of a rug are such that the expense of a proper repair cannot be justified, then one or another of these procedures may help extend its life of useful service.

Holes

Everyone knows what a hole is, but the cause of a hole has a direct bearing on the type and extent of the repair required. If a hole has been chewed or burned into a rug that is in otherwise very good condition, it should be professionally rewoven, not only because of the gratifying improvement in appearance but because its restored value will, in most cases, compensate for the cost of the repair.

Sometimes a repair person will suggest stitch-and-glue patching of a hole with a plug cut from a fragment of a similar rug. Although patching is less expensive than reweaving and a very tempting alternative if the match will be nearly exact, resist it. It is a shoddy and devaluing practice not worth considering for a collectible rug.

When a hole results from the wearing away of both the pile and foundation by hard use, it may be difficult to find adjacent warps sound enough to anchor the new foundation materials. In these cases, it is often necessary to enlarge the original hole before reweaving can begin, and the expense of the repair may overtake any value it could add to a rug that was in poor condition to begin with.

If a hole is the first visible sign of an extensive area of dry rot in a cotton foundation, reweaving may not be possible; if it is, the cost may be prohibitive for all but rugs of great historical or sentimental value. In cases of damage this extreme, backing the affected area with an adhesive tape in the hope of consolidating the rotting fibers may be your only alternative. Although this will not solve the problem—nothing can—it can delay the inevitable disintegration. However, since taping is irreversible, do not proceed without confirmation by an experienced dealer or repair person that dry rot is, in fact, the underlying problem. In that unhappy case, *and in that case only*, the use of an adhesive tape can be justified.

Splits and Tears

Tears may be the result of rough or careless handling, but since it isn't easy to rip through the foundation threads of a hand-knotted rug in sound condition, tears or splits may indicate either a hardened spill that has made the fibers stiff or brittle or a dry-rotted cotton warp, weft, or both.

If the tear is clean, affecting only a few foundation threads and pile knots, carefully realign the edges. Insert a needle threaded with button or linen thread an inch above and beyond the tear and work it through the foundation and across the tear, emerging about an inch beyond it on the other side. Continue working your needle back and forth as closely as possible along the tear's entire length. Then tack a *nonadhesive* backing strip to the foundation over the joining. Although reweaving is always the preferred solution, if the rug is not distorted by your mend, it can probably continue in service if placed in a lightly trafficked area.

A split occurring at the site of a hardened spill may resist being joined; indeed, it may be impossible to work a needle through the stiffened fibers without enlarging the split. If this is the case, either try to pick out or, if you know what substance was spilled, dissolve the hardened residue (see the section on stain removal) and proceed as described above. If the substance resists removal, the affected area will have to be removed and rewoven.

Removal and reweaving will also be required when foundation fibers have been weakened by dry rot or mildew, unless the rot proves on examination to be extensive, in which case an adhesive backing tape may be your last, if worst, resort.

CONSERVATION MEASURES

Conservation "repairs" are, without exception, reversible. This rules out such things as adhesive tapes, glued patches, and the cutting of weft reversals at rug edges.

Since they are largely intended for rugs planned to be hung, none of the measures described below are suitable for rugs expected to withstand heavy foot traffic. In all cases, however, they are preferred to turning a blind eye.

Kashmiring

An embroidery technique known as kashmiring is sometimes employed to minimize the insult to a rug's appearance by carrying wool yarns around the warps in a figure-eight stitch. This can be used either as a simple wrapping stitch to strengthen areas along the edges or can be chained around the foundation threads in areas where the pile is either very low or missing. The success of the effect depends largely on how well the colors are matched to the pile.

Because it is reversible, kashmiring has been employed extensively for museum collections so that pile replacements could be easily distinguished from the original on close inspection yet not be so obvious as to distract from the overall harmony of design when seen from a normal viewing distance.

Today purists frown upon even this minor degree of manipulation of original materials. They claim this warp-wrapping technique, which is similar to that used in flat-woven soumaks, creates tensions dissimilar to those set up by the original weaving and may in time weaken the structure. Whether or not one agrees, this is a serious danger in fact as well as in theory. It must be conceded that even the most elegantly accomplished kashmiring provides no more than a cosmetic masking of severe wear and should not be considered a permanent substitute for pile replacement except for rugs you intend to hang on a wall.

Fabric Patches

When a hole is rewoven, the damaged ends of the warps and wefts protruding into the hole are removed, including any loose knots, and the hole is enlarged. This is done to remove irregularities so that the alignment of the new foundation threads and subsequent knotting of new pile wool can be more precisely accomplished. For a temporary conservation repair, the loose knots can be removed, but the damaged warps and wefts should be drawn through to the back and securely tacked all around the perimeter of the opening. If the rug is finely woven or densely packed, a pliers may be needed to pull the needle through the foundation.

Once the broken threads have been secured, the hole may be backed with a heavyweight fabric of a color and texture that will be both harmonious and relatively inconspicuous—for example, a coarsely woven wool homespun for a tribal rug, a sturdy ribbed cotton or wool for flat weaves, and an upholstery-weight, smooth-surfaced wool or velvet for a fine, low-piled Persian carpet.

Cut the fabric into a patch about 2 inches larger in all dimensions than the hole to be backed. Overcast the edge to prevent fraying, and attach it to the foundation with strong thread.

If used as a floor furnishing, a rug temporarily patched in this fashion should be placed on a dense underlayment in a low-traffic area.

Silk-Screened Patch

An interesting new technique combining photography and silk screening enables visual duplication of damaged or missing areas of historically significant textiles with a minimum of fiddling with the original materials.

As reported in a recent issue of *Hali*, the international magazine devoted to carpets and textiles, this technique is best suited to flat weaves, but wall-hung low-pile rugs, especially those with finely detailed patterning, would seem candidates for this approach, too.

In brief, an area similar to the missing section in pattern and coloration is photographed, and the image is silk-screened onto a backing fabric matched as closely as possible to the thread count and weave structure of the original. The patch is then carefully incorporated into the damaged piece. For the benefit of those who do not themselves possess the necessary skills and equipment, the conservation workshop cited in the *Hali* article is listed at the end of this chapter.

Although the creation and attachment of a silk-screened patch is undoubtedly expensive—all first-class conservation services are—it would probably cost less than expert restoration of the same area. As always, let your decision be guided by the use expected of the rug in question.

MATERIALS NEEDED FOR REPAIRS MADE AT HOME

The tools required to execute the simple repairs discussed in this chapter are inexpensive and easily assembled. None is traditional, but their use is familiar, and they will allow you to perform the described tasks satisfactorily.

1. Large-eyed, sharp- and blunt-ended tapestry needles (needlepoint, crewel) in a variety of sizes.

2. Thimble.

3. Small pliers for pulling needles through rug foundations.

4. Tweezers for removing pile knots and damaged edge overcastings.

5. A small, stiff brush—a toothbrush will do—and a fine-toothed comb to separate, straighten, or align pile fibers. (If you can find one, a little gadget known as an embroidery fluffer, with fine, hooked, wire teeth, is ideal.)

6. Scissors: (a) a pair of medium-size shears; (b) curved-blade scissors (the type manufactured for shearing pile are expensive; for the procedures described here, a good-quality cuticle scissors will prove quite adequate).

7. A magnifying device of the hands-free type used by needlepointers is useful and sometimes essential when working with finely woven rugs.

8. A wooden mallet for flattening new edge cords and blending other kinds of new work with the original structure.

9. Wooden kitchen matches for singeing the fuzz from new overcastings.

10. An adjustable work light of the extensible-arm, multipositional type. Art supply stores often stock several varieties.

THREADS AND WOOLS

Closely matched fibers, colors, and textures are essential to a satisfactory repair. Although the use of any material is acceptable in an emergency

to arrest disintegration, there are a few basic fibers you would be wise
to have always on hand:

Threads

A *linen thread* is the best choice for overcasting rug ends, attaching
curling corner reinforcements and Velcro strips, anchoring loose edge
wrappings, and securing raw edges of holes and tears. Linen thread is
very strong and rot-resistant, and being a natural fiber itself, it is com-
patible with other natural fibers found in rugs. Unfortunately, it is expensive and difficult to find. A reliable mail order source is listed in the
Resource Guide. Because of the expense, I settle for a medium-weight
thread (#25) in neutral beige, dark red, brown, and blue, which I have
found to be the most commonly needed colors. Depending on the type
of rug you decide to collect, your needs may be somewhat different.

Button and carpet threads are an acceptable, much less costly alternative to linen. They are usually a cotton-and-synthetic blend and are
widely available in a range of colors at sewing and notions counters.

Transparent synthetic threads and small-diameter fishing lines are a
tempting choice because of their ability to blend with any color. But their
unyielding quality makes for uneasy partnering with natural fibers, and
they grow less resistant to breakage over time, especially if exposed to
heat or sunlight.

Wools

There is, theoretically, a wool available to match every conceivable
repair need; practically speaking, you will find your choice limited to
the wool yarns made for needlepoint, crewel, and tapestry work unless
you live in or near a large urban area. The goat-hair still used in edge
finishes by many tribal weavers is not available, so far as I can determine,
from any source here. Sometimes yarns hand-spun from natural brown
sheep's wool can be reasonably well matched in color, but none have the
wiry texture and gloss of Middle Eastern goat hair.

Purists advocate using only hand-spun wools colored with natural dyes
matched to a particular repair job, but this may not be a practical choice.
Vegetable dyes change over time, too, and the colors so painstakingly
and expensively matched may age in such a way that the once invisible
repair becomes apparent.

Old-time rug dealers with repair facilities on the premises often display
hanks of wool yarns in an awesome range of muted colors. They were
obtained years ago directly from the rug-producing areas, but there are
no retail suppliers of these wools in the United States. If you are on very
cordial terms with such a dealer, he might spare you a length or two of
his precious dusty bounty, but I wouldn't count on it.

For emergency repairs it is useful to have a black wool and two or three shades of ivory, brown, red, and blue in your work basket. These wools and the linen or button threads discussed earlier will allow you to perform relatively inconspicuous temporary repairs on just about any rug.

MATCHING WOOLS FOR COLOR AND DENSITY

Assuming you have access to a well-stocked needlework shop, take your *clean* rug with you and match the colors to the yarns in daylight. If the rug is too large, the shopkeeper may allow you to borrow packets of yarns in promising colors—or even the yarn sample books—over a weekend.

Pile colors are matched to the cut ends of the yarns because fibers seen on end absorb light and thus appear darker than the same yarn lying in a flat, light-reflective strand. It is, therefore, important always to keep in mind the use to which repair wools will be put when matching colors. If you are choosing yarns for the edge and flat-weave repairs discussed here, match the original to a flat-lying strand.

When deciding between closely matching colors, bear in mind that a repair requiring, for example, a blue-toned red wool will be more successful if done with yarns of the same tone, even if lighter or darker, than an orange-toned wool with the same intensity of color. If, however, a yarn of the same tonality as the original is not available, choose a lighter-colored yarn of the nearest tonality. A lighter yarn's tone can be drabbed with a solution of potassium permanganate (see below), but nothing much can be done to lighten a darker wool except mixing it with lighter-colored strands.

Matching by Mixing

If you look closely at the wools in an old, naturally dyed rug, you will often be able to distinguish strands of varying values and tones that, at a distance, your eye sees as a single, pleasantly vibrant color. This is especially true of colors achieved by overdyeing, like greens and aubergine. To approximate this effect or to match an unusual color, yarns can be separated into single strands and combined with strands of lighter, darker, or different tones.

Needlepoint, crewel, and tapestry yarns are made up of three, two and four strands of wool, respectively, which are plied or twisted together. Since the strands tend to curl up on each other like agitated snakes in the process of untwisting, I suggest you hold a length of the yarn tautly between your teeth and one hand while with the other you wind the threads down one by one in the direction opposite to the original ply.

For edge and flat-weave repairs the strands can be used without re-plying, either singly or in combinations up to about six, depending on the color and density required. But since unplied wool is easily pulled apart when subjected to the strain of being repeatedly drawn through a rug foundation, it's advisable to work with short lengths.

Although edge and flat-weave repairs can often be accomplished with unplied or home-plied wools, the warp cords used for rug edges are generally denser and more firmly plied than the other fiber threads used in rug construction. If sections of these cords are missing, it may be necessary to have them replaced by a professional.

Matching by Drabbing

Even the brightest colors found in rugs are, more often than not, less bright than the closest match available with commercial wools, despite the enormous range of hues available in the various lines of fine needle-work yarns. A concentrated brew of tea or coffee, often recommended to darken or "sadden" colors, will fade in time or with washing, but a permanent drabbing may be effected with a solution of potassium per-manganate ($KMnO_4$), an oxidizing agent used as an antiseptic.

This dark purple crystalline salt is available only by medical prescrip-tion. It is poisonous if ingested, and the label warns that the chemical renders textiles highly inflammable. Not wishing to advise the use of anything that might cause a cherished rug to burst into flame, I wrote the manufacturer of the brand I purchased and received a reassuring reply from the manager of their science products laboratory.

The compound is so highly colored, he wrote, that if the yarn is rinsed until there is no purple color deposited in the water, it can be safely assumed that there would not be enough left to be of any danger, as appreciable amounts have to be present to cause spontaneous combus-tion.

After expressing interest in this unusual use of the chemical, he went on to say that what probably occurs is a reaction between the $KMnO_4$ and the oil in the wool itself, producing the dioxide of manganese (MnO_2), which is dark brown and may even be self-mordanting.

Assuming you obtain a prescription from your doctor or dentist, about 4 ounces of the crystalline form of potassium permanganate should be sufficient for a lifetime of anything short of frenzied home repair activity. The solution will impart to wool yarns an ecru to brown coloration, but its use is so inexact that to obtain the degree of drabbing desired you will have to experiment with the strength of the solution and duration of immersion for each type and color of yarn to be treated. In general, however, the following guidelines should be observed.

Equipment

1. Two glass bowls for preparing the solution and for wetting and rinsing the wool.

2. A metal tray or aluminum foil roasting pan.

3. A pair of metal tongs or long fork and a mixing spoon.

4. Rubber gloves and a large apron to protect hands and clothes from stains.

Procedure

1. Place bowls in tray next to sink.

2. Dissolve 1 teaspoon of the crystals in 2 cups of warm water in one of the bowls. Mix well.

3. Fill the other bowl with lukewarm water, immerse the yarn and gently squeeze until the fibers are evenly wetted. (A drop or two of detergent will facilitate absorption.)

4. Transfer the yarn to the permanganate solution. Stir only long enough—seconds, not minutes—to ensure even absorption of the purple color.

5. Immediately remove the yarn with tongs or fork and rinse under running water until the water runs clear. (If the sink is not stain-proof, place a large bowl under the faucet to catch and further dilute the rinsed-out solution.)

Color Matching. If, after the purple color is rinsed away, the resulting brown drabbing is too pale, repeat the process. If it seems too dark, remember that a color dries lighter than it appears when wet.

Even quite a dark shade can result from a surprisingly short immersion time, so I suggest you proceed with caution, drabbing the wool a few strands at a time. If successive batches do not quite match, wools can be blended to minimize the variations.

Store any remaining solution in a screw-top glass jar. *Be sure to place both the leftovers and the unused crystals out of the reach of children.*

Note: If you have a number of rugs requiring extensive edge overcasting, the cost of the yarns can mount up; so if you fancy yourself a kitchen Dr. Frankenstein, you may wish to experiment with bargain bin yarns. Unlike the doctor's poor monster, truly repellent colors can often be tamed and rendered eminently usable through treatment with the permanganate solution.

RUG PAINTING: PROS AND CONS

The easiest but least acceptable treatment for a faded or worn rug is painting the altered colors, eroded pile, or exposed foundation. You might think that this cosmetic subterfuge would be obvious upon even the most casual inspection, but a reasonable amount of care in matching and applying color can achieve magical results, although whether that magic should be considered black or white depends on the circumstances and one's point of view.

The conservative view is that painting is never acceptable, not only because it is employed by unscrupulous dealers to mask major defects but also because little is known about the long-term effect of the pigments and solvents on rug fibers. Rugs painted with the specific intent of deceiving the unwary are quite commonly encountered at auctions, especially the type known in the trade as "short notice," typically held on weekends at motels. For this reason alone, no one should bid on a rug unless it has been inspected carefully beforehand, preferably in daylight.

There are, however, a few cases in which it can be argued that painting is acceptable both ethically and aesthetically. These include (1) old, expertly executed repairs performed with wools colored with dyes that, although they matched the original colors at the time of the repair, have subsequently faded or altered; (2) spots bleached noticeably paler than surrounding pile; and (3) the bright white tufts that occasionally work up through the pile from the knots of joined weft or warp threads of rugs with cotton foundations. Finally, there are the rugs that for one reason or another—primarily visible wear—possess little or no market value, yet with "freshened" colors or partially repainted designs could continue to serve as decorative furnishings for years to come, albeit in a dark corner or hallway.

Owners of classic antique rugs should, of course, adopt the conservative view and leave well enough alone. Wear may dim a fine old piece, but a faded beauty will always command greater respect than a painted floozy.

MATERIALS

Colored inks and felt marker pens are often used for rug painting, but neither is a good choice. The inks contain dyes that, although transparent and usually waterproof, have limited color-fastness in bright light. The brilliant marker-pen colors share this impermanency and in addition are glaringly incompatible with even poor rug dyes.

The most satisfactory coloring agent for home use is acrylic paint used as watercolor. The acrylics, also known as polymer paints, are made by dispersing colored pigments in an acylic emulsion. When thinned with water and applied to paper or cloth, the paint spreads out in a thin layer that, when the water evaporates, leaves a continuous, flexible, waterproof and virtually fadeproof film of plastic. I have used acrylics to paint designs on needlepoint canvas, and I know from experience that a modestly priced starter set can be used to mix and match an enormous range of colors and shades. For muting purposes, I suggest adding to your stock a few tubes of gray and brown shades. Avoid using white: it tends to make the colors chalky and clumps the wool fibers into stiff little tufts.

Because acrylics are so versatile and easy to use, they are usually available in stationery and variety stores as well as art supply outlets. One caution: it is not advisable to intermix different brands, as incompatible formulas may cause curdling.

Aside from the acrylic paints, very little equipment is required for achieving a satisfactory result:

1. A couple of stubby brushes—you may have to clip the tips—of the type used for oil painting. Watercolor brushes are too soft to push the paint into wool fibers.

2. A small brush or cotton swabs with which to mix the paint and water until you receive the right shade and consistency.

3. A medicine dropper for dispensing water.

4. A shiny white plate or two on which to mix colors.

PROCEDURE

Unless you are familiar with the mixing of colors, it may take a bit of experimentation before you get a feel for combining colors to achieve just the odd, subtle shade you need. Stick with it, and resist settling for approximate matches. Always mix and match colors in daylight, keep the paint quite thin—thick paint will clog the fibers—and work fast. Once the mixture you are working with dries, it will not redissolve. Depending on the condition of the rug, adequate coverage may require two or three thin applications of paint, each of which should be allowed to dry before adding the next.

When you have completed the touch-up, be sure the paint is entirely dry before walking on the rug or rolling it up. And keep in mind that although a well-worn rug may *look* better after painting, the foundation remains very vulnerable to breakage under normal conditions of daily use. To minimize the effect of stress, provide the rug with a well-cushioned underlayment.

After painting, wash your brushes immediately with soap and water. Never allow acrylic paint to dry on a brush; in fact, never allow it to dry on any textured or absorbent surface you don't want it on because it will be almost impossible to remove. It does, however, wash or peel off smooth, oily, or shiny surfaces like hands and paint-mixing plates.

To sum up, although rug-painting has its legitimate uses, it should never be used as a substitute on rugs for which pile replacement is obviously the preferred solution. By postponing minor repiling, which is a relatively easy and inexpensive repair, the risk of severe foundation damage is increased and the extent and cost of repairs multiplied.

RESOURCE
GUIDE

RUG BOOKS AND PERIODICALS

PERIODICALS

Hali, an international journal of carpets and textiles, with the emphasis on oriental rugs. Many fine color pictures of rugs in both the advertising and editorial sections; news of exhibits, conventions, rug societies; review of books and auctions; articles ranging from scholarly research reports to expressions of aesthetic appreciation. Published six times a year, 1991 U.S. subscription rates are $85 and $150 for one and two years, respectively. *Hali* Publications, Subscriptions Department, c/o I.M.D. Ltd., LUVS Container Station, 149-05 177th Street, Jamaica, NY 11434.

Oriental Rug Review, an American publication of more modest scope and size than *Hali*. Originally intended to focus on auction previews and reports, it has expanded to reflect primarily the dealer-scholar point of view in articles whose tone ranges from serious to tongue-in-cheek. Fewer color photos than *Hali* but more fun to read. Good coverage of news and events of interest to American collectors and dealers in collectible rugs. Published six times a year, 1991 subscription rates for first-class mail delivery are $60 and $110 for one and two years, respectively. Oriental Rug Auction Review, Inc., P.O. Box 709, Meredith, NH 03253.

BOOKS

Publications about oriental rugs sometimes offer a better return than the rugs themselves. The first issue of *Hali*, for example, now sells for 33 times its original 1978 price of $7.50.

Some of the recommended titles below are either out of print or difficult to obtain through conventional booksellers. If so, they are usually available from the sources noted at the end of the annotated listing of books. If the cost gives you pause, you might try your interlibrary loan service.

GENERAL

Bennett, Ian, ed. *Rugs and Carpets of the World.* New York: A&W Publishers, 1977.

A well-illustrated basic reference covering fine handmade rugs of all kinds but especially oriental rugs. There is more emphasis on old than new production; color reproduction is mediocre.

Denny, Walter. *Oriental Rugs.* New York: Cooper-Hewitt Museum, 1979.

This was the first volume of the Smithsonian Library of Antiques. Dr. Denny, an Islamic Arts scholar, has written and lectured widely on oriental rugs. Gracefully written, this book packs a lot of authoritative information into a relatively few, handsomely produced pages.

Eiland, Murray L. *Oriental Rugs.* Boston: NYGS/Little, Brown and Co., latest edition.

A complete, well-organized, and universally recommended introduction to the subject, including useful information about dyes and structure. A good selection of black-and-white photographs illustrates the no-nonsense prose; the color plates are dreadful.

Ford, P. R. J. *The Oriental Carpet.* New York: Harry N. Abrams, latest edition.

Lavishly illustrated in color, with good chapters on dyes and structures, the subtitle is *A History and Guide to Traditional Motifs, Patterns and Symbols.* The author is a knowledgeable member of the international trade; the rugs, including some Chinese examples, are largely late-19th and 20th century.

Hawley, Walter A. *Oriental Rugs, Antique and Modern.* 1913. Paperback reprint. New York: Dover, 1970.

The chief value of this venerable, inexpensively reprinted handbook is the lucidly presented information about rug structure and the line drawings illustrating the discussion of rug motifs. Hawley was one of the first Westerners to point out the importance of weave pattern in rug identification.

Jacobsen, C. W. *Oriental Rugs: A Complete Guide.* Rutland, VT: Tuttle, 1969.

If your library has only one book on oriental rugs, it is likely to be this one by an American dealer, since deceased, with a lively gift for self-promotion. It is an engaging book, liberally spiced with the author's pet peeves and dubious historical information. Although by no means a basic reference, it provides useful information about commercial carpets imported into the United States during the first six decades of the century.

Thompson, Jon. *Oriental Carpets.* New York: E. P. Dutton, 1988.

Acknowledged as one of the two best introductory books (Murray Eiland's *Oriental Rugs* is the other), it is peerless in terms of writing style and production. Its organization, in which rugs are grouped according to their purpose and the technical skill shown, rather than geographical origin, is illuminating, and the color illustrations are gorgeous.

HISTORICAL SURVEYS

Bode, Wilhelm von, and Kuhnel, Ernst. *Antique Rugs from the Near East*. Translated by C. G. Ellis. Ithaca, NY: Cornell University Press, 4th ed., 1984.

A classic scholarly introduction to early oriental carpets, with a very useful and updated annotated list of books about rugs made during the classical period. Well-chosen photographs, largely black-and-white.

Dimand, M. S., and Mailey, Jean. *Oriental Rugs in the Metropolitan Museum of Art*. New York: The Metropolitan Museum of Art, 1973.

"At once a comprehensive history of oriental rug weaving and a catalog." Illustrated with good black-and-white and color photographs accompanied by structural descriptions.

Ellis, Charles Grant. *Oriental Carpets in the Philadelphia Museum of Art*. Philadelphia: Philadelphia Museum of Art, 1988.

Another catalog of a distinguished museum collection, written by the quirky Grand Old Man of oriental rug studies. Good black-and-white and color photographs accompanied by complete structural analyses.

EXHIBITION CATALOGS

Adraskand, Inc. *Belouch Prayer Rugs*, 1983. Available through the Adraskand Gallery, cited below.

This exhibition catalog by Michael Craycraft and Anne Halley is long on good color photos, structural analyses, and speculative attributions; short on hard evidence. Mild quibbles aside, it is a boon to lovers of Baluch tribal rugs.

Eiland, Murray L., ed. *Oriental Rugs from Pacific Collections*. Available from author, 199 Hillcrest Road, Berkeley, CA 94705.

Produced in conjunction with the 1990 International Conference of Oriental Carpets held in San Francisco. A tribute to the discerning eyes of their collectors, this thoughtfully produced volume provides a beautifully photographed selection of superior oriental weavings of all types.

Herrmann, Eberhart. *Seltene Orienteppich*. Munich.

Issued annually since 1978 by one of the leading European dealers in collector pieces, these catalogs' lack of an English text is more than compensated for by the visual treat afforded by the rugs they include. Excellent color plates. Recommended particularly to collectors whose access to galleries and auction previews is limited.

SPECIALIZED BOOKS *(listed alphabetically by subject)*

Baluch Weavings

Boucher, Jeff W. *Baluchi Woven Treasures*, 1989. Available from author, 250 S. Reynolds, Alexandria, VA 22304

Baluch tribal rugs are notoriously difficult to photograph, a truism belied by this book displaying the best of Col. Boucher's distinguished collection. Conservative attributions, structural analyses, and superb color plates add up to a valuable resource for collectors of tribal weavings.

Caucasian Rugs

Bennett, Ian. *Oriental Rugs: Volume 1. Caucasian Rugs.* Woodbridge, Suffolk, England: Oriental Textile Press, Ltd., 1981.

An English text based on a German book with catalog illustrations from Nagel's, a German auction house. The color isn't accurate, but the many examples provided of almost every type of 19th- and early-20th-century Caucasian rug offers an unequaled wealth of detail.

Burns, J. D. *The Caucasus: Traditions in Weaving.* Seattle: Court Street Press, 1987.

The color could be better, but all in all an impressive selection from a well-known collection of 18th- and 19th-century Caucasian rugs and flat weaves. Few collectors can afford to assemble rugs of this quality, but they provide an ideal to approach as best we can.

Schurmann, Ulrich. *Caucasian Rugs.* 1990 reprint available from Old 99 Associates, P.O. Box 318, Poolesville, MD 20837.

First published in 1967, this book presents superior examples of 18th- and 19th-century rugs categorized by geographical origin. Some of the attributions are now questioned, but this classic work by a prestigious German dealer remains an important resource for collectors, if only for the sheer beauty of the color plates.

Chinese Rugs

Eiland, Murray L. *Chinese and Exotic Rugs.* Boston: NYGS/Little, Brown and Company, 1979.

Although spotty in its coverage, there is little else currently available that has information about Chinese rug dyes and structure. The so-called exotic rugs include those made in Tibet, Mongolia, East Turkestan, India, Morocco and also Balkan flat weaves.

East Turkestan Rugs

Bidder, Hans. *Carpets from East Turkestan.* Accokeek, MD: Washington International Associates, 1979.

The best single source of information about these handsome rugs, including dyes, structure, and motifs. Illustrated with numerous sketches and a good selection of color and black-and-white photographs.

Flat Weaves

Cootner, Cathryn. *Flatwoven Textiles: The Arthur D. Jenkins Collection.* Washington, DC: The Textile Museum, 1981.

A representative selection of flat-woven pieces discussed in the context of the social and cultural climates in which they were made. Detailed structural information; well illustrated, including good color plates.

Justin, Valerie. *Flat-Woven Rugs of the World.* New York: Van Nostrand Reinhold, 1980.

Although the structural descriptions do not please specialist collectors, who think them simplified to the point of being misleading, it remains a good choice for those starting from scratch.

Petsopoulos, Yanni. *Kilims.* New York: Rizzoli, 1979; reprinted 1982.

Newer research is said to cast doubt on some of the information given in this prize-winning, gorgeously produced book, but it will always be of value to collectors.

Indian Rugs

Gans-Ruedin, E. *Indian Carpets.* New York: Rizzoli, 1984.

Information about Indian rug weaving is frustratingly hard to come by. The first half of this handsomely produced volume deals with Indian carpet production, both past and present, and the materials and dyes used. Next is a section devoted to classical Indian carpets, followed by examples of 20th-century rugs. Very good color plates.

Kurdish Rugs

Eagleton, William. *An Introduction to Kurdish Rugs and Other Weavings.* New York: Interlink Publishing Group, 1988.

The author, a diplomat and rug collector, researched Kurdish weavings while stationed in the Middle East in the 1980s. The color illustrations are not of very good quality, but the information is unobtainable elsewhere. Recommended for collectors of tribal weavings.

Stanzer, Wilfried. *Kordi: Lives, Rugs, Flatweaves of the Kurds in Khorasan.* Vienna: Adil Besim OHG, 1988.

Another important book, also based on extensive fieldwork, of interest primarily to tribal weaving enthusiasts. Handsomely produced; good color plates.

Persian Rugs

Edwards, A. Cecil. *The Persian Carpet*. London: Duckworth, 1953; often reprinted.

The author's 50 years in the carpet business lends an authoritative tone to this account of commercial Persian rug production in the first half of this century. Down-to-earth and thorough, the presentation is flawed by the grayed and somewhat blurry black-and-white photo illustrations. A basic resource nevertheless.

Opie, James. *Tribal Rugs of Southern Persia*. Portland, OR: James Opie Oriental Rugs, 1988.

The author is a respected dealer-cum-scholar writing from personal knowledge of the weaving areas he specializes in. An informative, appealingly written text accompanies the beautiful color plates.

Tanavoli, Parviz. *Shahsavan*. New York: Rizzoli, 1985.

Extremely well-illustrated, meticulously researched survey of the rugs and trappings made by Turkic-speaking tribal peoples of what is now northwestern Iran. The author, a retired University of Tehran professor, is highly regarded in the rug world.

Structure and Repair

Emery, Irene. *The Primary Structures of Fabrics*, rev. ed. Washington, DC: The Textile Museum, 1980.

The standard reference for those interested in textile structure; a must for flat-weave collectors. The intelligently organized text is illuminated by clear, consistent, and concisely captioned photo diagrams.

Neff, Ivan, and Maggs, Carol. *Dictionary of Oriental Rugs*, 1977.

Both the front and back of 42 rugs of different types are illustrated in color. Although the weave pattern is indeed an important clue to the origin of a rug, the addition of structural analyses would have added enormously to this guide's value. Of limited interest to experienced collectors, beginners will find it useful when playing the identification game.

Stone, Peter. *Oriental Rug Repair*. Chicago: Greenleaf Company, 1981.

The one and only book of its kind, so good there is no need for another, although some of the photo diagrams are a bit hard to decipher due to the fuzziness of the rug fibers. A must for every collector: even if you do not plan to do repairs yourself, this sets forth in very clear terms what should be done in the way of repair and tips on how to avoid the need for it.

Turkish Rugs

Acar, Belkis Balpinar. *Kilim-Cicim-Zili-Sumak: Turkish Flatweaves*. Istanbul, 1983. English edition available.

Ms. Balpinar, who organized the permanent exhibit of Turkish flat weaves at the Sultan Ahmet Mosque in Istanbul, knows her subject very well. Good color plates.

Brüggemann, Werner, and Böhmer, Harald. *Rugs of the Peasants and Nomads of Anatolia*. Munich: 1983. English translation available.

Another prize-winning book that should be acquired by every collector regardless of specific interests. Excellent information on dyes and design development; first-rate color plates keyed to rug descriptions, accompanied by structural and dye analyses.

Cootner, Cathryn. *Anatolian Kilims: The Caroline & H. McCoy Jones Collection*. London: The Fine Arts Museums of San Francisco and Hali Publications, 1990.

Breathtaking examples in superb color compensate for a text overflowing with aesthetic appreciation at the expense of the scholarly commentary.

Yetkin, Serare. *Historical Turkish Carpets*. Istanbul: 1981.

A paperback publication available through specialist book dealers. A valuable, modestly priced scholarly resource for Turkish rug enthusiasts. The color illustrations are only fair; the black-and-whites are poor, but there are a lot of them, many of material unavailable elsewhere.

Zipper, Kurt, and Fritzsche, Claudia. *Oriental Rugs: Volume 4, Turkish*. Published in 1989 in German; English edition available.

Turkoman Weavings

Azadi, Siawosch. *Turkoman Carpets*. Hamburg: 1970. English edition published in 1975 by The Crosby Press, Wales.

Well-organized introduction to a widely collected group. Illustrated with detailed sketches and color plates of good rugs dully reproduced.

Loges, Werner. *Turkoman Tribal Rugs*. Atlantic Highlands, NJ: Humanities Press, 1980.

Another good introductory book. The color plates are better than those in the Azadi book; useful glossary and tables of rug structures and colors.

Mackie, Louise, and Thompson, Jon, eds. *Turkmen: Tribal Carpets and Traditions*. Washington, DC: The Textile Museum, 1980.

A collection of well-illustrated scholarly essays written in connection with a major exhibition of Turkoman weaving at the Textile Museum. Interesting material about tribal life. The color is quite good, and the structural analyses are notable for their completeness; but the keying of text to illustrations is confusing, and the lack of an index is regrettable.

Tzareva, Elena. *Rugs and Carpets from Central Asia: The Russian Collections.* New York: Penguin, 1984.

A selection from Russian collections, most never published before, with Uzbek, Kerghiz, Kazakh, and Karakalpak tribal rugs in addition to the more familiar Turkoman examples. The introduction discusses the place of weaving in tribal culture, the kinds of articles woven, and the significance of the motifs used. Good-quality color plates are accompanied by detailed structural analyses.

SOURCES FOR BOOKS ABOUT ORIENTAL RUGS AND RELATED TOPICS

Adraskand, Inc., 15 Ross Avenue, San Anselmo, CA 94960; (415) 459-1711. Principally tribal and village rugs, but books about rugs, too.

The East-West Room, Myrna Bloom, 3139 Alpin Drive, Dresher, PA 19025; (215) 657-0178. Large stock; book lists on request; discounts available.

George F. Gilmore, 2150 Newport Blvd., Costa Mesa, CA 92626; (714) 646-7847. *Hali* backlist in addition to rug books.

Oriental Rug Books, Denis B. Marquand, P.O. Box 1187, Culver City, CA 90232.

Paragon Book Gallery, Ltd., 2130 Broadway (in mezzanine of the Hotel Beacon), New York, NY 10023. Books on the Middle and Far East, including carpets and textiles. Write for catalog.

Renate Halpern Galleries, Inc., 325 East 79th Street, New York, NY 10021; (212) 988-9316. Rugs, tapestries, textiles, and books.

The Rug Book Shop, 2603 Talbot Road, Baltimore, MD, 21216-1621; (301) 367-8194. Large stock; book lists on request.

Strand Book Store, 828 Broadway (corner of 12th Street), New York, NY 10003; (212) 473-1452. "8 miles of books on all subjects; over 2 million in stock," including remainders and review copies at 50% off. I found here a mint copy of the 1974 reprint of Schurmann's *Caucasian Rugs* at half the list price. Worth a visit when in New York.

The Textile Museum, The Museum Shop, 2320 S Street, NW, Washington DC 20008; (202) 667-0441. A good selection of the best of the rug books as well as other textile arts; 10% discount to members.

DEALERS IN COLLECTIBLE ORIENTAL RUGS

GENERALISTS

The following dealers represent only a fraction of the reputable firms to be found nationwide and in Canada. The bulk of their business is in old and antique decorative carpets augmented by the best of the new productions, but most also have a good selection of collectible village and tribal weavings. Retailers who stock only new commercial goods are unlikely to have anything of collectible interest.

If you live far removed from the principal urban centers, I suggest you leave your name and wants with the dealers in your area, as pieces of unusual interest taken in on trade are apt to be shipped to the major auction houses, where, because of the exposure to the international trade, a good price can usually be obtained more quickly than from a local clientele.

In addition to a good selection of fine rugs, well-established dealers can supply rug repair and washing services either in-house or by recommendation. All are qualified to do appraisals, but the basis for determining the fee varies: in some cases it is a percentage of the rug's value; some dealers, like Washington, DC's Elsie Nazarian, who considers appraisals a courtesy service to her clients, charge a nominal flat fee.

Always call first: Some dealers have limited hours; others can be seen only by appointment; still others may have moved or gone out of business. This applies to all dealers on all lists.

CALIFORNIA

Ami Negbi Gallery Inc., 7736 Fay Avenue, Suite 102, La Jolla, CA 92037; by appointment: (619) 456-0131, 552-9328.

Baktiari Gallery, Arky Robbins, 2843 Clay Street, San Francisco, CA 94115; (415) 346-0437. Superior decorative rugs; fine collectibles.

Carpets of the Inner Circle, 444 Jackson Street, San Francisco, CA 94111; (415) 398-2988.

Claremont Rug Company, 6087 Claremont Avenue, Oakland, CA 94681; (415) 654-8661. Old decorative rugs in superb condition.

Emmett Eiland Gallery, 889 Ensenada Street, Berkeley, CA 94707; (415) 526-1087.

Oriental Carpet Gallery, 2150 Newport Boulevard, Costa Mesa, CA 92626; (714) 646-7847.

COLORADO

Phillips, Inc., Boulder, CO; by appointment only: (303) 444-0045.

CONNECTICUT

James Demorest, 1 Great Hammock Road, Old Saybrook, CT 06475; by appointment: (203) 388-9547.

Des Jardins, 4 Green Hill Road, Washington, CT 06794; (203) 868-9495.

Kebabian's, 73 Elm Street, New Haven, CT 06510; (203) 865-0567.

Oriental Rugs Ltd., 4 East Main Street, Mystic, CT; (203) 572-9233.

Tschebull Antique Carpets, 8 West Avenue, Darien, CT 06820; (203) 655-6610.

DISTRICT OF COLUMBIA

Nazarian Bros., Inc., 4801 Massachusetts Avenue, NW, Suite 200, Washington DC; (202) 364-6400.

David Zahirpour, 4918 Wisconsin Avenue, NW, Washington DC 20016; (202) 338-4141, 244-1800.

ILLINOIS

Karnig A. Demirdjian & Sons, Inc., 620 N. Michigan Avenue, Suite 330, Chicago, IL 60611; (312) 337-7847.

Joseph W. Fell, Ltd., 3221 North Clark Street, Chicago, IL 60657; (312) 549-6076.

The Nomad's Loom, 3227 North Clark Street, Chicago, IL 60657; (312) 248-5544

INDIANA

Antique Oriental Rugs & More, 2602 East 62nd Street, Indianapolis, IN 46220; (317) 255-3066.

KENTUCKY

D. Kelly's–Karkouti Oriental Rugs, Chevy Chase Place, 870 East High, Lexington, KY 40502; (606) 266-7802/9274.

MASSACHUSETTS

Thomas Caruso, Belmont, MA 02178; (617) 484-7452. Antique and classical carpets and textiles.

John J. Collins, Jr., 8 Newbury Street, Boston, MA 02116; (617) 267-4353. Gallery with decorative and collectible rugs.

Arthur T. Gregorian, Inc., 2284 Washington Street, Newton Lower Falls, MA 02162; (617) 244-2553.

Lawrence Kearney, P.O. Box 302, Newton, MA 02161; by appointment: (617) 964-0012.

Louise Woodhead, 300 Kent Street, Brookline, MA 02146; by appointment: (617) 566-2132. Antique rugs and textiles, more likely than most to have classical pieces.

Yenian Oriental Rugs, 57 Pearl Street, Springfield, MA 01101; (413) 737-0368.

MICHIGAN

Azar's, 251 Merrill, Birmingham, MI 48009; (313) 644-7311.

MINNESOTA

Persia International Carpets, 111 Washington Avenue North, Minneapolis, MN 55401; (612) 339-4771.

Shahidi Oriental Rug Co., 4253 Bryant Avenue South, Minneapolis, MN 55409; (612) 827-5977.

MISSOURI

Bendas Oriental Rug Co., 7505 Delmar Boulevard, St. Louis, MO 63130; (314) 862-4410.

NEBRASKA

Souq, Ltd., 421 South 11th Street, Omaha, NE 68102; (402) 345-1762.

NEW HAMPSHIRE

Peter Pap Oriental Rugs, Inc., Route 101, Box 286, Dublin, NH 03444; (603) 563-8717. Gallery with decorative and collectible rugs.

NEW JERSEY

Ronnie Newman, P.O. Box 14, Ridgewood, NJ 07451; by appointment: (201) 825-8775. International dealer in rare and esoteric village, tribal, and decorative pieces.

Sandler & Worth, Oriental Rug Galleries, 160 Route 22, Springfield, NJ 07081; (201) 376-5500.

NEW YORK

Berdj Abadjian, 201 East 57th Street, New York, NY 10021; (212) 688-2229.

Bergi Andonian, 102 Madison Avenue (at 29th Street), New York, NY

10016; (212) 532-4688. International dealer in classical, collectible, and decorative rugs.

A Beshar & Co., Inc., 611 Broadway, New York, NY 10014; (212) 529-7300.

Doris Leslie Blau, 15 East 57th Street, New York, NY 10021; (212) 759-3715. More likely than most to have classical carpets.

The Ghordian Knot, 136 East 57th Street (3rd floor), New York, NY 10022; (212) 371-6390. More likely than most to have classical rugs.

Renate Halpern, 325 East 79th Street, New York, NY 10021; by appointment: (212) 988-9316. Gallery with rugs, tapestries, and textiles.

K. Kermani Oriental Rugs, Inc., 3905 State Street, Schenectady, NY 12304; (518) 393-6884.

NORTH CAROLINA

Boone's Antiques, Highway 301 South, P.O. Box 3796, Wilson, NC 27893; (919) 237-1508.

Fargo-Hanna Oriental Rugs, 324 West Geer Street, Durham, NC 27707; (919) 419-0963.

The Persian Carpet, Durham-Chapel Hill Boulevard, Chapel Hill, NC 27514; (919) 968-0366.

OHIO

House of Davidian, Inc., 7 North Franklin Street, Chagrin Falls, OH 44022; (216) 247-3868.

Richard Markarian, 610 Walnut Street, Cincinnati, OH 45202; (513) 621-4122.

PENNSYLVANIA

Ani Oriental Rugs, 107 South Monroe Street, Media, PA 19063; (215) 565-4556.

George O'Bannon Oriental Carpets, 5666 Northumberland Street, Pittsburgh, PA 15217; (412) 422-0300. Reliable source for good examples of the new rug productions as well as fine antiques.

Peter Scholten, Oriental Rugs, 117 West Main Street, Boalsburg, PA 16827; (814) 466-7576/7506.

TENNESSEE

Ro's Oriental Rugs, Inc., 6602 Highway 100, Nashville, TN 37205; (615) 352-9055, 665-0094.

TEXAS

Caravanserai Ltd., Austin, TX 78765; by appointment: Casey Waller, (512) 459-2118.

Goravanchi Co. Persian Rugs, Pavilion Saks Fifth Avenue, 1800 Post Oak Boulevard, Suite 110, Houston, TX 77056; (713) 622-1023.

Post Oak Gallery, 2809 Fondren Road, Houston, TX 77063; (713) 965-0922.

VERMONT

Vincent J. Fernandez, Route 2, Box 79, Richmond, VT 05477; by appointment: (802) 434-3626.

VIRGINIA

Edgeworth-Trent Oriental Rug Co., 13 West Grace Street, Richmond, VA 23220; (804) 782-9666.

John Murray, 10 Horseshoe Drive, Williamsburg, VA 23185; by appointment: (804) 220-2114.

Salem M. Eways, Inc., 1417 N. Emmet Street, Charlottesville, VA 22901; (804) 295-3136.

WISCONSIN

Edward S. Gulesserian, 8 South Breese Terrace, Madison, WI 53711.

CANADA

Ararat Rug Company, Ltd., 3457 Park Avenue, Montreal, Quebec, Canada H2X 2H6; (514) 288-1218.

Uno Langman Ltd., 2117 Granville Street, Vancouver, BC V6H 3E9.

SPECIALISTS IN VILLAGE AND TRIBAL RUGS AND TRAPPINGS

CALIFORNIA

Adraskand, Inc., 15 Ross Avenue, San Anselmo, CA 94960; (415) 459-1700. Nirvana for the tribal weavings collector.

Anahita Gallery, Santa Monica, CA; by appointment: (213) 455-2310.

Michael Andrews, San Francisco, CA; by appointment: (415) 641-1937.

Armen Gallery, 6015 College Avenue, Oakland, CA 94618; (415) 655-0167.

Blackmon Gallery, 2140 Bush Street, No. 1, San Francisco, CA 94115; by appointment: (415) 922-1859.

Alex Chis Oriental Rugs, P.O. Box 2944, Niles Station, Fremont, CA 94536; (415) 489-8554. Tribal rugs, Islamic textiles.

Geissmann, 143 Cedros Avenue, Suite B 103, Solana Beach, CA 92075; (619) 481-3489.

Hazara Oriental Rug Gallery, 6251 College Avenue, Oakland, CA 94618; (415) 655-3511.

Noori Gallery, 2340 Polk Street, San Francisco, CA 94109; (415) 441-8468. Rugs, textiles, Middle Eastern art objects.

Rugs and Art, 7 East Anapamu Street, Santa Barbara, CA 93101; (805) 962-2166. Emphasis on Turkoman and Baluch weavings.

James D. Waterbury Oriental Rugs, P.O. Box 681, Camarillo, CA 93011; (805) 388-9901. Currently specializes in old Caucasian rugs.

COLORADO

Shaver-Ramsey, 2414 East 3rd Avenue, Denver, CO 80206; (303) 320-6363. Rugs, kilims, textiles.

FLORIDA

Steven Maeck, P.O. Box 1408, Key West, FL 33041; by appointment: (305) 293-3045.

GEORGIA

Afghanistan's Nomadic Rugs, 3219 Cains Hill Place, NE, Atlanta, GA 30305; (404) 261-7259.

ILLINOIS

Connoisseur Oriental Rugs, 1000 Chicago Avenue, Evanston, IL 60202; (708) 866-6622/7722.

Michael Cuccello, Chicago, IL; by appointment: (312) 348-3988.

MAINE

A. E. Runge, Jr., 106 Main Street, Yarmouth, ME 04096; (207) 846-9000.

MASSACHUSETTS

Yayla Tribal Rugs, 308 Broadway, Cambridge, MA 02139; (617) 576-3241. Specializes in Turkish and Afghan (Turkoman; Baluch) material; active wholesaler.

NEW HAMPSHIRE

Art Rug, 74 North Main Street, Concord, NH 03301; (603) 224-3099.

NEW YORK

Maqam/Dennis R. Dodds, 19 West 55th Street, #6A, New York, NY 10019; (212) 977-3603. Specializes in early village rugs, textiles.

OHIO

The Rug Collector's Gallery, 2460 Fairmount Boulevard, Cleveland Heights, OH 44106; (216) 721-9333.

OREGON

James Opie Oriental Rugs, Inc., 214 SW Stark Street, Portland, OR 97204; (503) 226-0116. Specializes in fine old Southwest Persian rugs and trappings.

PENNSYLVANIA

Peter Scholten, Oriental Rugs, 117 West Main Street, Boalsburg, PA 16827; (814) 466-7576/7506.

Woven Legends, 4700 Wissahickon #106, Philadelphia, PA 19144; (215) 849-8344.

TEXAS

Caravanserai. Ltd., P.O. Box 4725, Austin, TX 78765; (512) 459-2118. Specializes in Central Asian and Tibetan rugs and textiles.

VIRGINIA

Sun Bow Trading Company, 108 Fourth Street NE, Charlottesville, VA 22901; (804) 293-8821.

FLAT WEAVES

Most of the dealers in these lists stock at least a few old kilims and soumaks; those listed alphabetically below deal in flat weaves either exclusively or to an extent that qualifies them as better than average mentors for beginning collectors.

George Fine Kilims, 1 Cottage Street, Easthampton, MA 01027; by appointment: (413) 527-8527. A wide range of flat weaves, mostly Anatolian.

Marian Miller Kilims, 148 East 28th Street, New York, NY 10016; (212) 685-7746. Kilims only: good stock of antique, old, and fine new pieces.

Mark Shilen Gallery, 201 Prince Street, New York, NY 10012; (212) 777-3370. Specializing in antique Persian and Turkish kilims.

John Wertime, 4633 34th Street, South Arlington, VA 22204; by appointment: (703) 379-8528. Scholar/consultant/dealer in flat weaves.

Yayla Tribal Rugs, 308 Broadway, Cambridge, MA 02139; (617) 576-3249. Very large stock of old Turkish kilims.

AUCTION HOUSES

During 1990, collectors had an unprecedented opportunity to inspect and bid on two distinguished groups of carpets: the classical carpets consigned to Sotheby's by the Getty Museum in Malibu, California, and the Meyer-Müller collection from Zurich offered at Christie's East.

The following five houses hold sales devoted to oriental rugs as well as sales in which rugs are offered together with fine furnishings. The number of rug-only sales varies from house to house and year to year, but all hold previews of from two days to a week in length immediately prior to the sale, and all offer a variety of services.

Catalog subscriptions: All of the houses offer subscriptions to catalogs pertaining to specific interests. The price includes postsale results and the illustrated bulletins published several times a year.

The detail provided in catalog descriptions of condition not only varies from house to house but from rug to rug and should always be double-checked either in person or by phone with the rug experts.

Estimates of values: As a courtesy to potential consignors, the auction house experts will supply free verbal estimates of what your property may bring at auction. Call the rug department to inquire how this may best be done. Clear photographs of the front and back, the ends and edges, and close-ups of details may suffice; sometimes it may be necessary for a rug to be shipped to the auction house for a hands-on inspection.

Appraisals: The cost of a formal written appraisal varies from house to house, but in all cases it is more than the fee most dealers charge.

Packing and shipping: All of the houses can arrange for the packing and shipping of items bought at auction. This charge, which can be considerable, should be figured into the total price you are willing to pay. It would be wise to ask for an estimate before deciding to bid.

Absentee and phone bids: As a courtesy to buyers who are unable to attend, verbal or written bids may be left prior to a sale. For important rugs, it may be possible to arrange to bid during the sale over the telephone through an auction house representative. There are no fees for these services.

Butterfield & Butterfield, 220 San Bruno Avenue, San Francisco, CA 94103. For catalogs and information about buying and selling at auction and related fees, call (415) 861-7500; call the same number, ext. 292, for the rug department.

Seventy to eighty percent of the buyers at Butterfield's rug auctions are dealers, and the majority of rugs offered fall into the decorative commercial carpet category. The catalogs have fewer photographs than others do, and the descriptions are bare bones: no dating is provided, and only major repairs and significant reductions in size are reported. However, the Butterfield rug department is knowledgeable and happy to provide detailed information at previews—held in Los Angeles as well as San Francisco—and over the phone.

Christie's East, 219 East 67th Street, New York, NY 10021. For rug department, call (212) 606-0550; for catalogs, call (718) 784-1480; for a brochure about buying and selling at auction, call Customer Service, (212) 606-0440.

On the heels of two successful auctions of important collections of rugs in New York at its East 67th Street facility, Christie's cut back on its Islamic Arts departments both here and in London. In the future, except for a rug-only sale in January, rugs will be offered through the year at furniture sales at Park Avenue and Christie's East "when warranted." It is hoped that Christie's will continue to have the same high proportion of old and interesting estate rugs that have over the years distinguished their offerings. Their well-illustrated rug-only sale catalogs (color and black-and-white; condition reports included) are a must for the reference library of every collector.

Grogan & Company, 890 Commonwealth Avenue, Boston, MA 02215. Call (617) 566-7715 for catalog sales and buying and selling information. For rugs, ask for decorative arts specialists.

Michael Grogan, founder and president of this up-and-coming auction house, cut his teeth in Sotheby's rug department in New York. Grogan & Company cannot yet compete in numbers with the established houses, but the quality of the rugs being offered, usually together with silver or other fine furnishings, is attracting more and more collector attention, and the house is small enough to be both friendly and flexible. The catalog descriptions are basic; the photographs, although few in number, are good.

Skinner, Inc., 357 Main Street, Bolton, MA 01740. Call (508) 779-6241 for catalog sales, calendar of events flyers, and buying and selling information. For rugs, ask for rug department.

Skinner's holds rug-only sales each spring and fall and offers a good selection throughout the year at furniture sales. The rugs-as-art preview presentations pioneered by Louise Woodhead are far superior to those of any other house, and the gallery's location in a small town easily accessible by major highways makes the auction-day trip a pleasant outing. The selling style here is relaxed and informal, and the staff friendly and helpful. A subscription to the well-illustrated rug sale catalogs (both color and black-and-white; condition reports given) is a worthwhile investment.

Sotheby's, 1334 York Avenue, New York, NY 10021. Call (212) 606-7000 for catalogs, auction newsletters, and information about buying and selling. Call (212) 606-7996 for the rug department.

Sotheby's offers rugs at three to four major rug-only sales each year and at arcade sales when warranted. Collectors should consider as essential a subscription to the well-illustrated catalogs: the major sales provide structural analyses for the important collector pieces and condition reports for all rugs; the arcade sale catalogs, which offer only basic information, are generously illustrated in black and white. The rug experts here are knowledgeable and willing to be helpful to all comers, but beginning collectors unable to enter the competition at a fairly high level should not expect much in the way of TLC from this powerhouse organization as a whole.

Oriental rugs are offered from time to time by other auction houses as well, but reliable information about age, type, and dyes is usually lacking except for those able to afford expert advice from consultants. Since auction services come and go, collectors may wish to subscribe to a weekly journal that, although New England in origin and emphasis, provides current information about nationwide offerings:

Antiques and Arts Weekly, The Bee Publishing Company, Inc., 5 Church Hill Road, Newtown, CT 06470. For subscription information call (203) 426-3141.

Publishes previews and reviews of antique shows and auctions of unusual interest, editorial features on notable collections, and auction and antique show promotional advertising and listings by date.

ORIENTAL RUG SOCIETIES IN THE UNITED STATES AND CANADA

UNITED STATES

CALIFORNIA

The San Diego Rug and Textile Society, 143 South Cedros Avenue E, Solano Beach, CA 92075.

San Francisco Bay Area Rug Society, 4139 Coralee Lane, Lafayette, CA 95549; (415) 284-5605.

Textile Group of Los Angeles, 894 South Bronson Avenue, Los Angeles, CA 90005; (213) 931-4987.

Textile Museum Associates of Southern California (TMA/SC), P.O. Box 3893, Manhattan Beach, CA 90266; (213) 379-5048.

CONNECTICUT

The Connecticut Rug Society, P.O. Box 2842, Westport, CT 06880.

DISTRICT OF COLUMBIA

Armenian Rugs Society, 4505 Stanford Street, Chevy Chase, MD 20815; (301) 654-4044.

The International Hajji Baba Society, Inc., 6500 Pinecrest Court, Annadale, VA 22003.

The Washington Textile Group, 900 Turkey Run Road, McLean, VA 22101.

FLORIDA

For information about a newly formed rug society meeting in the Orlando/Winter Park area, call or write Larry Bergman, P.O. Box 1845, Winter Garden, FL 34787; (407) 656-9508.

ILLINOIS

The Chicago Rug Society, 126 East Lincoln, Palatine, IL 60067; (708) 358-1747.

KANSAS

Oriental Rug Society of Kansas City, 4200 West 83rd Street, Suite 210, Prairie Village, KS 66208.

MASSACHUSETTS

The New Boston Rug Society, 24 Oak Meadow Road, Lincoln, MA 01773.

NEW JERSEY

Princeton Rug Society, 24 Armour Road, Princeton, NJ 98540.

NEW YORK

New York Rug Society, 155 East 72nd Street, New York, NY 10021.

NORTH CAROLINA

Triangle Rug Society, 3100 Cornwall Road, Durham, NC 27707.

OHIO

Cleveland Rug Society, 3140 N. Martadale Drive, Akron, OH 44333.

RHODE ISLAND

The Oriental Rug/Textile Society of New England, 145 Grotto Avenue, Providence, RI 02906; (401) 272-0765.

CANADA

MONTREAL

Montreal Oriental Rug Society, 1451 Sherbrooke Street W, Montreal H3G 2S8, Quebec; (514) 937-6273.

TORONTO

Oriental Rug Society of Toronto, 235 Yorkland Boulevard, Willow Dale M2J 4Y8, Ontario.

NOTABLE NORTH AMERICAN RUG COLLECTIONS

MUSEUMS

The following museums have collections worth seeing, but not all rugs are on view at any one time. *Hali* and *Oriental Rug Review* provide their subscribers with news of special exhibitions at these and other institutions, and the catalogs prepared for these events are usually a relatively inexpensive source of up-to-date, authoritative information. Since they are subject to change, days open and hours are not given. (Regrettably, the important collections held by the Getty Museum in Malibu, California, and the Baltimore Museum of Art, which you might see mentioned elsewhere, had been largely deaccessioned as of January 1991.)

CALIFORNIA

Berkeley Lowie Museum of Anthropology
Los Angeles County Museum of Art
San Francisco M. H. de Young Memorial Museum
The H. McCoy and Caroline Jones collection of tribal rugs and kilims was donated to this museum in 1980; additional items have been added since. An endowed center for the study of rugs and textiles is planned.

DELAWARE

Wilmington Winterthur Museum (rug tours by appointment)

DISTRICT OF COLUMBIA

Washington The Textile Museum, (202) 667-0441.
Membership (tax-deductible) should be considered a priority by every collector. The only institution of its kind in the United States, it supports a conservation laboratory and research library, publishes scholarly publications, and mounts frequent and superior exhibitions. The TM also sponsors special-interest tours here and abroad.

MASSACHUSETTS

Boston–Cambridge Museum of Fine Arts
Fogg Art Museum, Harvard University

Deerfield Historic Deerfield

Springfield George Walter Vincent Smith Art Museum (exceptional Turkoman examples)

MISSOURI

St. Louis The St. Louis Art Museum

OHIO

Cincinnati The Cincinnati Art Museum

PENNSYLVANIA

Philadelphia Philadelphia Museum of Art

NEW YORK

New York The Brooklyn Museum
The Frick Collection
Hispanic Society of America
The Metropolitan Museum of Art

NORTH CAROLINA

Asheville Biltmore Estate
New Bern Tryon Palace Restoration

VIRGINIA

Williamsburg The Williamsburg Restoration

CANADA

Toronto Royal Ontario Museum

OTHER COLLECTIONS

California The Ahwahnee Hotel (completed 1927)
National Historic Landmark, Yosemite National Park. Decorated with oriental flat weaves by the noted Persian art scholars, Phyllis Ackerman and Arthur Upham Pope.

Canada Museum for Textiles, Toronto; (416) 599-5515

New York Olana, New York State Historic Site, Hudson; Islamic-style estate of the Hudson River School artist, Frederic Church; (518) 828-0135

Pennsylvania Glencairn Museum, Bryn Athyn; (215) 947-9919 or 947-4200

South Carolina Liberty Textile Collection, Greenville; Liberty Corporation, (803) 268-8096

CARE AND REPAIR SERVICES AND SUPPLIES

Most dealers in old rugs employ workers able to make serviceable repairs but who may or may not be sufficiently skilled to provide restoration services. The restoration specialists listed below may not wish to do basic repairs and may have work backed up for as much as a year. However, since good craftspeople invariably know who the other good ones are, additional names can probably be provided on request. To help you decide what level of skill will best serve your particular needs, please first read or review the sections dealing with rug care and repair.

RESTORATION

FLAT WEAVES

Barnett, Ronee, 430 West 14th Street, New York, NY 10011; (212) 807-9630.

Kane, Tina, 8 Big Island Road, Warwick, NY 10990; (914) 986-8522.

Sanford Restoration Works: Emily Sanford, 451 Gould Avenue, Hermosa Beach, CA 90254; (213) 374-7412.

Sany and Company: S. Ahmad Sany, 219 East 31st Street, New York, NY 10016; (212) 685-6603.

Zahirpour, David, 4918 Wisconsin Avenue NW, Washington, DC 20016; (202) 338-4141, 244-1800.

PILE

Altay Tribal Rugs, 213A Highland Avenue, Somerville, MA 02143: (518) 623-5526. Restoration and hand-washing.

Atenian, Vartanoush, 38 East 57th Street, New York, NY 10022; (212) 755-0374; (718) 263-0049 (home).

Buckland-Rasmussen: Mary Rasmussen, 1451 Sherbrooke Street W., Montreal, Canada H3G 2S8; (514) 937-6273.

Costikyan Cleaning and Restoration, 32-16 37th Avenue, Long Island City, NY 11101; (212) 786-9684.

Thomas J. Dwyer Ltd., 304 East Genesee Street, Fayetteville, NY 13066; (315) 637-4988.

Huggins, James A., c/o Salem M. Eways, Inc., 1417 N. Emmet Street, Charlottesville, VA 22901; (804) 295-3136.

Newman, Richard E., 337 East 81st Street, New York, NY 10028; (212) 249-9797. Tribal and village rug specialist: reweaving, custom spinning, hand-washing.

Sanford Restoration Works: Emily Sanford, 451 Gould Avenue, Hermosa Beach, CA 90254; (213) 374-7412.

  Note: Ms. Sanford informed me at the time of writing that an international referral service to craftspeople qualified to do rug restoration is in the planning stage. Assuming all goes as hoped, please do not call the number given above for a list; instead, direct your requests to P.O. Box 925, Hermosa Beach, CA 90254.

Sany and Company: S. Ahmad Sany, 219 East 31st Street, New York, NY 10016; (212) 685-6603.

Shallcross & Lorraine: Beacon Hill, Boston MA 02114; (617) 720-2133.

Talisman: David Walker, Santa Cruz, CA; (408) 425-7847.

Zahirpour, David, 4918 Wisconsin Avenue NW, Washington, DC 20016; (202) 338-4141, 244-1800.

TEXTILE CONSERVATION

Buckland-Rasmussen: Mary Rasmussen, 1451 Sherbrooke Street W., Montreal, Canada H3G 2S8; (514) 937-6273.

Chevalier Conservation: Stan Olshefski and Dominique Chevalier, 500 West Avenue, Stamford, CT 06902; (203) 969-1980.

Restoration Works: Emily Sanford, 451 Gould Avenue, Hermosa Beach, CA 90254; (213) 374-7412.

The Textile Conservation Workshop: Main Street, South Salem, NY 10590; (914) 763-5805.

The Textile Museum, 2320 S Street NW, Washington, DC 20008.

  Note: Textile conservation is a rapidly growing field of specialization. Although the TM workshop is not available for private work, it may have publications of interest to private collectors and suggestions as to where services may be obtained. Call the Education Department at (202) 667-0441.

CLEANING SERVICES

If a rug is clearly in need of washing and you have neither the time nor the place to do it properly yourself, be prepared to ship it to a facility experienced in the washing of oriental rugs. The local carpet steam cleaner will not do. This is a case where a penny saved can result in many dollars lost; besides, the cost of washing a rug in average condition is relatively modest. Request that an estimate be supplied to you in writing when the rug is received, and make sure it will be adequately insured just in case something goes wrong. Experts can make mistakes, too.

A. Beshar and Company, 5 Canal Place, Bronx, NY 10451; (212) 292-3301. For rug washing call above number; for repairs, (212) 529-7300.

Danbury Rug Works, 13 Summit Street, Danbury, CT 06810; (203) 743-1691. Wool rugs washed; only very basic repairs.

Fred Remmers Rug Cleaners, 2186 Central Avenue, Memphis, TN 38104; (901) 278-3704.

Kouri's, 95 North Clinton Street, Poughkeepsie, NY 12601; (914) 471-4909/4968.

Nazarian Bros., Inc., 4801 Massachusetts Avenue NW, Washington, DC 20016; (202) 364-6400. This respected old-line firm of rug dealers also operates a washing establishment. Call this number for further information about cleaning, repair, and restoration services.

Oriental Cleaning Services, 3907 Ross Avenue, Dallas, TX 75204; (214) 821-9135. Offers rug washing, cleaning of silk rugs, repairs.

Rug Renovating Company, 532 North Grove Street, East Orange, NJ 07017; (201) 675-8313. Offers rug washing, cleaning of silk rugs, repairs.

Shishadeh (formerly Jerrehian), 116 Cricket Avenue, Ardmore, PA 19003; (215) 649-2000.

CLEANING AND REPAIR SUPPLIES

Orvus Paste, low pH anionic detergent. Available from Talas Conservation Supplies, 213 West 35th Street, New York, NY 10001; (212) 736-7744.

Crispell's Mothproofing Solution. Read the section on rug storage first. Order from Chatalbash (below) or call Crispell, (914) 454-5500, for local suppliers.

Chatalbash Rug Co., Inc., 20 East 30th Street, New York, NY 10016; (212) 532-5260. Write or phone for catalog. Source for Paternayan and Appleton wool rug yarns, linen carpet thread, replacement edgings, stair rods and clips, rug hanging clips, cotton fringing (special catalog on request), rug underlayments, Crispell's Mothproofing Solution, and other supplies.

BIBLIOGRAPHY

AUCTION CATALOGS

Butterfield and Butterfield. Sale #4367R, 9/21/90.

Christie's East. Sale #6786, 4/8/89; sale #6829, 6/6/89; sale #6894, 9/12/89; sale #6919, 11/29/89; sale #7056, 4/7/90; sale #7055, 9/11/90; sale #7135, 1/22/91.

Skinner's. Sale #1264, 6/4/89; sale #1293, 12/2/89; sale #1328, 6/10/90; sale #1357, 12/1/90; sale #1375, 2/15/91.

Sotheby's. Sale #5868, 6/3/89; sale #5893, 9/13/89; sale #5974, 1/20/90; sale #6035, 6/9/90; sale #1333, 9/11/90; sale #6112, 12/8/90; sale #6124, 12/8/90.

PERIODICALS, JOURNALS, BULLETINS, AND EXHIBITION CATALOGS

"All About Oriental Rugs." *Rug News*, Vol. 8, No. 10, January 1987.

Badische Co. Catalog of dye materials, 128 Duane Street, New York, NY, no date, c. 1900.

Baker, George P. OCM Catalog, 1886.

Bogle, Michael M. "The Mounting of Textiles for Storage and Display." *Textile Conservation Center Notes, No. 15*. North Andover, MA: Merrimack Valley Textile Museum, 1979.

————. "The Storage of Textiles." *Textile Conservation Center Notes, No. 14*. North Andover, MA: Merrimack Valley Textile Museum, 1979.

————. "Technical Data on Moth-Proofing." *Textile Conservation Notes, No. 10*. North Andover, MA: Merrimack Valley Textile Museum, 1979.

————. "Technical Data on Silk Textiles." *Textile Conservation Center Notes, No. 1*. North Andover, MA: Merrimack Valley Textile Museum, 1979.

————. "Technical Data on Wool Textiles." *Textile Conservation Center Notes, No. 2*. North Andover, MA: Merrimack Valley Textile Museum, 1979.

Böhmer, Harald. Notes titled "Dyeing of Wool with Natural Dyes," 1984.

_____. "The Revival of Natural Dyeing in Two Traditional Weaving Areas of Anatolia." *Oriental Rug Review*, Vol. 3, No. 9, December 1983.

Bulbach, Stanley. "The Weaving Arts: An Ancient Technology." Reprinted in *Rug News*, Vol. 10, No. 8, January 1989.

Columbus, Joseph V., ed. "Principles of Practical Cleaning for Old and Fragile Textiles." *Museum News Technical Supplement*, Conservation Department, Textile Museum. Washington, DC: American Association of Museums, 1956.

"The Decorative Rug." Rug Basics Series, updated reprint. *Oriental Rug Review*, Vol. 10, No. 3, 1990.

Diyarbekirli, Nejat. "New Light on Pazyryk Carpet." Translated by Alan Mellaart. *Hali*, Vol. 1, No. 3, 1978.

Eiland, Murray. "A Look at the Word Tribal." *Oriental Rug Review*, Vol. 9, No. 5, 1989.

Engerisser, Franz. "Ornamentale Kufi-Schrift und Flechtbandmotive in Borduren von Orientteppichen." *Hali*, Vol. 3, No. 1, 1980.

Ford, P. R. J. "Kelardasht Weaving." *Rug News*, Vol. 7, No. 8, pp. 16–17, October 1985.

Gardiner, Roger F. *Oriental Rugs in Canadian Collections*. Catalog of 1975 exhibition. Toronto, Canada: The Oriental Rug Society, 1975.

Gross, Laurance. "Reducing the Perils of Textile Display," *Museum News*, Vol. 38, No. 1, September 1979.

Gupta, Dr. D. K. "Carpet Trade in India," *Rug News*, Vol. 19, No. 8, 1987.

"Hand-Laundry Detergents." *Consumer Reports*, February 1982.

Mailand, Harold F. *Considerations for the Care of Textiles and Costumes*. Indianapolis, IN: Indianapolis Museum of Art, 1980.

Mast, Ted. *Oriental Rug Review*, Vol. 10, No. 4, pp. 25–26, 1990.

_____. "Rethinking Caucasian Soumak Production," *Oriental Rug Review*, Vol. 10, No. 4, 1990.

Merritt, Jane. "A Considered Choice: Selecting a Conservator." *Hali*, Vol. 12, No. 2, April 1990.

Moore, William G. "Collecting Rugs: The Great Middle Class Thing," *Oriental Rug Review*, Vol. 9, No. 3, 1990.

Mushak, Paul. "Dye Use in Caucasian Rugs," *Oriental Rug Review*, Vol. 10, No. 4, 1990.

Myers, George Hewitt. "Rugs: Preservation, Display and Storage." *Textile Museum Workshop Notes*, Paper No. 5. Washington, DC: Textile Museum, June 1952.

O'Bannon, George. "Caucasian Rug Nomenclature and Structure," *Oriental Rug Review*, Vol. 10, No. 4, 1990.

————. "Interview of Collectors Ralph and Linda Kaffel," *Oriental Rug Review*, Vol. 10, No. 4, 1990.

————, ed. Auction reports and previews. *Oriental Rug Review*, issues dated 1989 through February/March 1991.

————, ed. "Price Guide to Five Caucasian Rug Types from 1983 to 1990," *Oriental Rug Review*, Vol. 10, No. 4, 1990.

Palmai, Clarissa. "Caring for Your Rugs." *Rug News Digest*, Vol. 2, No. 1, 1980.

————. "Textile Mounting." *Textile Museum Journal*. Washington, DC: The Textile Museum, 1979.

Pinner, Robert, and Stanger, Jackie. "Kufic Borders on Small Pattern Holbein Carpets." *Hali*, Vol. 1, No. 4, 1978.

Rice, James W. "The Conservation of Historic Textile Colorants." *Principles of Textile Conservation Science*, No. 4. Washington DC: Textile Museum, n.d.

Ruters, Nils, et al. "Cleaning and Restoring Oriental Carpets." *Hali*, Vol. 1, No. 4, 1978.

Sakisian, Armenag. "Dragon Rugs and Their Armenian Origin." *Rug News Digest*, Vol. 33, March 1980.

Schetky, EthelJane McD., ed. "Dye Plants and Dyeing." *Plants and Gardens*, Vol. 20, No. 3. Brooklyn, NY: Brooklyn Botanic Garden, 1964.

Shelley, Louise, and Wright, Richard E. "Caucasian Rugs in the Late Nineteenth Century." *Hali*, Vol. 3, No. 1, 1980.

Sherrill, Sarah B. "The Islamic Tradition in Spanish Rug Weaving: Twelfth through Seventeenth Centuries." *The Magazine Antiques*, March 1974.

Steinert, Stefan. "Coloring Antique Woollen Fabrics with Water and Lightfast Colors." *Hali*, Vol. 1, No. 4, 1978.

Stroh, Leslie. "Traditional Sizes and Shapes in Oriental Rugs." *Rug News*, Vol. 8, No. 12, March 1987.

Tschebull, Raoul. "The Development of Four Kazak Designs." *Hali*, Vol. 1, No. 3, 1978.

Weigle, Palmy, ed. "Natural Plant Dyeing." *Plants and Gardens*, Vol. 29, No. 2. Brooklyn, NY: Brooklyn Botanic Garden, 1973.

Wertime, John T. "Flat-Woven Structures Found in Nomadic and Village Weavings from the Near East and Central Asia." *Textile Museum Journal*, Vol. 18. Washington, DC: Textile Museum, 1979.

Whiting, Mark. "The Dyes of Turkoman Rugs." *Hali*, Vol. 1, No. 3, 1978.

————. "Dye Analysis in Carpet Studies." *Hali*, Vol. 1, No. 1, 1978.

Wilber, Donald N. "Heriz Rugs." *Hali*, Vol. 6, No. 1, 1983.

Wright, Richard E. *Rugs and Flatweaves of the Transcaucasus.* A catalog for the Pittsburgh Rug Society exhibition, 1980.

U. S. Department of Agriculture. "Controlling Household Pests." *Home and Garden Bulletin*, No. 96, 1976 revision.

————. "How to Prevent and Remove Mildew." *Home and Garden Bulletin*, No. 68, 1971 revision.

————. "Protecting Woolen Clothes against Clothes Moths and Carpet Beetles." *Home and Garden Bulletin*, No. 113, 1980 revision.

————. "Removing Stains from Fabrics." *Home and Garden Bulletin*, No. 62, 1978 revision.

BOOKS

Acar, Belkis Balpinar. *Kilim-Cicim-Zili-Sumak: Turkish Flatweaves.* Istanbul: Eren Yayinlari, 1983.

Allane, Lee. *Oriental Rugs: A Buyer's Guide.* New York: Thames and Hudson, 1988.

Alsop, Joseph. *The Rare Art Traditions.* New York: Harper and Row, 1982.

Alth, Max, and Alth, Simon. *The Stain Removal Handbook.* New York: Hawthorn Books, 1977.

Azadi, Siawosch. *Turkoman Carpets.* Fishguard, Wales: The Crosby Press, 1975.

Bacharach, Jere L., and Bierman, Irene A. *The Warp and Weft of Islam.* Seattle: Henry Art Gallery, University of Washington, 1978.

Bayer, Friedr. and Co., dye catalog, 1898.

Beattie, May H. *Carpets of Central Persia.* Kent, England: World of Islam Festival Publishing Co., 1976.

Bennett, Ian. *Complete Illustrated Rugs and Carpets of the World.* New York: A&W Publishers, 1977.

Beresneva. L. *The Decorative and Applied Art of Turkmenia.* Leningrad: Aurora Art Publishers, 1976.

Bidder, Hans. *Carpets from Eastern Turkestan.* New York: Zwemmer, 1964.

Birrell, Verla. *The Textile Arts.* New York: Harper Brothers, 1959.

Blake, Wendon. *Acrylic Watercolor Painting.* New York: Watson-Guptill, 1970.

Bosly, Caroline. *Rugs to Riches.* New York: Pantheon, 1980.

Boucher, Jeff W. *Baluchi Woven Treasures.* Alexandria, VA: Jeff W. Boucher, 1989.

Brüggemann, Werner, and Böhmer, Harald. *Rugs of the Peasants and Nomads of Anatolia.* Munich: Kunst & Antiquitäten, 1983.

Bukhardt, Willy. *Alte Teppiche aus dem Orient*. Basel: Gewerbemuseum, 1980.

Calvert, Dr. F. Crace. *Coal Tar Colors and Recent Improvements in Dyeing and Calico Printing*. Philadelphia: Henry Carey Baird, 18—.

Clarke, Leslie J. *The Craftsman in Textiles*. London: G. Bell and Sons, 1968.

Collingwood, Peter. *The Techniques of Rug Weaving*. New York: Watson-Guptill, 1969.

Croot, Ann. *A Step-by-Step Guide to Woven Carpets and Rugs*. London: Hamlyn Publishing Group, 1974.

Davis, Don R. "Clothes Moth," *Encyclopedia Britannica*, Vol. 7, p. 99, 1973.

Denny, Walter B. *Oriental Rugs*. New York: Cooper-Hewitt Museum, The Smithsonian Illustrated Library of Antiques, 1979.

"Detergents and Detergency." *Encyclopedia Britannica*, Vol. 7, pp. 311–13, 1973.

Dimand, M. S. *A Handbook of Muhammadan Art*. 3rd ed. New York: Metropolitan Museum of Art, 1944; revised and enlarged 1958.

Dimand, M. S., and Mailey, Jean. *Oriental Rugs in the Metropolitan Museum of Art*. New York: The Metropolitan Museum of Art, 1973.

"Dyes and Dyeing." *Encyclopedia Britannica*, Vol. 7, pp. 814–21, 1973.

Eagleton, William. *An Introduction to Kurdish Rugs*. New York: Interlink Publishing Group, 1988.

Edwards, A. Cecil. *The Persian Carpet*. London: Duckworth, 1953.

Eiland, Murray L. *Chinese and Exotic Rugs*. Boston: New York Graphic Society/Little, Brown and Co., 1979.

————. *Oriental Rugs*, 3rd edition. Boston: New York Graphic Society/Little, Brown and Co., 1981.

Ellis, Charles Grant. *Early Caucasian Rugs*. Washington, DC: The Textile Museum, 1976.

————. *Oriental Carpets in the Philadelphia Museum of Art*. Philadelphia: Philadelphia Museum of Art, 1988.

Emery, Irene. *The Primary Structure of Fabrics*. Washington, DC: The Textile Museum, 1966.

Erdmann, Kurt. *The History of the Early Turkish Carpet*. London: Oguz Press, 1977.

————. *Seven Hundred Years of Oriental Carpets*. London: Faber and Faber, 1970.

Fichter, George S. *Insect Pests*. New York: Golden Press, 1966.

Finch, Karen, and Putnam, Greta. *Caring for Textiles*. New York: Watson-Guptill, 1977.

Ford, P. R. J. *The Oriental Carpet: A History and Guide to Traditional Motifs, Patterns and Symbols*. New York: Harry N. Abrams, 1981.

Franses, Jack. *European and Oriental Rugs for Pleasure and Investment.* New York: Arco Publishing Co., 1970.

Gans-Ruedin, E. *Indian Carpets.* New York: Rizzoli, 1984.

_____. *The Splendor of Persian Carpets.* New York: Rizzoli, 1978.

Hall, A. J. *A Handbook of Textile Dyeing and Printing.* London: Woodbridge Press, 1955.

Hardingham, Martin. *The Fabric Catalog.* New York: Pocket Books, Simon and Schuster, 1978.

Hawley, Walter A. *Oriental Rugs, Antique and Modern.* 1913. Reprint. New York: Dover Press, 1970.

Herbert, Janice Summers. *Affordable Oriental Rugs.* New York: Praeger, 1970.

Hoffmeister, Peter. *Turkoman Carpets in Franconia.* Edinburgh: The Crosby Press, 1980.

Hubel, Reinhard C. *The Book of Carpets.* New York: Praeger, 1970.

Jacobsen, Charles W. *Oriental Rugs: A Complete Guide.* Rutland, VT: Charles E. Tuttle Company, 1962.

Jerrehian, Aram K., Jr. *Oriental Rug Primer.* Philadelphia: Running Press, 1980.

Joseph, Marjory L. *The Essentials of Textiles.* New York: Holt, Rinehart and Winston, 1976.

Justin, Valerie S. *Flat-Woven Rugs of the World.* New York: Van Nostrand Reinhold, 1980.

Kendrick, A. F., and Tattersall, C. E. C. *Handwoven Carpets, Oriental and European.* 1922. Reprint. New York: Dover Press, 1970.

Knecht, Edmund; Rawson, Christopher; and Loewenthal, Richard. *A Manual of Dyeing.* London: Charles Griffin and Co., 1893.

Konieczny, M. G. *Textiles of Baluchistan.* London: British Museum Publications, 1979.

Kuløy, Hallvard Kåre. *Tibetan Rugs.* Bangkok: White Orchid Press, 1982.

Landreau, Anthony N., and Yohe, Ralph S. *Flowers of the Yayla: Yörük Weaving of the Toros Mountains.* Washington, DC: The Textile Museum, 1983.

LeFevre, Jean. *The Persian Carpet.* Catalog. London: LeFevre and Partners, 1977.

_____. *Turkish Carpets from the 16th to the 17th Century,* Catalog. London: LeFevre and Partners, 1977.

Linton, George C. *Applied Basic Textiles.* New York: Duell, Sloan and Pearce, 1966.

Loges, Werner. *Turkoman Tribal Rugs.* Atlantic Highlands, NJ: Humanities Press, 1980.

Loughlin, James E. "Dyeing." *McGraw-Hill Encyclopedia of Science and Technology,* Vol. 4, pp. 348–51, 1971.

Lucius and Bruning. *Coal Tar Colours of Farbwerke Vorm. Meister.* Germany, 1908.

Lutz, Frank E. *Field Book of Insects.* New York: G. P. Putnam's Sons, 1918.

Macauley, David. *The Way Things Work.* New York: Houghton Mifflin, 1988.

Mackie, Louise, and Thompson, Jon, eds. *Turkmen Tribal Carpets and Traditions.* Washington, DC: The Textile Museum, 1980.

Maerz, A., and Paul, M. Rea. *A Dictionary of Color.* New York: McGraw-Hill Book Co., 1930.

Maritz-Iten, J. *Turkish Carpets.* New York: Harper and Row, 1977.

Mayer, Ralph. *The Artist's Handbook of Materials and Techniques.* New York: Viking Press, 1970.

Mills, John. *Carpets in Pictures.* London: National Gallery, 1975.

Minnis, Wesley. "Dye." *McGraw-Hill Encyclopedia of Science and Technology*, Vol. 4, pp. 336–47, 1970.

Moore, Alma Chestnut. *How to Clean Everything.* New York: Simon and Schuster, 1968.

Neff, I. C., and Maggs, C. V. *Dictionary of Oriental Rugs.* London: A. D. Donker, 1977.

Opie, James. *Tribal Rugs of Southern Persia.* Portland, OR: James Opie Oriental Rugs, 1981.

Petsopolous, Y. *Kilims.* New York: Rizzoli, 1979.

Pluckrose, Henry. *Introducing Acrylic Painting.* New York: Watson-Guptill, 1968.

Proud, Nora. *Textile Printing and Dyeing.* New York: Reinhold Publishing, 1965.

Quick, John. *Artist's and Illustrator's Encyclopedia.* New York: McGraw-Hill, 1977.

Rattee, Ian D. "Dye." *Encyclopedia Americana*, Vol. 9, pp. 508–12, 1973.

Russ, Stephen. *Fabric Printing by Hand.* New York: Watson-Guptill, 1965.

Schorsch, Anita, ed. *The Art of the Weaver.* New York: Universe Books, 1978.

Schurmann, Ulrich. *Caucasian Rugs.* 1974 reprint; distributed by Washington International Associates, Accokeek, MD.

_____. *Central-Asian Rugs.* Frankfort: Verlag Osterrieth, 1969.

Schwartz, Anthony. "Detergent." *Encyclopedia Americana*, Vol. 9, p. 21, 1973.

Singer, Max. *La Teinture Moderne.* Paris: Adolphe Delmee, 1875.

Swan, Lester A., and Papp, Charles S. *Common Insects of North America.* New York: Harper and Row, 1972.

Swezey, Kenneth. *Formulas, Methods, Tips and Data for Home and Workshop*. New York: Popular Science Publishing Co./Harper and Row, 1969.

Tanavoli, Parviz. *Shahsavan: Iranian Rugs and Textiles*. New York: Rizzoli, 1985.

Tattersall, C. E. C. *Notes on Carpet Weaving and Knotting*. London: Victoria and Albert Museum, 1969.

Thompson, Jon. *Oriental Carpets: From the Tents, Cottages and Workshops of Asia*. Rev. ed. New York: E. P. Dutton, 1988.

Tschebull, Raoul. *Kazak*. New York: The Near Eastern Art Research Center, Inc., and the New York Rug Society, 1971.

Turkish Ministry of Culture and Tourism. *Turkish Handwoven Carpets*. Catalogs 1 and 2. Ankara: Turkish Republic Ministry of Culture and Tourism, 1987.

Weigle, Palmy. *Ancient Dyes for Modern Weavers*. New York: Watson-Guptill, 1974.

"Wool, Worsted and Woollen Manufactures." *Encyclopaedia Britannica*, Vol. 28, pp. 805–17, 1911.

Wright, Vera Penick. *Pamper Your Possessions*. Barre, VT: Barre Publishers, 1972.

Yetkin, Şerare. *Early Caucasian Carpets in Turkey*. Atlantic Highlands, NJ: Humanities Press, 1978.

———. *Historical Turkish Carpets*. Istanbul: Türkiye iş Bankası Cultural Publications, 1981.

INDEX